lone[ly planet]

TRAV[EL]

BELIZE

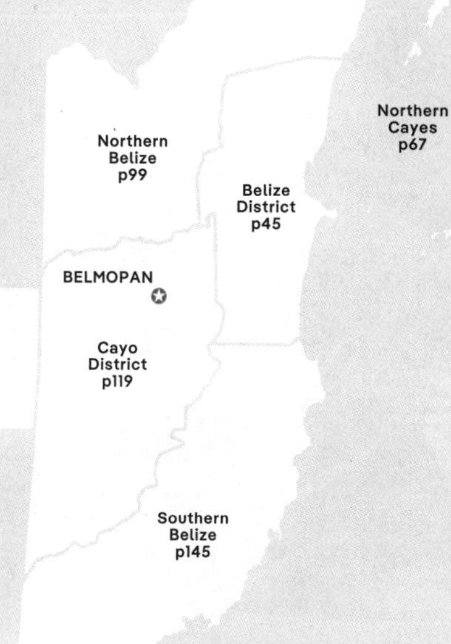

Paul Harding, Ray Bartlett, Carolee Chanona, Anna Kaminski, Ali Wunderman

KRISTY VIERA/SHUTTERSTOCK ©

Ambergris Caye (p70)

CONTENTS

Plan Your Trip

The Guide

Egret, Crooked Tree Wildlife Sanctuary (p64)

Toolkit

Storybook

Belize City (p48)

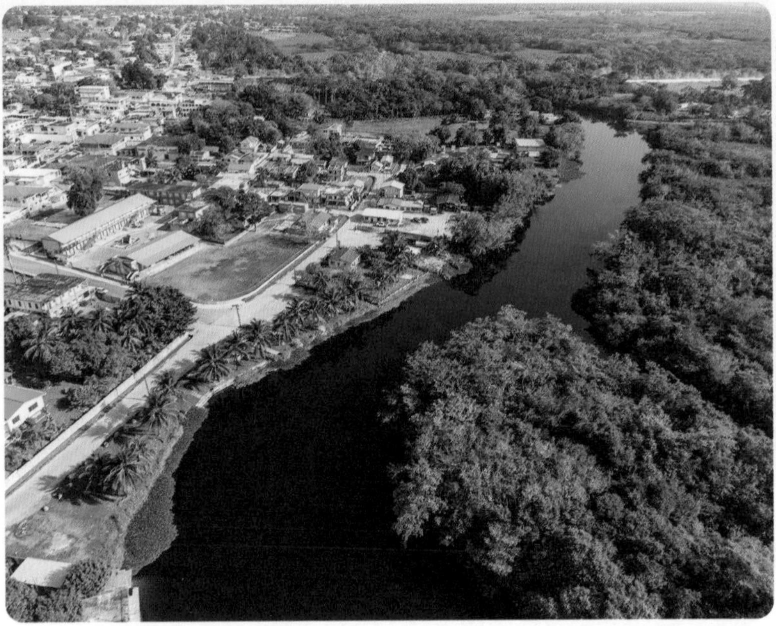

TOP: PAUL HARDING/LONELY PLANET ©, BOTTOM: MEHDI KASUMOV/SHUTTERSTOCK ©

New River, Orange Walk Town (p102)

BELIZE

THE JOURNEY BEGINS HERE

Belize may be Central America's best-kept secret. It flies under the radar but those who dip their toe in its Caribbean waters can't help but be captivated by the country's eclectic makeup, from jungle and reef to culture and history. Part Caribbean, part Latin American, Belize carries the legacy of British colonization in its language and traditions but is a proud mix of Creole, Mestizo, Garifuna, Maya, Mennonites and expats.

I love the untouristed mainland, the Orange Walk and San Ignacio markets, the Crooked Tree birdlife, Placencia beaches, Garifuna drum culture at Hopkins and the Maya sites all over the country. But if I had to throw a dart and stay in one place it would be Ambergris Caye and Caye Caulker. The two islands are different in character but only a short hop apart; both are the epitome of laid-back Caribbean island life with good food, good times and the glorious barrier reef on your doorstep. It may be corny, but as the locals say, it's unbelizable!

Paul Harding

@phtravel

Paul is a writer and photographer specializing in travel, from Belize to Borneo and beyond.

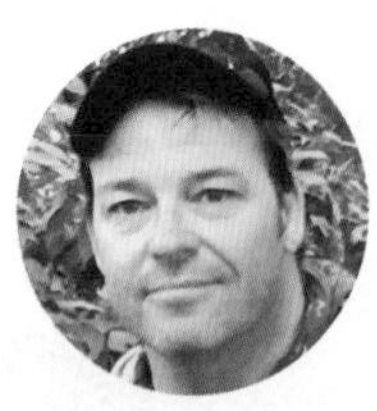

My favourite experience is the boat ride down New River from Orange Walk to Lamanai. Stepping ashore at New River Lagoon, the thick jungle parts to reveal one of Belize's most beautiful Maya sites.

WHO GOES WHERE

Our writers and experts choose the places that, for them, define Belize.

The wonder of **Tikal** (p184) and its surrounding jungle has to be seen to be believed. It's a spectacular site and often a highlight of any visitor's journey to Guatemala. I've been there so many times and each time leaves me more in awe and more admiring than the last. The more I learn about the Maya culture, the more upset I am that the Conquistadors destroyed so much of it without a moment's thought to what that might mean for future generations.

Ray Bartlett

@kaisoradotcom or at www.kaisora.com

Ray Bartlett is an acclaimed travel writer, novelist, and photographer.

Mountain Pine Ridge Forest Reserve (p132) holds an otherworldly reverence for me, with 100,000 gobsmacking acres of protected native pine forests revealing a treasure trove of geological and archaeological wonders. Crashing waterfalls (including one of Central America's tallest), steep ravines and yawning caves all evoke a feeling of personal Eden. Its vastness is a solace: problems feel trivial when you're face-to-face with this force of nature.

Carolee Chanona

@car.elix

Freelance journalist Carolee writes about travel, food, and eco-adventures from her home base in Belize

I find **Punta Gorda** (p166) utterly beguiling. This laid-back, spread-out town on the Gulf of Honduras draws you in with its unique vibe: the locals, happy to chat with you for hours; the lack of mass tourism found in Belize's north; the rich mix of cultures that call PG and its environs home; and the wealth of find-your-own adventure attractions beyond PG's borders, from half-forgotten Maya ruins and cacao farms to water-filled caves.

Anna Kaminski

@ACkaminski

Anna is a travel writer who majored in the history and culture of the Caribbean and Central and South America, and who specializes in adventure travel.

San Ignacio (p122) is the home of Belize's adventurous spirit, a hub from which exploration blossoms. It's a place where the curious can gather, where wildlife-lovers can be charmed by local animals. Belize's roots run deep here, from the towering monuments of the ancient Maya still visible today, to the modern collaboration of cultures forming their own ecosystem that is so uniquely Belize.

Ali Wunderman

@aliwunderman

Ali is an award-winning journalist who writes about travel and food, as well as a guidebook author for Belize and Iceland.

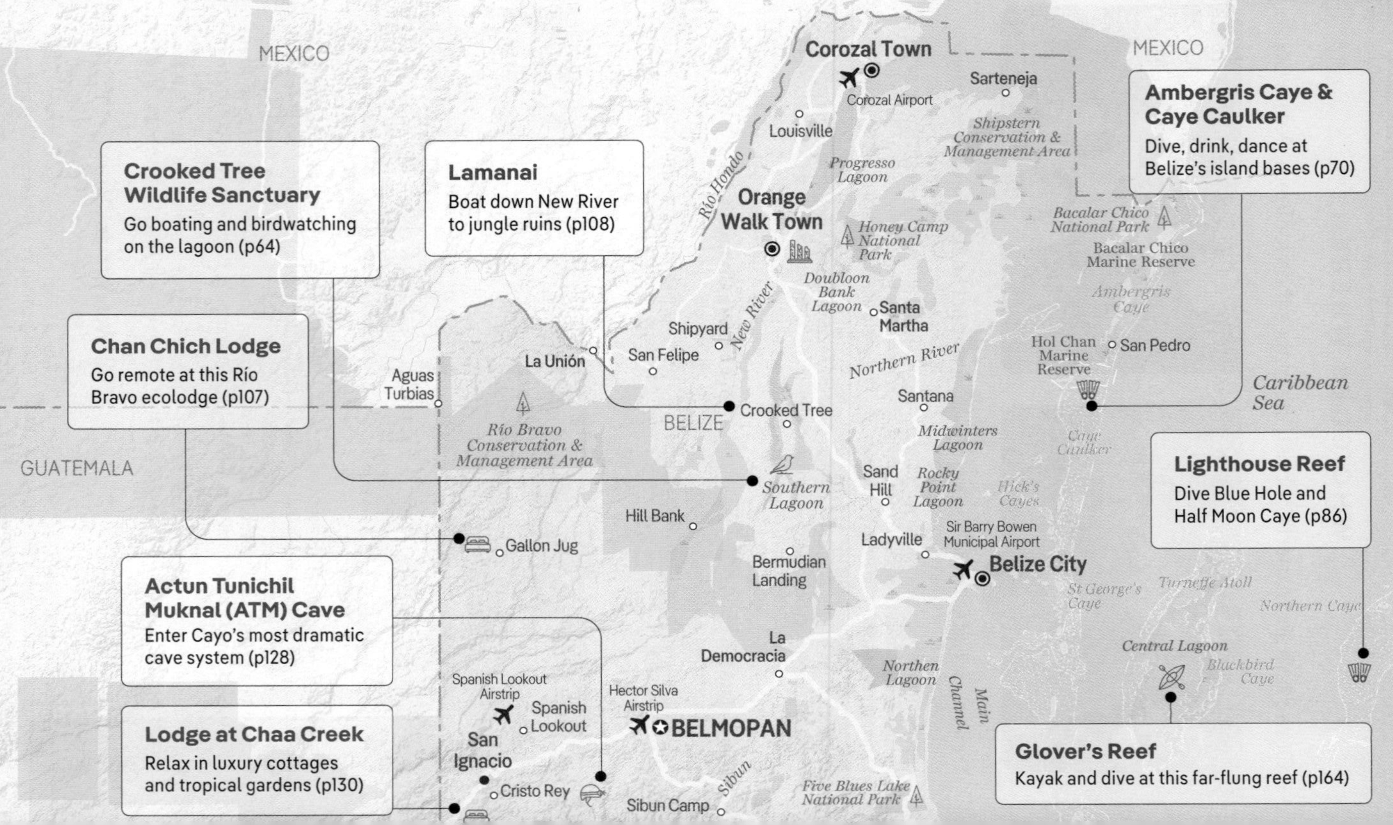
Crooked Tree Wildlife Sanctuary
Go boating and birdwatching on the lagoon (p64)
Lamanai
Boat down New River to jungle ruins (p108)
Chan Chich Lodge
Go remote at this Río Bravo ecolodge (p107)
Actun Tunichil Muknal (ATM) Cave
Enter Cayo's most dramatic cave system (p128)
Lodge at Chaa Creek
Relax in luxury cottages and tropical gardens (p130)
Ambergris Caye & Caye Caulker
Dive, drink, dance at Belize's island bases (p70)
Lighthouse Reef
Dive Blue Hole and Half Moon Caye (p86)
Glover's Reef
Kayak and dive at this far-flung reef (p164)
MEXICO
MEXICO
GUATEMALA
BELIZE
Corozal Town
Corozal Airport
Sarteneja
Louisville
Shipstern Conservation & Management Area
Progresso Lagoon
Río Hondo
Orange Walk Town
Honey Camp National Park
Bacalar Chico National Park
Bacalar Chico Marine Reserve
Ambergris Caye
Doubloon Bank Lagoon
Santa Martha
New River
Shipyard
San Felipe
La Unión
Aguas Turbias
Northern River
Hol Chan Marine Reserve
San Pedro
Caribbean Sea
Santana
Crooked Tree
Río Bravo Conservation & Management Area
Midwinters Lagoon
Caye Caulker
Sand Hill
Rocky Point Lagoon
Hick's Cayes
Southern Lagoon
Hill Bank
Gallon Jug
Ladyville
Sir Barry Bowen Municipal Airport
Belize City
Bermudian Landing
St George's Caye
Turneffe Atoll
Northern Caye
La Democracia
Central Lagoon
Blackbird Caye
Northen Lagoon
Main Channel
Spanish Lookout Airstrip
Spanish Lookout
Hector Silva Airstrip
BELMOPAN
San Ignacio
Cristo Rey
Sibun
Sibun Camp
Five Blues Lake National Park

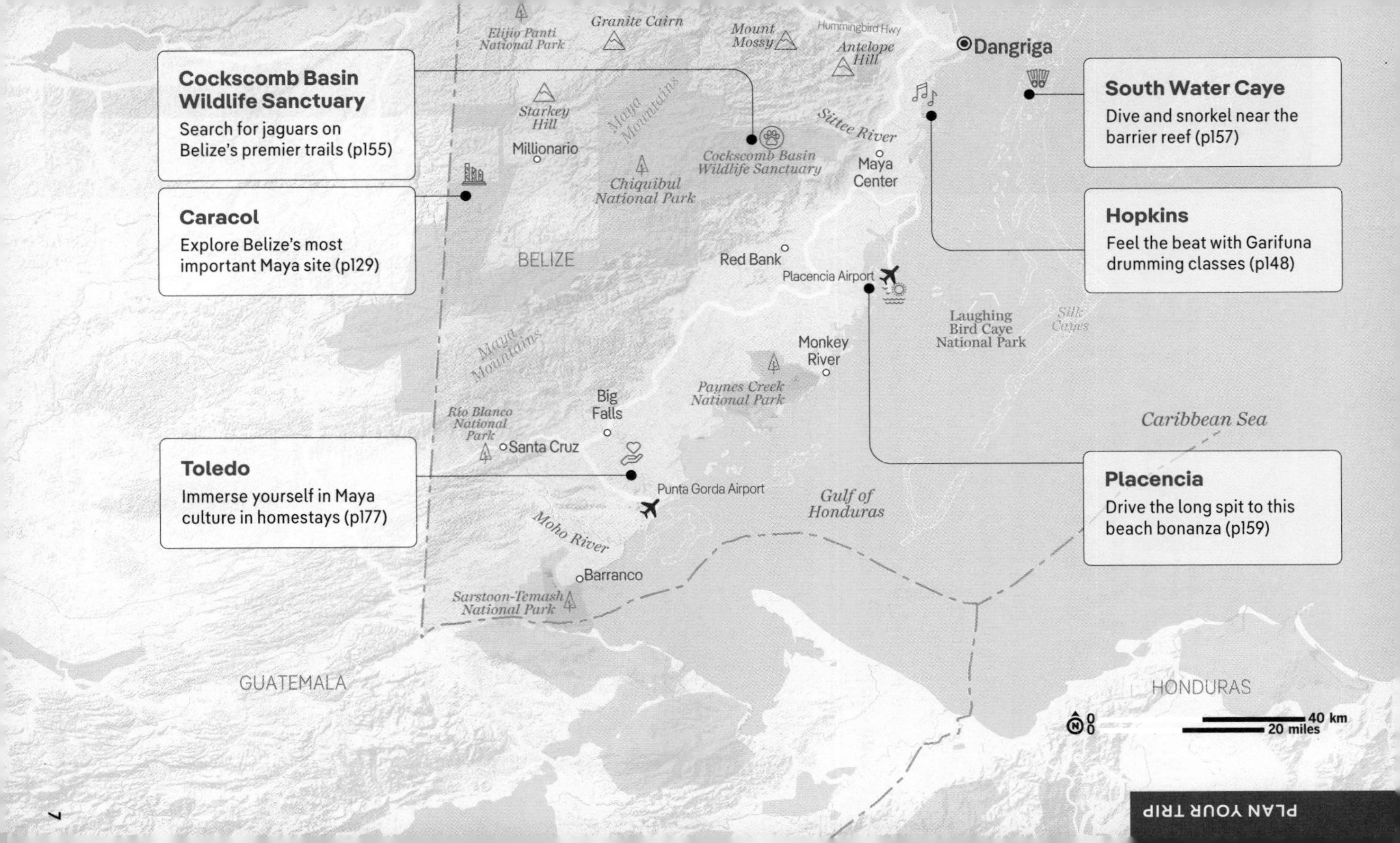

Cockscomb Basin Wildlife Sanctuary
Search for jaguars on Belize's premier trails (p155)

Caracol
Explore Belize's most important Maya site (p129)

Toledo
Immerse yourself in Maya culture in homestays (p177)

South Water Caye
Dive and snorkel near the barrier reef (p157)

Hopkins
Feel the beat with Garifuna drumming classes (p148)

Placencia
Drive the long spit to this beach bonanza (p159)

Elijio Panti National Park
Granite Cairn
Mount Mossy
Hummingbird Hwy
Antelope Hill
Dangriga
Starkey Hill
Maya Mountains
Millionario
Chiquibul National Park
Cockscomb Basin Wildlife Sanctuary
Sittee River
Maya Center
BELIZE
Red Bank
Placencia Airport
Laughing Bird Caye National Park
Silk Cayes
Monkey River
Paynes Creek National Park
Big Falls
Río Blanco National Park
Santa Cruz
Caribbean Sea
Punta Gorda Airport
Gulf of Honduras
Moho River
Barranco
Sarstoon-Temash National Park
GUATEMALA
HONDURAS
0 40 km
0 20 miles

UNDERWATER ADVENTURE

Belize is justifiably renowned in the diving world for its easily accessible barrier reef and three famous offshore atolls – Lighthouse Reef, Turneffe Atoll and Glover's Reef. Life under the sea here is dramatic and diverse, from the fantastical coral formations and kaleidoscopic fish to the massive marine life lurking in deeper waters. You don't need to be a certified diver to enjoy the reef though, with snorkelers in for a treat at sites like Shark Ray Alley.

RIGHT: GLOBE GUIDE MEDIA INC/SHUTTERSTOCK ©, FAR LEFT: ETHAN DANIELS/SHUTTERSTOCK ©, LEFT: MICHAEL BOGNER/SHUTTERSTOCK ©

Out at Sea

The barrier reef is so close that many boat trips are just five to 15 minutes away. Access Lighthouse Reef and Turneffe Atoll (pictured) from San Pedro, and Glover's Reef from Placencia/Hopkins.

Get Certified

There's plenty for snorkelers on the reef but to get among the marine life you need to scuba dive. Operators offer Discover Scuba and PADI courses.

Snorkel the Reef

Swim with sharks and stingrays at Hol Chan Marine Reserve on a day trip from San Pedro or Caye Caulker, aboard a catamaran or yacht.

Blue Hole Natural Monument (p86)

BEST UNDERWATER EXPERIENCES

Take a day trip to **Lighthouse Reef ❶**, famous for the Blue Hole and the Wall at Half Moon Caye. (p86)

Experience underwater life at **Turneffe Atoll ❷**, the largest in the Americas, with coral, fish, mangroves, dolphins and large rays. (p85)

Swim and snorkel with sizable but harmless nurse sharks and stingrays in an unforgettable experience at **Hol Chan Marine Reserve ❸**. (p76)

Dive, snorkel and kayak at the most remote of Belize's Caribbean cayes, far-flung **Glover's Reef ❹**, with a few castaway resorts. (p164)

Snorkel and dive straight from your cabaña on **South Water Caye ❺**, part of a marine park right on the reef. (p157)

Sip N'Dip beach bar (p91), Caye Caulker

ISLAND HOPPING

There's a Belizean island out there for everyone, with more than 400 cayes (islands) scattered around the Caribbean Sea. The northern cayes, best reached from Belize City, include Ambergris Caye and Caye Caulker; the central cayes are a boat ride from Dangriga, Hopkins or Placencia; and the southern cayes are off the coast of Punta Gorda.

Sailing Away

There's no better way to island-hop than aboard a yacht or catamaran. Book a live-aboard adventure or a day trip with snorkeling at an uninhabited island.

Water Taxis

Regular scheduled water taxis visit the northern cayes from Belize City or Corozal. Regular charter boats go from Dangriga to Tobacco Caye and other central cayes..

BEST ISLAND EXPERIENCES

Relax on mellow **Caye Caulker ❶**, the most laid-back developed caye, where life moves to an easy reggae beat. (p89)

Dive, dine and dance the night away at the largest island in Belize, **Ambergris Caye ❷**. (p70)

Go cheap on tiny **Tobacco Caye ❸**, the budget island of choice with the barrier reef just a few flipper kicks away. (p158)

Stay at the twin private-island resorts on **Thatch & Coco Plum Cayes ❹**, stunning castaway islands off the southern coast. (p158)

Dive, snorkel and sea-kayak at remote **Glover's Reef ❺**, one of the best places to get away in the Caribbean. (p164)

CULTURE & FESTIVALS

With a mix of Creole, Maya, Garifuna, Mestizo and some British traditions, Belize has its share of culture which inevitably spills over into food and festivals. Carnival comes to Belize City and other towns during September celebrations, San Pedro and Placencia food tours offer a culinary cultural expedition, while Toledo homestays enable you to experience Maya village life.

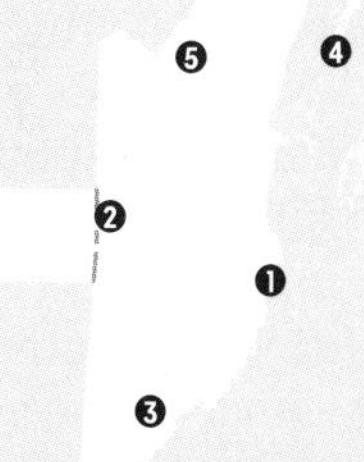

Garifuna Drummin'

The drum beat is central to the Garifuna people's music, reflecting their African heritage. The *primero* (tenor) and *segundo* (bass) drums are locally made from hardwoods like mahogany or mayflower.

Holy Holidays

Belizeans celebrate Christian holidays like Easter with church services and street parades. At Christmas, homes are decorated with colored lights and Christmas Day includes family feasts.

Why September?

The huge September celebrations occur between two important dates: Battle of St George's Caye on September 10 and Belize's Independence Day on September 21.

BEST CULTURAL EXPERIENCES

See, hear and learn about Garifuna drumming with the masters at **Hopkins** ❶. (p148)

Delve into the Maya chocolate-making process at **AJAW Chocolate** ❷ in San Ignacio in an immersive experience. (p135)

Stay with a Maya family in Toledo District through the **Toledo Ecotourism Association (TEA)** ❸ village homestay network. (p177)

Dive into a **San Pedro** ❹ food tour and learn about local culture through culinary delights. There's a similar tour in Placencia. (p71)

Visit the Mennonite communities of **Shipyard** ❺ or Spanish Lookout, where locals get around by horse and buggy. (p110)

LAND OF THE MAYA

For almost 3000 years the ancient Maya civilization flourished in Belize, building towering temples as tributes to their god-like rulers. The remains of these once-mighty city-states are scattered throughout the country – some in remote locations, others easily accessible, but all are rewarding, photogenic and humbling in their historic scale and beauty. The Toledo District in southern Belize is home to the largest modern Maya communities in the country.

Journey to the Ruins

Get to Lamanai on a scenic wildlife-spotting speedboat ride down the New River. Xunantunich (pictured) is reached via a cable ferry across the Mopan River.

Into Guatemala

Across the border, the Maya ruins of Tikal (pictured) are amazingly preserved, jungle-shrouded ancient structures. There are day tours from San Ignacio – bring your passport.

Jade Head & Crystal Skull

Of the many treasures unearthed at Maya sites, the Jade Head at Altun Ha is the largest jade carving found, while the mysterious Crystal Skull was found at Lubaantun

Temple, Caracol (p129)

BEST MAYA EXPERIENCES

Cruise by boat to New River Lagoon and jungle-covered **Lamanai** ❶, an enthralling nature and cultural day trip. (p108)

Take in the epic views of **Xunantunich** ❷ from towering El Castillo, one of Belize's most impressive Maya archaeological sites. (p129)

Cross into Guatemala to explore **Tikal** ❸, one of the great Central American Maya sites where you can also stay overnight. (p184)

Schedule a day at remote **Caracol** ❹, Belize's largest and most important Maya site, with stops at Mountain Pine Ridge waterfalls. (p129)

Feel the history at one of Belize's best-kept sites, **Altun Ha** ❺, home of the Jade Head and immortalized on Belikin beer. (p63)

LEFT: AL ARGUETA/ALAMY STOCK PHOTO ©, RIGHT: WOLLERTZ/SHUTTERSTOCK © FAR RIGHT: SHARON K. ANDREWS/SHUTTERSTOCK ©

Bar at Chaa Creek (p130)

JUNGLE ECOLODGES

Belize has long been blessed with an under-the-radar charm which has encouraged ecotourism pioneers to build remote or stunningly located ecolodges with easy access to nature. Some of the best are in the Cayo District in the hills and valleys south of San Ignacio, but there are luxury jungle hideaways scattered around the country.

Jungle Life

Most lodges are luxurious but part of the appeal is nature and adventure on your doorstep – canoeing, hiking, birdwatching or relaxing on your deck to the cicada symphony.

Celeb Spotting

Celebrities are drawn to Belize's seclusion, both the cayes and inland. Director Francis Ford Coppola owns Blancaneaux Lodge in Mountain Pine Ridge, Turtle Island in Placencia and Coral Island Caye.

BEST LODGE EXPERIENCES

Relax at one of Belize's top lodges, **Chaa Creek** ❶, with tropical gardens, thatched cottages above the river and luxurious treetop suites. (p130)

Hike pristine trails, ride a horse to Vaca Falls or canoe down the Macal at **Black Rock Lodge** ❷, in the Cayo hills. (p130)

Feel like a star at Francis Ford Coppola's **Blancaneaux Lodge** ❸ in Mountain Pine Ridge, with cabañas and luxury villas. (p133)

Go remote at Belize's most isolated ecolodge, **Chan Chich Lodge** ❹, set in a 200-sq-mile private bird and wildlife reserve. (p107)

Sleep in jungle splendor at hilltop **Copal Tree Lodge** ❺, north of Punta Gorda, with cable tramways and a jungle restaurant. (p168)

NATURE & WILDLIFE

Belize packs a surprising array of wildlife sanctuaries and reserves into its relatively small land area, protecting everything from jaguars to black howler monkeys and manatees. The Maya Mountains are the source of the country's most dramatic waterfalls around Mountain Pine Ridge, as well as the largest wildlife sanctuary. In the north, rivers and lagoons provide excellent birdwatching.

Wild Things

Native Belizean animals and birds include the jaguar (pictured), Baird's tapir (national animal), jaguarundi, gibnut, ocelot, black howler monkey, West Indian manatee, green iguana, toucan (national bird), scarlet macaw and jabiru stork.

Manatee Spotting

Belize has some of the largest populations of endangered West Indian manatees in the Caribbean. See them at Gales Point and Swallow Caye. Swimming with manatees is prohibited.

Birds of a Feather

Belize is a birdwatcher's paradise. On the coast look out for frigate birds and heron; inland is the rare harpy eagle, toucans, jabiru storks, hummingbirds and the scarlet macaw.

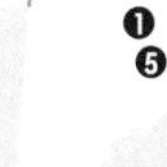

BEST WILDLIFE EXPERIENCES

Search for rare jaguars and tapirs at **Cockscomb Basin Wildlife Sanctuary** ❶ along hiking trails and even a mountain-biking trail. (p155)

Go in search of noisy black howler monkeys in the wild at the **Community Baboon Sanctuary** ❷, northwest of Belize City. (p62)

Point your binoculars at bird-filled lagoons at the **Crooked Tree Wildlife Sanctuary** ❸, a remarkable conservation project. (p64)

Come face to face with Belize's most elusive native animals at **Belize Zoo** ❹ a remarkable conservation project. (p57)

Be enthralled by flocks of vibrant scarlet macaws which descend on the forest near **Red Bank** ❺ to feed on seasonal fruit. (p165)

INLAND ADVENTURE

They don't call Cayo District the adventure capital for nothing. This is the place for subterranean caving, canoeing on the Macal and Mopan rivers, horseback riding and ziplining from a base in San Ignacio or Belmopan. Southern Belize has its fair share of adventures with waterfall rappelling at Mayflower-Bocawina, hiking in the Maya Mountains and river tubing in Toledo, while in the north there's remote wildlife-watching and river tours.

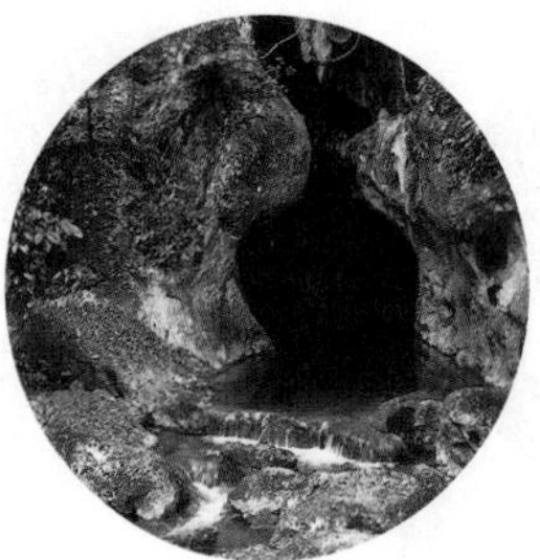

RIGHT: KARA ARCENEAUX/SHUTTERSTOCK ©, FAR LEFT: JOHN PIEKOS/SHUTTERSTOCK ©, LEFT: BLUE ICE/SHUTTERSTOCK ©

Why the Caves?

Most Cayo District cave geology is limestone karst. Over millennia, rivers and streams have carved extensive cave systems, including Río Frio Cave (pictured; p128), from porous rock and many caves still have underground rivers.

Enter the Underworld

The ancient Maya believed caves were the abode of the gods and the entrance to the Underworld – Xibalba. Some caves were used in ritual sacrifices, most famously the Actun Tunichil Muknal cave (pictured).

Maya Mountains

Belize's only mountain range separates Cayo District from southern Belize. The highest peak is Doyle's Delight (3688ft/1124m). More accessible to climbers is Victoria Peak (3680ft/1122m) in Cockscomb Basin.

Waterfall, Mayflower-Bocawina National Park (p154)

BEST ADVENTURE EXPERIENCES

Explore the stunning **Actun Tunichil Muknal Cave** ❶, an adventure squeezing deep into the Cayo cave system by guided tour. (p128)

Float through the underground river system on tubes to **Crystal Cave** ❷, or go ziplining in the jungle at Nohoch Che'en. (p128)

Go horseback riding with professional outfits like **Mountain Equestrian Trails** ❸ in Cayo cowboy country. (p133)

Float on a pontoon boat and chase waterfalls on a boat tour to **Vaca Lake** ❹. (p130)

Hike to waterfalls, or rappel down one, at **Mayflower-Bocawina National Park** ❺, where you'll find Belize's longest zipline. (p154)

REGIONS

Find the places that tick all your boxes.

Northern Belize

MAYA RUINS AND REMOTE SEASIDE COMMUNITIES

The least-visited region of Belize, bordering Mexico to the north, has some outstanding attractions and no crowds. From Orange Walk Town, take the sublime river trip to the extraordinary ruins at Lamanai. In Corozal District explore coastal ruins, the birdlife of Shipstern Lagoon and the dreamy fishing village of Sarteneja.

p99

Northern Cayes

ISLAND LIFE AND THE DEEP BLUE

Tourists head here for sun, fun and underwater adventures. Ambergris Caye, with its culinary and nightlife-capital San Pedro, draws travelers like bugs to a flame. Smaller and mellower Caye Caulker is no less a tropical idyll. The barrier reef and beyond brings world-class diving topped by the big one – the Blue Hole.

p67

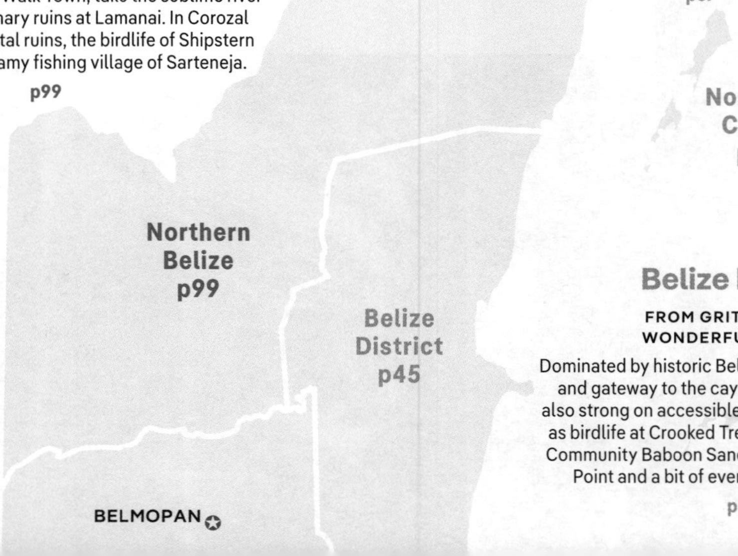

Northern Cayes
p67

Northern Belize
p99

Belize District
p45

BELMOPAN

Tikal & Flores (Guatemala)

WELCOME TO THE JUNGLE

Hot, sweaty and fascinating, the El Petén region of northern Guatemala is scattered with Maya ruins including the big one – Tikal. Fly or take a bus from Belize to the pretty Guatemalan island town of Flores, where hotels and restaurants abound, and get your exploring boots on.

p181

Belize District

FROM GRITTY CITY TO WONDERFUL WILDLIFE

Dominated by historic Belize City, the former capital and gateway to the cayes, this central district is also strong on accessible wildlife experiences such as birdlife at Crooked Tree, howler monkeys at the Community Baboon Sanctuary, manatees at Gales Point and a bit of everything at Monkey Bay.

p45

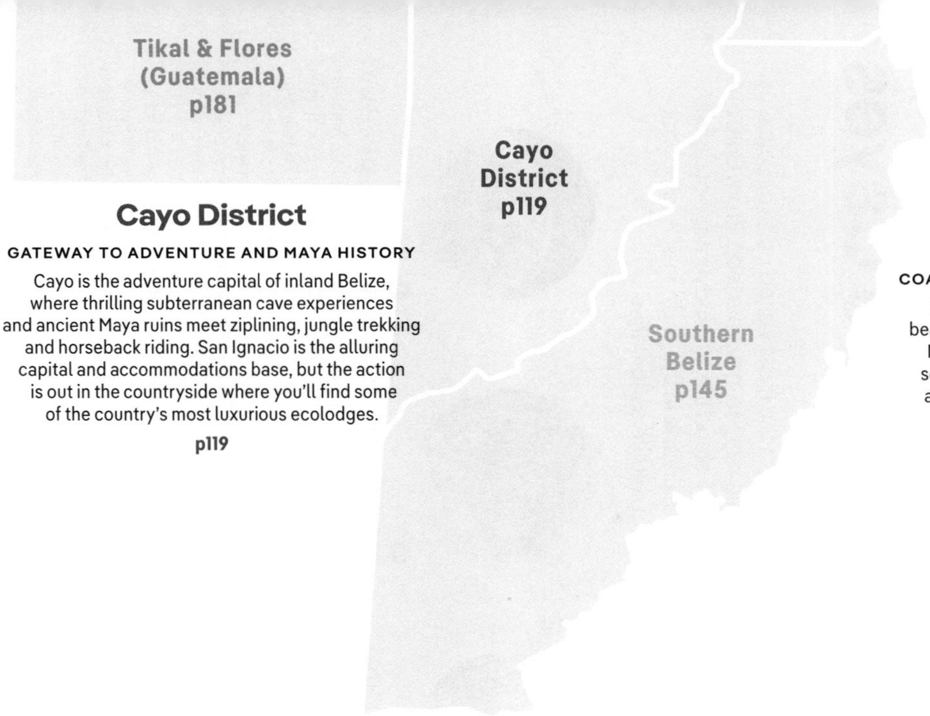

Tikal & Flores (Guatemala)
p181

Cayo District
p119

Southern Belize
p145

Cayo District

GATEWAY TO ADVENTURE AND MAYA HISTORY

Cayo is the adventure capital of inland Belize, where thrilling subterranean cave experiences and ancient Maya ruins meet ziplining, jungle trekking and horseback riding. San Ignacio is the alluring capital and accommodations base, but the action is out in the countryside where you'll find some of the country's most luxurious ecolodges.

p119

Southern Belize

COASTAL TOWNS, JUNGLE ADVENTURE AND DIVING

South Belize is a cultural melting pot with Garifuna beats around Hopkins and Dangriga and Belize's largest Maya population down in Toledo. Placencia and the southern cayes will satisfy your beach, diving, sailing and watersports needs, while inland are some of the country's best wildlife parks and sanctuaries.

p145

ROB CRANDALL/SHUTTERSTOCK ©

Belize City (p48)

ITINERARIES

The North & the Cayes

Allow: 10 days **Distance:** 140 miles (225km)

This northern itinerary takes in both the most visited parts of Belize and the least visited region in an easy-to-navigate loop. From Belize's major city to the barrier reef and island life, take advantage of regular daily boat travel to rejoin the mainland in the north then explore back down through Maya ruins and wildlife sanctuaries.

1 BELIZE CITY 1 DAY

Spend a day getting acquainted with Belize's urban life and colonial past at the former capital, **Belize City** (p48). Don't miss the Museum of Belize, wander along the waterfront to the Baron Bliss Lighthouse and browse the markets and murals outside the Fort Street Tourism Village (pictured). Head south to Government House and stop for a drink at Bird's Isle Restaurant or take a taxi for lunch at Di Bruwry.

45 mintues

2 CAYE CAULKER 2 DAYS

Catch an early water taxi to **Caye Caulker** (p89) for some laid-back island life. Swim at the Split or ferry across to North Side Beach, snack at the beach barbecues and wade with the visiting stingrays at Iguana Reef Inn beach. On day two, snorkel at one of the marine reserves, relax on a sunset sailing tour and mingle with locals at Barrier Reef Sports Bar or I&I Reggae Bar.

30 mintues

3 AMBERGRIS CAYE 3 DAYS

Make the short hop to **Ambergris Caye** (p70). Sample local dishes with Belize Food Tours in San Pedro, visit the Eco Iguana Sanctuary and recline at over water *palapa*-covered (open-air shelter with a thatched roof) bars or the excellent Truck Stop. If you're a diver, consider a full-day trip to Lighthouse Reef or Turneffe Atoll or local barrier-reef dives. Hire a golf cart and ride out to Secret Beach for an afternoon of swimming and rum punch.

1 hour 30 mintues

FROM LEFT: YINGNA CAI/SHUTTERSTOCK ©, PAUL HARDING/LONELY PLANET ©, TOP PHOTO CORPORATION/SHUTTERSTOCK ©

4

COROZAL TOWN ⏱1 DAY

Take the morning water taxi to **Corozal Town** (p111), an appealing northern community on Corozal Bay with a strong Mexican influence. Spend the afternoon visiting the local museums, Santa Rita ruins and sampling Mexican street food. Ask at the boat dock about a trip to Cerros Maya ruins across the bay. With an extra day to spare you could stop at Sarteneja on the way.

1 hour

5

ORANGE WALK TOWN & LAMANAI ⏱2 DAYS

Make an early start for **Orange Walk Town** (p102) to get on a prebooked boat tour (pictured) down the New River to the magnificent Maya ruins at **Lamanai** (p108). After touring the site and an exhilarating ride back, spend the evening exploring Orange Walk Town and dining on local street food, then enjoy a beer and sunset at Palm Island Bar on the New River.

2 hours

6

CROOKED TREE ⏱1 DAY

Off the main highway south of Orange Walk, **Crooked Tree** village (p64) sits beside a lagoon within the wildlife sanctuary. The main attraction is the birdlife, but with some good budget accommodations and walking trails it's also a peaceful place to overnight. Hire a kayak or take a boat trip on the lagoon. From here it's an easy trip back to Belize City, Cayo or the south.

ITINERARIES

Best of the West

Allow: 7 days
Distance: 198 miles (319km)

The Cayo District is Belize's adventure capital with its network of underground caves, Maya Mountains and some of the best preserved Maya archaeological sites in the country. This itinerary allows you to take in some of the best activities from a base in Belmopan, San Ignacio or one of the excellent jungle ecolodges.

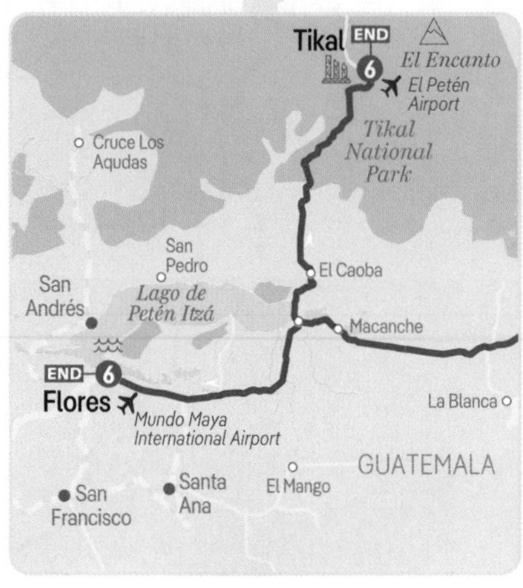

1

BELMOPAN 1 DAY

Start at the national capital, **Belmopan** (p137), a good base for cave tubing on the Caves Branch River, horseback riding at Banana Bank Lodge or caving and ziplining adventures along the Hummingbird Hwy such as St Herman's Blue Hole National Park. Grab a cheap meal and absorb the atmosphere at the central-market food stalls. Consider staying in a jungle ecolodge along the Hummingbird Hwy.

1 hour

2

SAN IGNACIO 2 DAYS

San Ignacio (p122) is the archetypal budget base for exploring central Cayo, though some of Belize's best ecolodges are in the surrounding hills and forest. The town is always buzzing with travelers, locals, street-food vendors and cave-bound tour groups. Don't miss the Saturday farmers market, learn how to make Maya chocolate, visit the Green Iguana Conservation Project or trek up to the Cahal Pech hilltop ruins.

30 minutes

3

XUNANTUNICH & AROUND SAN IGNACIO 2 DAYS

Start early for the half-hour trip to the Maya ruins at **Xunantunich** (p129), across the river from San Jose Succotz, 6miles (10km) from San Ignacio. Other activities within easy reach of San Ignacio include canoeing through Barton Creek Cave, the pontoon-boat tour on Vaca Lake, and communing with nature at the Belize Botanic Gardens and Chaa Creek Nature Reserve. Horseback-riding tours are also popular in 'cowboy country'.

2 hours return

FROM LEFT: CAVAN-IMAGES/SHUTTERSTOCK ©, WIRESTOCK CREATORS/SHUTTERSTOCK ©, LOES KIEBOOM/SHUTTERSTOCK ©

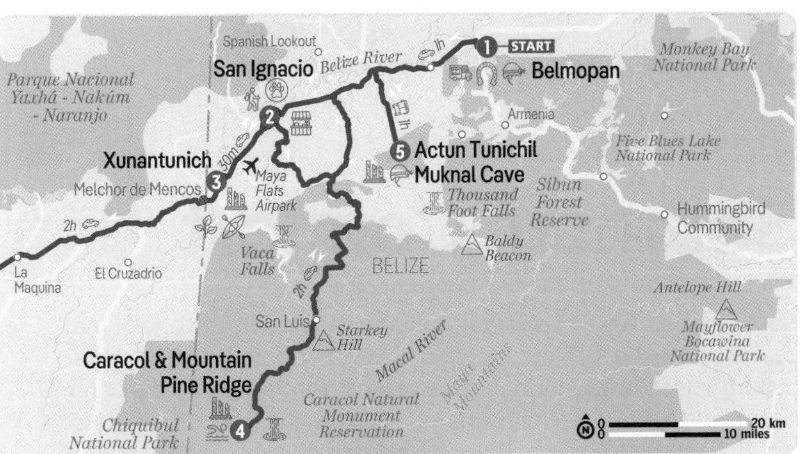

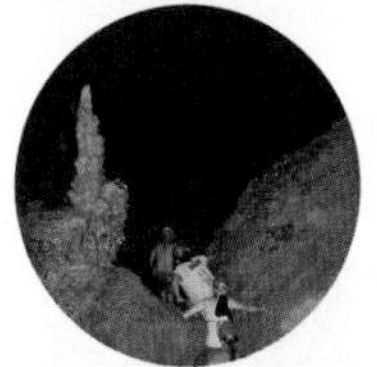

4

CARACOL & MOUNTAIN PINE RIDGE ⏱ 1 DAY

The trip to **Caracol** (p129), the mother of all Belizean Maya sites, is a full-day trip from San Ignacio or your lodge accommodations (51miles/82km), two hours each way). The rugged road trip (now partly sealed) is usually done in convoy and passes through beautiful **Mountain Pine Ridge** (p132); most tours stop at the waterfalls and swimming holes, along with the Río Frio Cave.

1 hour return (tour)

5

ACTUN TUNICHIL MUKNAL CAVE ⏱ 1 DAY

Another full-day trip from San Ignacio, **Actun Tunichil Muknal** (p128) is the most thrilling organized caving adventure in Belize. It involves a 45-minute trek, a river crossing and climbing, clambering and squeezing through watery caverns, culminating in a shimmering Maya burial chamber. It's a long and exhilarating day that will linger in your memory well after you leave Belize.

/ 2 hours (from San Ignacio)

6

GUATEMALA ⏱ 1 DAY

The famous Maya ruins of **Tikal** (p184) and lakeside town of **Flores** (p188) are tantalizingly just across the border in Guatemala. Tour operators in San Ignacio offer this as a day trip, but with your own vehicle (or public buses) it's not difficult to go alone. It's 9 miles (15km) from San Ignacio to the border and another 62 miles (100km) to Tikal and about the same to Flores.

DUYAN/SHUTTERSTOCK ©

Beach, Hopkins (p148)

ITINERARIES

Southern Comfort

Allow: 9 days **Distance:** 205 miles (330km)

Southern Belize is a captivating cultural melting pot and one of the country's most under-appreciated highlights. Experience Garifuna culture in Hopkins, Caribbean beach fun in Placencia and the central cayes, and Maya hospitality and village life in the Deep South. This trip also features some of Belize's best wildlife sanctuaries and national parks.

❶

HOPKINS ⏱ 2 DAYS

Start your southern journey in **Hopkins** (p148), a sweet little beachfront village with a strong Garifuna culture. Try your hand at Garifuna drumming lessons, enjoy local Creole food, visit Kalipuna Island and dance the night away at Driftwood Beach Bar. On day two head out to the barrier reef, or inland for adventure and wildlife at Mayflower-Bocawina National Park.

30 minutes

❷

DANGRIGA & THE CAYES ⏱ 1 DAY

Dangriga (p153) is the gritty seaside regional capital and transportation hub where you'll find Pen Cayetano's gallery and a Garifuna museum, but the main reason to visit is to arrange boat transportation to the central cayes. At South Water Caye (pictured) or Tobacco Caye you can snorkel or dive on the reef, with day trips available from Hopkins.

45 minutes

❸

COCKSCOMB BASIN WILDLIFE SANCTUARY ⏱ 1 DAY

Back on the highway, turn off at the village of Maya Center to access **Cockscomb Basin Wildlife Sanctuary** (p155), one of Belize's biggest and best protected wildlife areas, home to jaguars and other wild cats. Part of the eastern Maya Mountains, there are walking trails, waterfalls, river-tubing and accommodations. You can also stay with the Mopa Maya villagers in Maya Center.

1 hour 30 minutes

FROM LEFT: ROI BROOKS/SHUTTERSTOCK ©, DUARTE DELLAROLE/SHUTTERSTOCK ©, KEVIN WELLS PHOTOGRAPHY/SHUTTERSTOCK ©

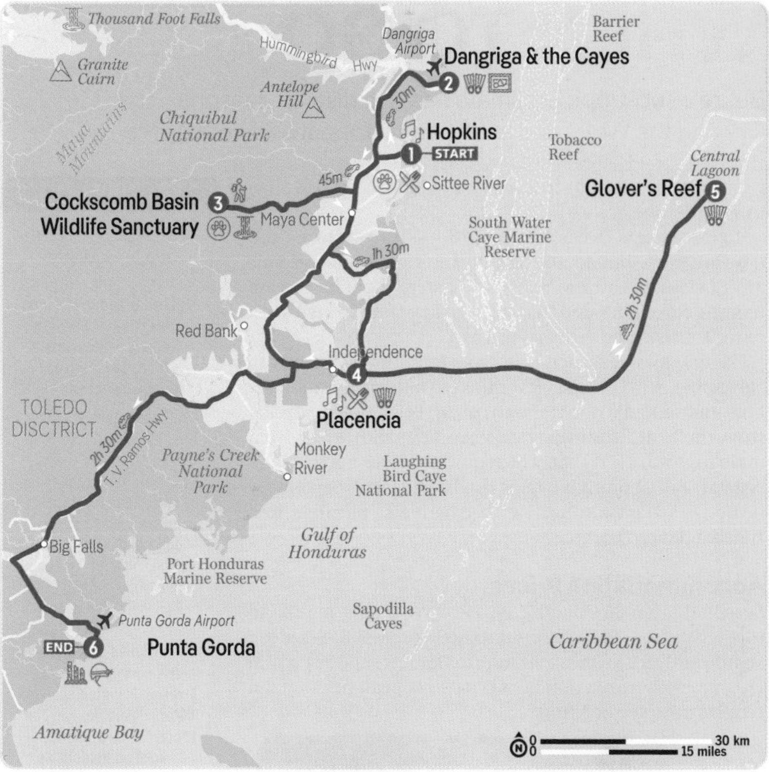

4 PLACENCIA ⏱2 DAYS

About an hour south of Maya Center, at the end of a long narrow, sandy peninsula, **Placencia** (p159) is the darling of southern Belize beach tourism and boasts the 'caye you can drive to'. Spend a couple of days snorkeling or sailing, sampling food with Taste Belize Tours or hanging out at the Sidewalk beach bars, listening to live music. It's also a good base for Glover's Reef.

2 hours return (tour)

5 GLOVER'S REEF ⏱1 DAY

The southernmost of Belize's three offshore atolls, **Glover's Reef** (p164) is a paradise for diving, snorkeling and sea kayaking adventures. There are island resorts here so you can easily spend a week, but if time is short, tour operators in Placencia offer fabulous day trips. This is one not to be missed.

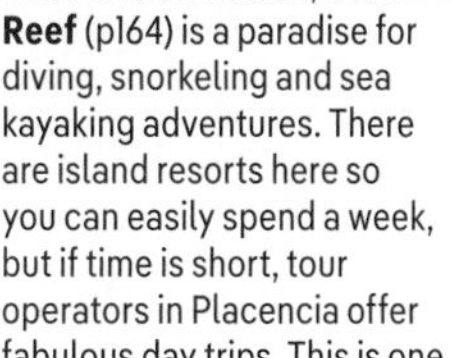

2 hours 30 minutes

6 PUNTA GORDA & TOLEDO DISTRICT ⏱2 DAYS

Take the Hokey Pokey Water Taxi from Placencia to Independence and an onward bus to the Deep South capital **Punta Gorda** (p166) – if you're driving you'll have to take the long way around. From here you can explore **Toledo** (p177) with tours, caves, Maya villages, chocolate-making families and the outstanding Maya ruins of Lubaantum.

WHEN TO GO

Belize's sub-tropical climate has two distinct seasons – the Dry and the Wet – and each has its appeal and drawbacks.

Unless you get caught in a hurricane, there's no bad time to visit Belize.

High season is December to April – skies are sunny and days are warm but not too humid. Additional peak seasons are Christmas to New Year and Easter. Shoulder season months November and May are a prime time to visit with fewer tourists and reduced prices.

The muggy wet season runs from late June/early July to November, with the heaviest rains in October. Humidity is high and sporadic rains (often at night) bring welcome relief from the heat. However, roads can be muddy away from main highways (4WD may be required), caves flooded, and coastal sailing or diving trips can be canceled. September is Belize's party month with carnivals, parades and Independence Day.

Accommodation Prices

Seasonal prices are notable on the cayes and at mainland tourist places, including upmarket lodges. Rates drop significantly for low season (June to October) and rise again December to April. Holiday periods hit peak pricing and require advance booking.

I LIVE HERE

SAIL AWAY

Neftali & Tammy Lemus operate Xsite Belize Sailing Adventures from San Pedro. @xsitebelizesailing

'The best time for sailing the cayes is April to June, when the wind drops and before rainy season starts. Diving clarity peaks from April into June and July but we sail year-round. The best thing about sailing from San Pedro is meeting new people and creating memories that last a lifetime for our guests. The reef is incredible – so clear it feels like you can touch the bottom though it might be 100ft deep.'

Kitesurfing

EASTER WINDS

The so-called 'Easter winds' are strong gusts that blow in over the Caribbean Sea from the east around late March/early April, bending palm trees and creating choppy waters on the coast and cayes. Not perfect for diving or fishing but prime for wind sports like kitesurfing.

Weather through the year

JANUARY	FEBRUARY	MARCH	APRIL	MAY	JUNE
Avg daytime max: **28°C**	Avg daytime max: **29°C**	Avg daytime max: **30°C**	Avg daytime max: **31°C**	Avg daytime max: **32°C**	Avg daytime max: **32°C**
Days of rainfall: **5.2**	Days of rainfall: **2.8**	Days of rainfall: **1.5**	Days of rainfall: **2.3**	Days of rainfall: **4.4**	Days of rainfall: **8.2**

SUNNY DAYS

Dry season is high season from January to April; the latter has a reported average of 258 hours of sunshine, which is welcome on the coast and the cayes. Strong winds start to blow in before Easter. October is the wettest with an average 11 inches (279mm) of rain.

Carnival Time

September Celebrations (p52) are the biggest event on the calendar, starting with the Battle of St George's Caye Day on September 10 and culminating with Independence Day on September 21. Throughout the country there are carnival street parades, elaborate costumes, outdoor concerts and ceremonies.

September

San Pedro has its own carnival in February with **El Gran Carnaval** (p83) bringing music, dancing and street parades.

February

The **Costa Maya Festival** (p83) is a three-day extravaganza in San Pedro focusing on international Maya culture. Live music and dance performances, theater, food and a beauty pageant draw crowds to Belize's favorite caye.

August

Holy Week is a popular religious celebration with services and processions leading up to Easter Sunday throughout the country. Good Friday and Easter Monday are public holidays.

March/April

I LIVE HERE

CAYO CLIMATE

David Hernandez, adventure guide and leader at Come Explore Belize in San Ignacio. @comeexplorebelize

'The best time for adventure activities in Cayo is February to May – the rains have dried so it's perfect for caving. Belize is a birding hub so we get a lot of migrating birds in Cayo from November to May. September and October are the slow season, when some caves close. It's a good time for visiting archaeological Maya sites and we offer immersive cultural tours with nearby Maya communities.'

Culture & Sports

La Ruta Maya (pictured right; p52) is a grueling annual four-day canoe race on the Macal and Belize rivers from San Ignacio to Belize City, ending with a big party.

March

The end of the race often coincides with **National Heroes & Benefactors Day** (formerly Baron Bliss Day, p52) on March 9, a big celebration in Belize City featuring a sailing regatta.

March

In Deep South San Antonio, the **Deer Dance Festival** (p169) features ritual dancing reenacting the hunting of deer, accompanied by Maya violins and harps.

August

In Hopkins and Dangriga, **Garifuna Settlement Day** (p153) is a unique celebration of Garifuna culture on November 19. Reenactments of the 'coming ashore' ceremony are played out, along with plenty of Garifuna drumming and dancing.

November

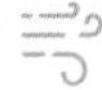

HURRICANE WATCH

Hurricane season in Belize is generally August to November. Tropical cyclones develop over the Atlantic Ocean several times a year but don't always make landfall with any intensity. When they do the results can be catastrophic (p58).

JULY	AUGUST	SEPTEMBER	OCTOBER	NOVEMBER	DECEMBER
Avg daytime max: **32°C**	Avg daytime max: **32°C**	Avg daytime max: **32°C**	Avg daytime max: **31°C**	Avg daytime max: **29°C**	Avg daytime max: **28°C**
Days of rainfall: **7.4**	Days of rainfall: **6.8**	Days of rainfall: **7.8**	Days of rainfall: **11**	Days of rainfall: **8.2**	Days of rainfall: **4.9**

Xunantunich (p129)

GET PREPARED FOR BELIZE

Useful things to load in your bag, your ears and your brain

Clothes

Light clothing: Belize's tropical climate is warm or humid year-round. For the cayes or south-coast resorts bring shorts, T-shirts, skirts, summer dresses and sandals or casual footwear.

Swimwear: Pack swimwear, including a rash vest. Bikinis are inappropriate away from the beach.

Casual clothing: Apart from formal occasions, such as church, dress in Belize is casual even when heading out for food or drinks. Revealing outfits may be frowned upon in some areas.

Raincoat: Summer (June to December) is humid with frequent heavy showers. Pack a light rain jacket or umbrella.

Hiking boots: Boots help with serious trekking but a good pair of running shoes or sturdy sandals will do for most walks.

Long trousers: Bring a light pair of long trousers and a long-sleeve shirt for cooler winter nights and to protect against mosquitoes at Maya sites or jungle locations.

Manners

Greetings Don't be shy about making eye contact and greeting strangers. Belizeans are friendly. The most common greeting is the Kriol catch-all 'Aarait?' ('Alright?'), to which you might respond 'Aarait, aarait?'

Queues Belizeans are firm in respecting queues. Where there is a turn system for services, respect the order.

Tipping Although tipping is not a custom, tourists are expected to offer a small tip at restaurants and for guides.

READ

Beka Lamb (Zee Edgell; 1982) A heart-wrenching novel about a girl's coming-of-age amid political upheaval.

The Last Flight of the Scarlet Macaw (Bruce Barcott; 2008) An unflinchingly honest account of Sharon Matola's fight against the construction of the Chalillo Dam.

How to Cook a Tapir: A Memoir of Belize (Joan Fry; 2009) Memoir of an American woman who spent a year living among the Kekchí Maya with her anthropologist husband in 1960s British Honduras.

On Heroes, Lizards & Passion (Zoila Ellis; 1991) Collection of short stories by Garifuna writer Zoila Ellis, portraying the lives of everyday Belizeans.

Words

English is the official language of Belize and is widely spoken in Belize City and tourist areas, but the majority of Belizeans speak Kriol or Spanish as a first language, or are multilingual.

Belizean Kriol is a Creole patois that derives mainly from English, with influences from Maya and West African languages carried over from the slave trade, as well as Spanish. Linguists note that it has its own grammatical rules and a small body of literature, as well as speaking populations in different countries – criteria that determine the difference between a dialect and a language. Kriol is used by more than 70% of the population, not only by Creoles, but also many Garifuna, mestizos and Maya who speak it as their second language. In the far north and south of Belize, Spanish is often the first language.

Some Kriol phrases.

Aarait? Hello

Yuh aarite? How are you?

Weh gaan ahn? How's it going?

Weh yu naym? What's your name?

Mee naym... My name is...

Weh you gwein? Where are you going?

How much fi dis? How much does this cost?

Lata! Good bye (see you later)

(Gud) mawnin' (Good) morning

Tenk yu Thank you

Ekskyooz mi, mek ah paas Excuse me (let me pass)

Noh? Are you OK?

Ah peckish I'm hungry (let's eat)

Da weh time? What time is it?

You da Belize? Are you from Belize?

Fu chroo? Really? (Is that true?)

Mi luv Bileez! I love Belize!

WATCH

Mosquito Coast (Peter Weir; 1986; pictured) Harrison Ford stars as the father of an American family in search of a simpler life in Central America.

Curse of the Xtabai (Matthiew Klinck; 2012) Belizeans are proud of this feature-length horror film, the first to be 100% filmed and produced in Belize using local cast and crew.

Running with the Devil (Charlie Russell; 2022) Subtitled *The Wild World of John McAfee*, this documentary follows the fugitive years of the tech millionaire, much of it in Belize.

Apocalypto (Mel Gibson; 2006) Mel Gibson's visually arresting – if not historically accurate – Maya thriller.

My Father Belize (Leon Lozano; 2019) Short film following a Belizean man who discovers a few secrets when he returns home to scatter his father's ashes.

LISTEN

Aban (The Garifuna Collective; 2023) Look out for anything by this acclaimed Dangriga Garifuna outfit; their latest album is *Aban (One)*.

Wátina (Andy Palacio & the Garifuna Collective; 2007) The late Andy Palacio was a leading figure in modern Garifuna music.

Biama (Lebeha; 2023) New album from the legendary Hopkins Garifuna drum school.

Ah Wah Know Who Seh Creole No Gàh No Culture (Leela Vernon; 1991) The late *brukdown* queen released this song from her album *Kriol Kolcha* in 2001.

ANDY KORTELING/SHUTTERSTOCK ©

Grilled lobster

THE FOOD SCENE

Belizean cuisine is as eclectic as its people, spanning Creole, Mexican, Maya and British and American influences, with seafood playing a major role on the coast.

Belizeans love to eat and in the towns and tourist cayes there are plenty of opportunities to sample local dishes shaped by Caribbean, African, Latin American and Maya cultures.

The staple dish, served as a side with most Belizean meals and often partnered with stew chicken, is rice and beans. It comes in two varieties: 'rice and beans,' where the two are cooked together; and 'beans and rice,' where beans in a soupy stew is served separately. Both variations are prepared with coconut milk and red beans.

On the coast, seafood features prominently, while down south Garifuna and Maya specialties are a culinary treat. In the north and west (Cayo), Mexican street food such as tacos, empanadas, tamales and *salbutes* are common snacks – Orange Walk and San Ignacio are particularly renowned for their street-food stands.

Farmers markets are a great place to find fresh fruit, vegetables and local food stalls. The best are in San Ignacio, Belmopan, Orange Walk and Punta Gorda.

From the Sea

Lobster is the king of seafood in Belize. The claw-less Caribbean spiny lobster is delicious and widely available in the cayes and coastal towns, except mid-February to mid-June, when lobster season is closed.

Best Belizean Dishes

RICE & BEANS
Belize's staple national dish accompanies everything from seafood to stew chicken.

GRILLED LOBSTER
Lobster is barbecued, grilled and served in everything from ceviche to omelets.

CEVICHE
Appetizer of seafood marinated in lemon or lime juice, garlic and seasonings.

Conch (pronounced 'konk') is the large snail-like sea creature that inhabits conch shells. During conch season (October to June), it is often prepared as ceviche (seafood marinated in lemon or lime juice, garlic and seasonings) or conch fritters. The local waters are home to snapper, grouper, barracuda, jacks and tuna, all of which make a tasty filet or steak, often prepared 'Creole-style,' where seafood, peppers, onions and tomatoes are stewed together.

Regional Specialties

The Garifuna people brought their own unique traditions, recipes and even ingredients to Belize. Cassava, a sweet-potato starch, is used to make cassava bread and cakes, while 'boil-up' is a popular stew of root vegetables and beef or chicken. The most beloved Garifuna dish may be *hudut,* mashed plantain cooked in coconut milk with local fish such as snapper.

Down south, Maya meals include *caldo,* a hearty spicy stew, usually made with chicken, corn and root vegetables, served with tortillas. *Ixpa'cha* is steamed fish or shrimp, cooked inside a big leaf.

Cocktails & Beer

Fresh tropical-fruit drinks and coconut water are healthy ways to quench a thirst, but are also commonly mixed with Belize's national liquor, rum. Sugarcane is northern Belize's cash crop and it's used to make several types of Caribbean rum, including dark, white and coconut. Rum punch is a common mixer but bartenders, especially on the coast and islands, will tell you the national cocktail is the 'panty ripper', a straightforward mix of coconut rum and pineapple juice on ice.

When it comes to beer, *Belikin* (p50) is the national favorite and the most popular brand, with varieties including regular and light, a popular stout and a line of craft beers. Beer, rum and imported wines can be found at the ubiquitous grocery stores.

Rum cocktail

FOOD FESTIVALS

Lobster Festivals The reopening of the lobster season on June 15 is cause for big celebrations in coastal towns and islands, with festivals in Placencia (p159), Caye Caulker (p89) and San Pedro (p83).

Cashew Festival (p47) This festival in Crooked Tree in May celebrates the humble cashew harvest.

Chocolate Festival of Belize (p169) Celebrating all things to do with cacao and chocolate – the Maya food of the gods. This festival is held mainly in Punta Gorda (pictured above) in May.

Belize International Music & Food Festival (p52) In Belize City in July, this music festival also showcases food from around the country.

Taco Festival (p105) Orange Walk celebrates the humble taco in November.

HUDUT	SALBUTES	STEW CHICKEN	FRY-JACKS	CHIRMOLE
Garifuna specialty of whole fish and mashed plantain cooked in coconut milk and spices.	Deep-fried tortilla topped with chicken, lettuce and onion.	Staple dish of boiled chicken with spices, served with rice and beans.	Deep-fried dough stuffed and served sweet or savory; popular for breakfast.	A soup made with black *rechado* (charred spice paste), chicken and vegetables.

Local Speciaities

Dare To Try

Hot sauce Marie Sharp's famous hot sauce can be found on just about every dining table in Belize. Made from habanero peppers in Belize since 1981, the iconic sauces have names like Beware, Belizean Heat and the fiery Red Hornet – at 150,000 on the Scoville scale, we dare you.

Cowfoot soup A glutinous concoction of pasta, vegetables, spices – and a real cow's foot (or feet). It's said to be 'good for the back'; in other words, an aphrodisiac.

Street Food & Snacks

Tacos Cheap and tasty Mexican street food with a variety of fillings. Popular in tourist areas and northern Belize.

Salbutes Belizean take on the tasty fried corn tortillas topped with chicken, lettuce and tomato.

Fry-jacks Deep-fried dough, stuffed with meat, cheese, beans, eggs, or butter and jam for breakfast.

Fry-jacks

Tamales Corn dough steamed in banana leaves and filled with meat, cheese and spices.

Sweet Treats

Cacao chocolate Specialty of the Maya people and still handmade at a number of places in Toledo, Cayo District and San Pedro.

Johnny cakes Belizean breakfast biscuit best eaten hot from the oven with butter and jam, or cheese and ham.

MEALS OF A LIFETIME

Di Bruwry (p51) Modern dining in the famous Belikin brewery in Belize City.

Hidden Treasure (p79) Head south of San Pedro for Caribbean delights on Ambergris Caye.

Guava Limb Café (p123) Wood-fired pizza and creative cocktails in San Ignacio.

Wish Willy (p93) Simple Belizean fare in a rustic island setting on Caye Caulker.

Rumfish & Vino (p160) Romantic gastrobar in the heart of Placencia.

Belize Food Tours (p80) Sample San Pedro eateries with in-the-know guides.

Chef Rob's (p150) Imaginative seafood and hot-rock-grilled steak at a seafront institution in Sittee Point near Hopkins.

Miss Bertha's Tamales (p143) Stop on the Hummingbird Hwy for Belize's best tamales.

THE YEAR IN FOOD

SUMMER (WET)

The Wet season (mid-June to November) isn't prime time for crops, though cacao (pictured) and coconut are produced year-round and lobster and mangoes are in season.

WINTER (DRY)

Many vegetable crops, as well as sugarcane (pictured), are planted towards the end of the wet season and are available through winter. Get in early for lobster before the season closes in February. Conch season is October to June.

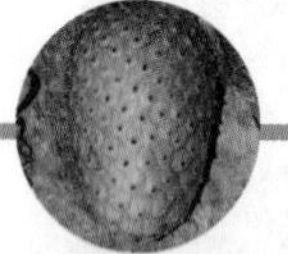

SEASONAL FRUITS

Bananas, pineapples and papaya are available year-round. Citrus (oranges, limes, grapefruit) grow best in early winter. Mangoes are harvested June to August, dragon fruit in May and soursop (pictured) in August and September.

LOBSTER SEASON

Lobster season is June 15 to February 15. Outside of this time, trapping, catching or consuming the local Caribbean spiny lobster is illegal, giving the crustaceans time to breed, spawn and enjoy life before they become dinner.

PAUL HARDING/LONELY PLANET ©

Lobster tail with beans and rice

Silk Cayes (p160)

TRIP PLANNER

DIVING & SNORKELING

Belize is a world-class destination for diving and snorkeling – after all, the world's second-longest barrier reef parallels the country's coastline and three of the four atolls in the Caribbean are here. From north, central and southern cayes to those stunning offshore atolls, whatever your level of underwater experience you'll find a place to explore and indulge in Belize.

Belize Barrier Reef

Belize has the second-longest barrier reef in the world after Australia's Great Barrier Reef. It stretches 190 miles (306km) from north to south and around the northern cayes it's as little as 1000ft (305m) offshore from the main islands.

NORTHERN CAYES

The most touristed part of Belize and accessible by a short flight or water taxi from Belize City, Ambergris Caye and Caye Caulker are the main bases for the reef and outer atolls.

Ambergris Caye is the largest and most-developed offshore island, so it attracts most divers. Ambergris also has the only two hyperbaric chambers in Belize.

LIVE-ABOARD BOATS

If you're a truly dedicated diver wanting to maximize the number of dives during your trip, a live-aboard boat is the way to go.

Your 'floating hotel' moves with you to the dive site, which gives you the opportunity to dive four or five times a day, including night dives. The boats that operate in Belizean waters are comfortable and well-equipped, and will even pamper you with hot showers on the dive deck.

All boats depart from Belize City. Live-aboard boats in Belize include the *Belize Aggressor III* and *IV* (aggressor.com). A seven-night all-inclusive package costs from BZ$6800 per person.

Popular Caye Caulker is smaller and more laid-back. Although accommodations prices are generally lower on Caulker than Ambergris, snorkeling and diving rates are comparable and there are only a handful of dive shops there.

The barrier reef is a few minutes by boat from either island. Diving here is quick and easy, though visibility is not always prime and the water can be somewhat surging. Between Ambergris and Caulker, Hol Chan Marine Reserve is the most popular snorkeling spot, thanks to renowned Shark Ray Alley.

CENTRAL CAYES

Best reached from Dangriga or Hopkins, the idyllic small isles and resorts of the central cayes are right on the barrier reef, with fewer dive boats than the northern cayes.

Hopkins is a good mainland base to explore the islands of the 62-sq-mile South Water Caye Marine Reserve, about a 30-minute boat ride away. There are resorts with dive centers on South Water Caye and Thatch Caye. Alternatively, daily boats from Dangriga depart for tiny 5-acre Tobacco Caye, only 10 miles (16km) from the coast, with budget accommodations and a dive outfit at Reef's End Lodge. This caye sits right on the edge of the barrier reef, providing excellent snorkeling straight from your cabaña, and is one of Belize's few beach-diving locations.

SOUTHERN CAYES

The southern cayes have developed into a diving hot spot, with excellent sites around Silk Caye and Laughing Bird Caye, reached from resort town Placencia. The sandy peninsula has some of Belize's best beaches, while laid-back restaurants and a range of accommodations make it an excellent base. Dive shops are scattered around town and connected with specific resorts.

Offshore Atolls

There are only four atolls in the Caribbean and three are right here off the coast of Belize. Lighthouse Reef, Turneffe Atoll and Glover's Reef lie offshore from the barrier reef, rising from great depths to just a few feet above sea level. You can enjoy day-trip dives from the main islands (most operators require at least 10 passengers), choose an atoll-based resort or take a live-aboard boat that concentrates on diving the atolls.

LIGHTHOUSE REEF

At about 50 miles (80km) offshore, Lighthouse Reef is the best-known atoll in Belize and the most popular, due to the

Loggerhead turtle

LEARNING TO DIVE

If you're not certified, dive shops on Ambergris Caye, Caye Caulker and at Hopkins and Placencia offer PADI courses. Open Water Diver qualification enables you to dive just about anywhere on the reef but Advanced Open Water is required for the Blue Hole and dives deeper than 59ft (18m) at outer atolls. A Discover Scuba course costs around BZ$350, and a three-day PADI certification course is BZ$1000.

Good spots for novice divers include: Mexico Rocks, off Ambergris Caye; Hol Chan Cut, south of Ambergris Caye; Faegon's Point and Tobacco Cut, near Tobacco Caye; Long Caye Lagoon and Long Caye Cut, Glover's Reef; any Placencia sites.

Blue Hole, an unfathomably deep sinkhole with stunning walls, swim-throughs and superb blue (and at depth inky-black) water that suits experienced and advanced open-water certified divers. Half Moon Caye Natural Monument has some fantastic dive sites, including Aquarium and Painted Wall.

Dive boats go to Lighthouse Reef from both Ambergris and Caye Caulker on long day trips. Serious divers should consider a live-aboard boat, offering the advantage of early-morning dives and fascinating night dives.

TURNEFFE ATOLL

Turneffe Atoll is the largest of the offshore trio, dominated by mangrove islands where juveniles of every marine species are protected until they make their way into wider waters. Sand flats, shallow gardens and life-filled walls are highlights of Turneffe dives.

The Elbow is the most beloved Turneffe dive site, with its enormous schools of pelagic fish and pods of dolphins. Visibility varies widely depending on the wind direction, but usually the deep water around the atolls guarantees excellent visibility and some of the most thrilling wall-diving you'll find anywhere.

The northwest site moorings such as Sandy Slope and Amber Head normally sit in 35ft to 40ft (10–12m) of water and the reef becomes a spur-and-groove system that leads to a vertical wall. East-side sites such as Grand Bogue II and Front Porch start a bit deeper, in the 40ft to 60ft (12–18m)range.

GLOVER'S REEF

Glover's Reef is the most remote and least visited atoll, but excellent island accommodations make it popular for extended stays.

First recognized as a bird sanctuary in 1954, it was declared a marine reserve in 1993, then a Unesco World Heritage Site in 1996. There's a marine research station on Middle Caye and the remains of an ancient Maya settlement are being studied on Long Caye.

About an hour's boat ride from the mainland, Glover's Reef rises from depths of well over 2000ft (610m); indeed, a dive site midway between Long Caye and Middle Caye is known as the Abyss. Several rustic ecofriendly outpost resorts here accommodate divers, kayakers and fishers. Otherwise, there's day-boat diving from Hopkins and Placencia, and live-aboard boats occasionally cruise this far south.

RESPONSIBLE DIVING

Consider the following tips when diving, and help preserve the ecology and beauty of reefs.

- Never use anchors on the reef, and take care not to ground boats on coral.
- Take home all your trash and any litter you find. Plastics are a serious threat to marine life.
- Avoid feeding fish. Rules are in place to prevent tour operators chumming or feeding fish.
- Minimize your disturbance of marine animals. Never ride on the backs of turtles.
- Practice and maintain proper buoyancy control. Major damage can be done by divers descending too fast and colliding with the reef.
- Take great care in underwater caves. Spend as little time within them as possible as your air bubbles may be caught within the roof and leave organisms high and dry. Take turns to inspect the interior of a small cave.
- Do not collect or buy coral or shells, or loot marine archaeological sites (mainly shipwrecks).
- Be conscious of your fins. Even without contact, the surge from fin strokes near the reef can damage delicate organisms. Avoid kicking up clouds of sand, which can smother organisms.
- Avoid touching or standing on living marine organisms or dragging equipment across the reef. Polyps can be damaged by even gentle contact. If you must hold the reef, only touch exposed rock or dead coral.

STUART WESTMORLAND/GETTY IMAGES ©

Scuba diver, Hol Chan Marine Reserve (p76)

Parasailing

THE OUTDOORS

From the Maya Mountains to the Caribbean Sea and from high on a zipline to deep in an underground cave, there's a Belizean adventure out there for everyone.

Belize is all about the great outdoors. Despite its small land area, there's an extraordinary variety of national parks and wildlife and marine reserves within its borders. Though not an especially mountainous country, the Maya Mountains and Mountain Pine Ridge areas provide enough elevation for some challenging jungle trekking, while the limestone karst topography around Cayo has formed some of the largest underground cave systems in Central America. Add the world's second-longest barrier reef and some epic inland rivers and you have a recipe for adventure.

Hiking

Inland Belize offers plenty of jungle trekking and many marked trails don't require a guide. If you're staying at an ecolodge, they often have their own jungle trails and may have guides.

In the foothills of the Maya Mountains, Cockscomb Basin Wildlife Sanctuary and Mayflower-Bocawina National Park, easily reached from Hopkins, have a network of walking routes, some leading to waterfalls and swimming holes. At Cockscomb you can climb Victoria Peak on a three- to four-day guided trek.

On the other side of the range, Mountain Pine Ridge is a cool, elevated region south of San Ignacio, with waterfalls, caves and swimming holes. You don't have to be a guest to hike at Chaa Creek nature reserve or walk through the Belize Botanic Gardens.

In the remote north, Río Bravo Conservation & Management Area offers nature trails from La Milpa Lodge and Hill Bank Field Station, while in the Deep South, Río Blanco National Park has forest trails and an awesome swimming hole.

HORSEBACK RIDING
Enjoy organized horse-back rides at ranches including **Banana Bank Lodge** (p139) and **Mountain Equestrian Trails** (p133).

WIND SPORTS
Kitesurfing, windsurfing and parasailing can be booked in **San Pedro** (p71), **Caye Caulker** (p89), **Hopkins** (p148) and **Placencia** (p159).

RIVER TUBING
Float in caves on a rubber tube on the **Caves Branch River** (p143), or down the Río Grande at **Big Falls** (p176).

FAMILY ADVENTURES

Children will enjoy the historical miniature train ride and waterslides of Kukumba Beach in **Old Belize** (p51).

There's plenty to do on **Ambergris Caye** (p70); swim off the dock, snorkel on the reef, meet the iguanas and bounce around at the Secret Beach Water Park.

Rubber tubing into caves on the **Caves Branch River** (p143) is a fun family experience.

The waterfalls of **Mountain Pine Ridge** (p132) are a great place to cool off with the kids. The best are Big Rock Falls and Five Sisters Falls.

Kids are welcome at drumming classes at **Hopkins** (p148) or book a half-day sailing and snorkeling adventure for the family.

San Ignacio has lots for families, including iguanas, chocolate-making classes, horseback riding and canoe trips into **Barton Creek Cave** (p128).

Caving

The Cayo District has extensive underground caves but only a few are open to the public. For most, you need a licensed guide so visits are usually on an organized tour. A popular trip near Belize City is the Nohoch Che'en Caves Branch Archaeological Reserve where you can float through a subterranean river in a rubber tube. The ultimate cave experience is the 3-mile-long Actun Tunichil Muknal where you wade, scramble and squeeze deep into the cavern to an ancient Maya burial site. Barton Creek Cave is entered by canoe and is filled with Maya artifacts. Near Belmopan, St Herman's Blue Hole National Park is one of few caves you can visit without a guide. Down south, remote Blue Creek Cave involves swimming and climbing.

Oriole

BEST SPOTS

For the best outdoor spots and routes, see map on pp40–41.

Kayaking & Canoeing

Belize has some important rivers that can be explored by kayak and canoe, while the Caribbean Sea offers virtually unlimited sea and lagoon kayaking opportunities.

At the Caves Branch River you can kayak interconnecting underground caves. Barton Creek Cave is also only accessible on a guided canoe tour. From San Ignacio, the Macal and Mopan rivers are great for paddling – the Mopan has a series of Class I and II (easy) whitewater rapids. San Ignacio and Belize City operators can get you out on the water. Inland canoeing and kayaking is also possible at Crooked Tree Wildlife Sanctuary's bird-filled lagoon and on guided trips on Shipstern Lagoon.

Sea kayaking is superb all along Belize's Caribbean coast with waters inside the barrier reef remaining calm during dry season. Kayaks can be rented at inhabited cayes such as Ambergris and Caulker, and at beach resorts like Hopkins and Placencia. Remote island resorts have kayaks for guest use. Glover's Reef Atoll is one of the great sea-kayaking destinations: Slick Rock Adventures is the premier kayaking outfit here, based on Long Caye. Island Expeditions is another sea-kayaking pioneer with base camps and trips on the outer atolls and Tobacco Caye.

FISHING
Fly-fish for tarpon, bonefish, barracuda and more from the **northern cayes** (p67), **Hopkins** (p148), or **Punta Gorda** (p166).

BIRDING
Spot migratory and endemic birdlife at sanctuaries including **Crooked Tree** (p64), **Shipstern** (p117), and **Red Bank** (p165).

SAILING
Sail into the sunset aboard a catamaran or yacht; best from the **northern cayes** (p67), **Hopkins** (p148) or **Placencia** (p159).

ZIPLINING
Zipline at a half-dozen courses, including **Nohoch Che'en** (p129) in Cayo and **Bocawina** (p154) in southern Belize.

ACTION AREAS

Where to find Belize's best outdoor activities.

Caving

1. Actun Tunichil Muknal (p128)
2. Nohoch Che'en Caves Branch Archaeological Reserve (p129)
3. Barton Creek Cave (p128)
4. Blue Creek Cave (p177)
5. St Herman's Blue Hole National Park (p141)

Hiking

1. Cockscomb Basin Wildlife Sanctuary (p155)
2. Mayflower-Bocawina National Park (p154)
3. Mountain Pine Ridge (p132)
4. Chaa Creek (p130)
5. Río Bravo Conservation & Management Area (p107)

National Parks

1. Cockscomb Basin Wildlife Sanctuary (p155)
2. Mayflower-Bocawina National Park (p154)
3. Crooked Tree Wildlife Sanctuary (p64)
4. Guanacaste National Park (p138)
5. Río Blanco National Park (p178)
6. Río Bravo Conservation & Management Area (p107)

Snorkeling/Diving

1. Lighthouse Reef (p86)
2. Hol Chan Marine Reserve (p76)
3. Glover's Reef (p164)
4. Turneffe Atoll (p85)
5. South Water Caye Marine Reserve (p157)

Kayaking/Canoeing

1. Glover's Reef (p164)
2. Ambergris Caye & Caye Caulker (p70 & p89)
3. San Ignacio (p122)
4. Crooked Tree (p64)
5. Placencia (p159)

THE GUIDE

Chapters in this section are organized by hubs and their surrounding areas. We see the hub as your base in the destination, where you'll find unique experiences, local insights, insider tips and expert recommendations. It's also your gateway to the surrounding area, where you'll see what and how much you can do from there.

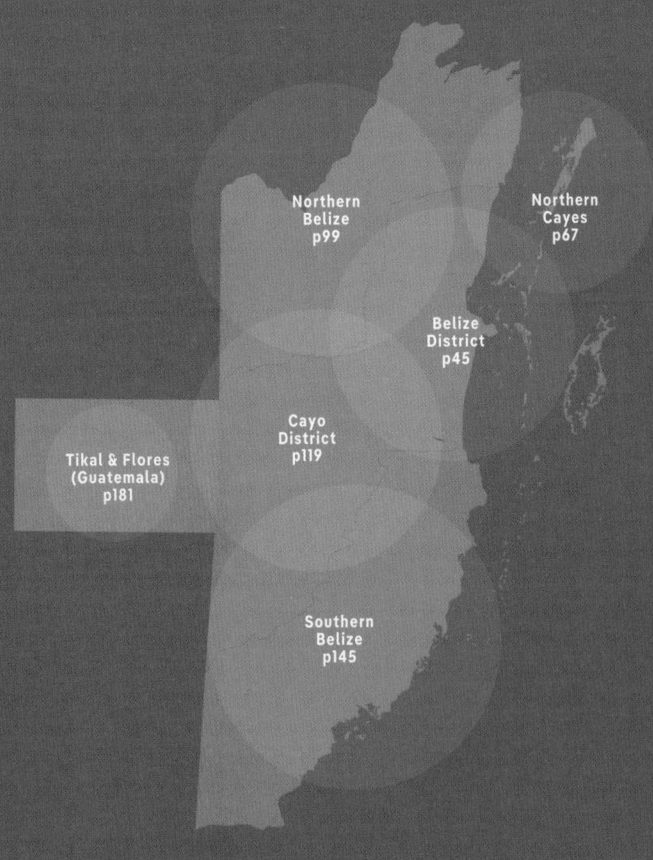

Horseback riding, Cayo District (p119)

Harbored boats, Haulover Creek (p48)

BELIZE DISTRICT

FROM GRITTY CITY TO WONDERFUL WILDLIFE

More than just an entry and exit point, Belize District is the historic heart of this country, an exotic swirl of cultures and surprisingly rich wildlife experiences.

Belize District is a tale of two regions. Belize City is the former capital, main city and the country's largest population center, but just a few dozen miles from the light urban sprawl in several directions brings you to some pristine tropical environs, wildlife sanctuaries and seemingly remote rural countryside.

Belize City gets a bad rap for its impoverished areas, some of which are plagued by crime and gang violence. But the seaside city also embodies the country's amazing cultural diversity and its colonial past, its neighborhoods are packed with people, restaurants, and shops that represent every ethnicity.

Beyond the city center, the gritty Caribbean urbanism crumbles, revealing a landscape of vast savanna that stretches to the north, dense tropical forest to the west, and lush marshland to the south. Many visitors never set foot in this region, preferring to fly straight from the airport to San Pedro or make a beeline for the water taxi, but there's enough to see and do in Belize District to easily fill a week, sampling the country's Maya heritage, including the museum at Altun Ha (pictured), Creole culture and luxuriant wildlife.

Belize District was the earliest colonial settlement from the mid-17th century; the Spanish had earlier driven out the Maya but never settled here themselves. The British settlers, known as Baymen, began the lucrative logging trade, floating mahogany and other hardwoods down the Belize River. The Spanish made several attempts to capture Belize City before they were finally defeated in the Battle of St George's Caye in 1798.

THE MAIN AREAS

BELIZE CITY
Former capital and cayes gateway.
p48

NORTHERN BELIZE DISTRICT
Birdwatching and Maya ruins.
p60

Find Your Way

All roads lead to Belize City: the main bus terminal is here, the international airport is just outside town and boats to the northern cayes leave from a central water-taxi terminal.

BUS

From Belize City's main bus terminal regular buses run to Belmopan via the Belize Zoo and Monkey Bay, and there are direct buses to Burrell Boom, Bermudian Landing and Crooked Tree.

CAR

A car will give you the most flexibility to explore the region and distances are relatively short. Both the Philip Goldson Hwy and George Price Hwy are in good condition. Some minor side roads are less well maintained.

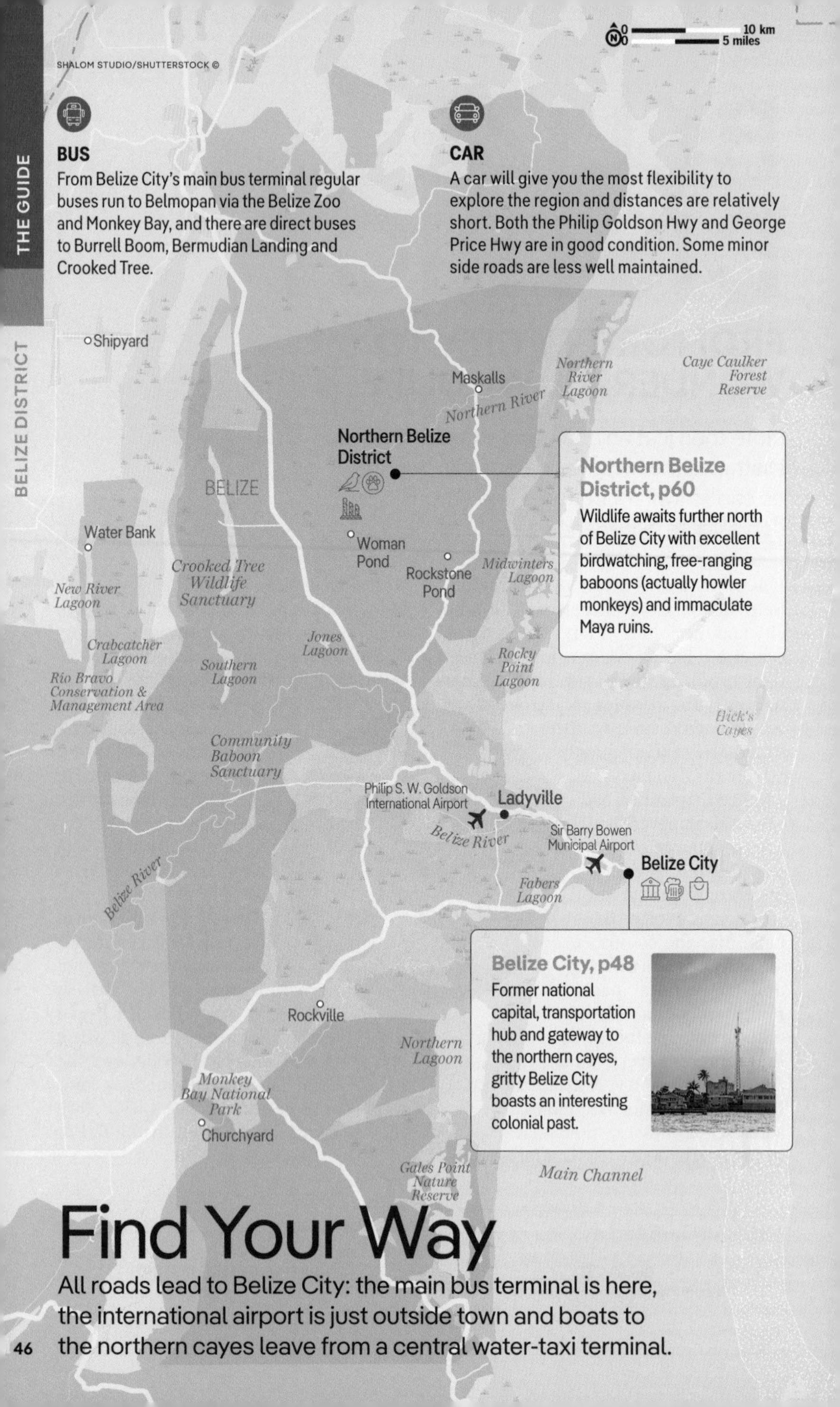

Northern Belize District, p60

Wildlife awaits further north of Belize City with excellent birdwatching, free-ranging baboons (actually howler monkeys) and immaculate Maya ruins.

Belize City, p48

Former national capital, transportation hub and gateway to the northern cayes, gritty Belize City boasts an interesting colonial past.

0 — 10 km
0 — 5 miles

Shipyard
Maskalls
Northern River Lagoon
Caye Caulker Forest Reserve
Northern River
Northern Belize District
BELIZE
Water Bank
Woman Pond
Rockstone Pond
Crooked Tree Wildlife Sanctuary
Midwinters Lagoon
New River Lagoon
Jones Lagoon
Crabcatcher Lagoon
Southern Lagoon
Rocky Point Lagoon
Rio Bravo Conservation & Management Area
Hick's Cayes
Community Baboon Sanctuary
Philip S. W. Goldson International Airport
Ladyville
Belize River
Sir Barry Bowen Municipal Airport
Belize City
Fabers Lagoon
Belize River
Rockville
Northern Lagoon
Monkey Bay National Park
Churchyard
Gales Point Nature Reserve
Main Channel

Temple of the Masonry Altars, Altun Ha (p64)

Plan Your Time

Belize District is a compact area that can be visited in a few days. It's best explored in your own vehicle but there are bus services to the towns along the two main highways and tours run from Belize City to main attractions.

Belize City & Beyond

Spend two days in urban Belize. Delve into history at the **Museum of Belize** (p49) and walk around the waterfront **Fort George** (p54) area. Taxi it south of Haulover Creek to **Government House** (p49). Head west for wildlife-spotting at **Monkey Bay Wildlife Sanctuary** (p57) and **Belize Zoo** (p57). Stop at **Belize Prison** (p56) to browse souvenirs or go manatee-spotting at **Gales Point** (p58).

Baboons, Birds & Maya Ruins

Head northeast of Belize City to **Burrell Boom** (p61). Further on, the real attraction is the **Community Baboon Sanctuary** (p62), home to noisy howler monkeys. The next day take the Old Northern Hwy to the beautifully preserved Maya ruins at **Altun Ha** (p63). Backtrack to **Crooked Tree Wildlife Sanctuary** (p64) for birdwatching on the lagoon.

Seasonal Highlights

MARCH

Belize City celebrates **National Heroes & Benefactors Day** with a regatta. **La Ruta Maya** finishes here.

MAY

Dry season ends and the **Crooked Tree Cashew Festival** celebrates the cashew harvest with music and dancing.

JULY

Humidity kicks in. In Belize City the **Belize International Film Festival** brings culture to town.

SEPTEMBER

September Celebrations (p52) are big in Belize City ending on September 21, Independence Day.

BELIZE CITY

Belize City
BELMOPAN

Belize City, historical former capital of British Honduras, is a lively, ramshackle waterfront city with a palpable colonial past. There's nothing particularly modern about this urban space, where narrow streets pass by dilapidated wooden houses, but it feels alive with colorful characters who represent every facet of Belize's ethnic makeup, especially the Creoles. Some handsome colonial houses, seaside parks and sailboats bobbing at the mouth of Haulover Creek give the city a photogenic quality. The Fort George area is well touristed, especially around the Tourism Village and water-taxi terminal, but some areas of the city southwest of Haulover Creek are less savoury.

The city was founded in the mid-17th century by British baymen (log-cutters) and grew with an influx of African enslaved people. It was from here in 1798 that the settlers elected to kick out the invading Spanish in the Battle of St George's Caye.

TOP TIP

Haulover Creek separates the downtown commercial area (focused on Albert St) from the more genteel Fort George district to the northeast. The Swing Bridge, which crosses Haulover Creek to link Albert St with Queen St, is the hub of the city.

Court House, Regent St (p50)

ROB CRANDALL/SHUTTERSTOCK ©

Colonial Belize City

A STEP BACK IN TIME

As the original British settlement and former capital, Belize City's colonial history dates to the 17th century and there are still remnants of the early days of British rule, along with museums offering an insight into Belizean history. The modern **Museum of Belize** (facebook.com/mobnich) in the Fort George District provides an excellent overview of the story of Belize, through exhibits housed in the country's former main jail (built in 1857). Fascinating displays, historical photos and documents bear testimony to the colonial and independence eras, along with an exhibit on slave history and a contemporary-art gallery. Upstairs is a gallery of the art of Belizian legend Pen Cayetano. Other sections are devoted to Belize's coins, bottles and birdlife.

Fronting the sea at the end of Regent St, **Government House** is a handsome white two-story colonial mansion that served as the residence of Britain's superintendents and governors of Belize from the building's construction in 1814 until 1996. Queen Elizabeth II stayed here on two royal visits in 1985

HOT SPOTS FOR A DRINK

Most partying around here is in San Pedro but Belize City has a few reputable places for a drink. Top-end hotel bars are one focus of social life where locals, expats and tourists mingle.

Bird's Isle
Island oasis at the southern tip of town; sea breezes, cocktails and cold beers.

Thirsty's
Local favorite with a balcony overlooking Digi Park (closed Monday).

Baymen's Tavern
Main bar at the Radisson with veranda and good food.

Riverside Tavern
Local beer, cocktails and decent food overlooking Haulover Creek.

Princess Hotel & Casino
Ageing waterfront hotel with lounge bar and small casino; rebranded as the Ramada.

WHERE TO SHOP IN BELIZE CITY

T-shirt Factory
Custom T-shirts, hats, bags and other printed souvenirs cheaper than at tourist shops.

Tourism Village
At the cruise terminal, lots of inflated souvenirs and a handicraft market outside.

Caribbean Spice
Small Fort St branch of the San Ignacio spice shop with spices, sauces, condiments and more.

CITY SAFETY

Belize City has a reputation for crime and some neighborhoods are best avoided, but if you take precautions and stay aware of your surroundings you shouldn't run into trouble.

The Southside district is known for gang-related crime, but north of Haulover Creek, the Fort George and King's Park districts are safe by day as is the waterfront and Regent St south of the Swing Bridge.

Be alert
Be wary of overly friendly strangers. Don't flash signs of wealth.

Main roads
Avoid deserted streets. Stay on main roads or take taxis to or from bus terminals and stops.

After dark
Always take taxis and don't go anywhere alone.

Di Bruwry

and 1994 and it was here, at midnight on September 21, 1981, that the Union Jack was ceremonially replaced with the Belizean flag to mark the birth of independent Belize. You can visit the grand exterior and grassy waterfront gardens though the interior was closed at the time of writing. There are plans to return various artifacts and furnishings stored at Belmopan to create the House of Culture museum here. Opposite Government House is **St John's Cathedral** (1820), the oldest Anglican church in Central America.

At the north end of Regent St, opposite Battlefield Park, the **Court House** (1926) is another impressive colonial building, complete with clock tower and central exterior staircase. It still serves as the High Court of Belize.

Iconic Beer & Brewery Restaurant

SAMPLE BELIKIN IN STYLE

Belikin is Belize's most iconic and best-known brand. Up there with Marie Sharp's hot sauce, the 'Beer of Belize' is everywhere in advertising – store fridges, bars, restaurants,

WHERE TO EAT IN BELIZE CITY

Bird's Island Restaurant
Burgers, steaks and seafood south of the center with a water view and a well-stocked bar. **$$**

Midtown Restaurant
North of Digi Park this modern restaurant-bar is well located and popular with locals for good international food. **$$**

Manatee Lookout
Overlooking the Belize River on the western edge of the city, known for kebabs and burgers. **$$**

and billboards. The name is from a Maya word meaning 'route to the East' and the label features a Maya temple from Altun Ha.

Belikin Brewery (aka Belize Brewing Company) is just outside Belize City in Ladyville (behind the international airport). The main reason to visit is for lunch or early dinner at the excellent **Di Bruwry** (dibruwry.bz; closed Mondays), a slick restaurant and bar within the brewery. As well as Belikin's offerings on tap, including craft beers, the menu ranges from burgers and pizzas, to tacos, burritos, chicken wings, steak and Belizean stewed chicken with rice and beans. Shiny steel brewing tanks form part of the backdrop behind the bar but the open-plan dining area peers into the brewery itself, with huge steel vats and pipes on show. Call the restaurant a day in advance to book a **brewery tour** (BZ$50 per person).

Along with the popular Belikin lager and stout, Belikin brews Lighthouse Lager, Landshark and a range of craft beers under the Two 5 label, including Coffee Lager, Valencia IPA and Bird Pepper Porter. All are on tap at Di Bruwry.

BOATS FROM BELIZE CITY

San Pedro Belize Express (belizewatertaxi.com) has regular daily boats to Caye Caulker and San Pedro from the San Pedro Water Taxi terminal daily between 8am and around 5:30pm. A one-way/return ticket to Caye Caulker costs BZ$41/73, and to San Pedro BZ$61/113.

Caribbean Sprinter (sprinter.bz) runs a similar service from a dock near the Swing Bridge on Front St between 8am and 4:30pm. Ticket prices vary but you can book or check prices on the website.

Belize in Miniature

MINI BELIZE AND A BEACH

Just 5 miles (8km) outside Belize City at the Old Belize Marina, **Old Belize** (oldbelize.com) is an odd museum and adventure park built to provide hurried cruise-ship tourists with a neatly encapsulated version of Belizean history and culture. To further attract cruisers the artificial **Kukumba Beach** was created next door, complete with lagoon, giant waterslide, *palapa*-covered (open-air shelter with a thatched roof) huts, beach bars and restaurants.

The **Old Belize Exhibit** attempts to pack the country's entire ecological, archaeological, industrial and political history into a 15-minute mini-train ride through a museum with various displays, dioramas and audio-visuals. It starts in the rainforest, with reproductions of the tropical trees and limestone caves that you'll find (for real) just a few miles west. A Maya exhibit has reproductions of temples and tombs, which you also might see for real a few miles north. There are displays on the timber, chicle and sugar industries, a reproduction of a Garifuna home interior, and a life-size model of an early-20th-century Belize Town street.

Old Belize and Kukumba can kill half a day. There are plenty of tour operators waiting to take you here from the Tourism Village in Belize City. The complex is closed on Monday.

Nerie's II
Belizean rice and beans with everything from curried lamb to stewed cow foot. Great value. **$**

Riverside Tavern
Great burgers, pasta and steaks and a popular riverfront bar. **$$**

Celebrity Restaurant
Swanky independent restaurant with extensive international menu; near Museum of Belize. **$$**

BEST CAFES

Spoonaz Photo Cafe
Quality coffee and breakfast best enjoyed under the green cloth umbrellas out the back, watching the sailboats bobbing on Haulover Creek. $$

Moon Clusters Coffee House
Cool, quirky cafe serving great frappes, many types of espresso, and pastries, donuts and muffins. $

Le Petite Cafe
Excellent bakery treats and fresh brewed or espresso coffee at the Radisson. $

Martha's Cafe
Vegetarian/vegan cafe in a fine old building overlooking the harbor with a great reputation for fresh healthy food and good coffee, juices and smoothies. $$

Festive Belize

CARNIVAL IN THE CITY

Belize City hosts a number of annual festivities that really bring the city to life. Even if you're staying in the cayes it's worth popping over for these events.

Formerly called Baron Bliss Day, **National Heroes & Benefactors Day** on March 9 features events including a regatta in front of **Baron Bliss Lighthouse**. It regularly coincides with the epic **La Ruta Maya** canoe race (larutamaya.bz), which finishes in Belize City. Born Henry Edward Ernest Victor Bliss in Buckinghamshire, England, in 1869 (the title 'Baron' was hereditary), Bliss was a wealthy self-made man with a powerful love of the sea and sailing who spent years living aboard his yacht *Sea King II* in the Caribbean, eventually dropping anchor off the coast of Belize. Though he reportedly never set foot on land in Belize, on his death in 1926 he created and bequeathed his considerable fortune to the Baron Bliss Trust Fund to aid community projects in then British Honduras. He stipulated that only the interest on the fund be used for these projects, so to this day the fund continues to provide grants for approved projects throughout Belize. As a result Bliss is a much-loved benefactor of the Belizean people and he is buried beside the lighthouse bearing his name in Belize City.

- **September Celebrations** start on September 10 (Battle of St George's Caye) and culminate on Independence Day on September 21, with two weeks of city-wide patriotic celebrations keeping the locals dancing in the streets. The Belize Carnival, a street festival held during this time, sees Belizeans don colorful costumes and dance to Caribbean beats.
- **Belize International Film Festival** showcases films produced in Belize and other Central American and Caribbean countries. It takes place at the **Bliss Center for the Performing Arts** usually in July (belizefilmfestival.com).
- The two-day **Belize International Music & Food Festival** on the last weekend in July features local and international performers and food from around Central America and the Caribbean at the city's Marion Jones Stadium.

Snorkeling on Goff's Caye

A SHORT BOAT RIDE AWAY

For island life most travelers base themselves on Ambergris Caye or Caye Caulker, but some of the southernmost of the

WHERE TO STAY IN BELIZE CITY

Harbour View
Boutique hotel and apartments and yoga retreat close the Tourism Village and water-taxi terminal. **$$**

Villa Boscardi
Charming eight-room midrange guesthouse with pool in the safe Buttonwood Bay area. **$$**

Radisson Fort George
The city's swankiest top-end hotel, well-located on the Fort George waterfront. **$$$**

Belize Carnival

northern cayes are much closer to Belize City. **Goff's Caye**, a tiny speck of powder-white sand right on the barrier reef southeast of Belize City, is one such gem. With nothing but some palms and a couple of *palapa*-covered picnic tables, the idyllic island offers good snorkeling and the amenities were renovated in 2022. It's essentially a cruise-ship day trip though and minimum numbers are required to make the trip. Try **Splash Wave Tour** (splashwavetour.com) in Belize City.

Fort Street Tourism Village

CRUISE SHIP SHOPPING

Cruise ships regularly visit Belize but don't dock in Belize City port. They anchor a couple of miles offshore in deeper waters and passengers are ferried into the **Fort Street Tourism Village** (Terminal 1) for shopping and land-based activities. The village has duty-free shops, bars, restaurants and souvenirs but it's all designed around cruise-ship passengers; outside travelers must present a passport to enter and most shops and restaurants are closed if the cruise ships aren't in. Since the village is beside the water-taxi terminal (which also has shops and eateries) and an outdoor craft market, the whole area is sometimes called the 'Tourism Village'.

BATTLE OF ST GEORGE'S CAYE

The Battle of St George's Caye is a nationally famous sea battle that occurred in 1798 between invading Spanish forces and a small band of British colonist Baymen, crucially assisted by their slaves.

The British and Spanish faced off on September 10 just off St George's Caye, about 8 miles (12.9km) northeast of Belize City. The settlers defeated the Spanish, forcing them to retreat within a few hours. It was the last time the Spaniards would attempt to invade Belize, ensuring it would remain the only English-speaking country in Central America.

September 10 has been a national public holiday since 1898, and is celebrated by proud Belizeans as a significant day in the nation's history.

GETTING AROUND

Belize City is small by city standards and easy to get around. The Fort George waterfront area is walkable. There's no local bus transportation but the main bus terminal for buses to elsewhere in Belize is 1.5km west of the Tourism Village. Taxis cost around BZ$10 for rides within the city and from BZ$60 to the airport. Confirm prices in advance with your driver. Most restaurants and hotels will call a taxi for you.

If you need to park on the street, try to do so right outside the place you're staying. If you're heading to the cayes, there's a large overnight parking area next to the San Pedro water-taxi terminal. Boats depart regularly for Caye Caulker and San Pedro from the terminal.

EXPLORING FORT GEORGE

This 2km walk follows the Caribbean seafront and passes several local landmarks and attractions. Allow half an hour for the walk and half a day for stops and lunch.

Start at the **1 Museum of Belize** (p49) for an excellent overview of Belizean history. Walk east along Goal Lane, past Celebrity Restaurant to the waterfront and turn right on Marine Parade Blvd. It's a couple of blocks to **2 Memorial Park**, dedicated to the soldiers of WWI. Continue south on Marine Parade Blvd, past the swanky **3 Radisson Fort George Hotel** until it becomes Fort St. Here you'll find the red-and-white **4 Baron Bliss Lighthouse**, built with funds from the Baron Bliss estate – his granite tomb is at the foot of the lighthouse. There's also a much-photographed Belize sign here and a small park across the road.

It's 100m to the **5 Fort Street Tourism Village** (p53) with its small collection of bars, restaurants and souvenir shops aimed at cruise-ship passengers. Look for murals showing Belizean life along the wall on Fort St. Further along is the terminal for the **6 San Pedro water-taxi service**. Keep going along North Front St to **7 Image Factory** (closed weekends), the country's most innovative art gallery. It stages changing exhibitions, usually of work by Belizean artists. Next door, call in for a coffee or a beer on the deck at the riverfront **8 Spoonaz Photo Cafe** (p52).

From here it's a short walk to the landmark **9 Swing Bridge** over Haulover Creek, separating Fort George from Southside. The 1923 road bridge is said to be the only remaining manually operated bridge of its type in the world. These days, it's rarely opened except to allow tall boats through before a serious storm. It's a good spot to photograph boats on the creek.

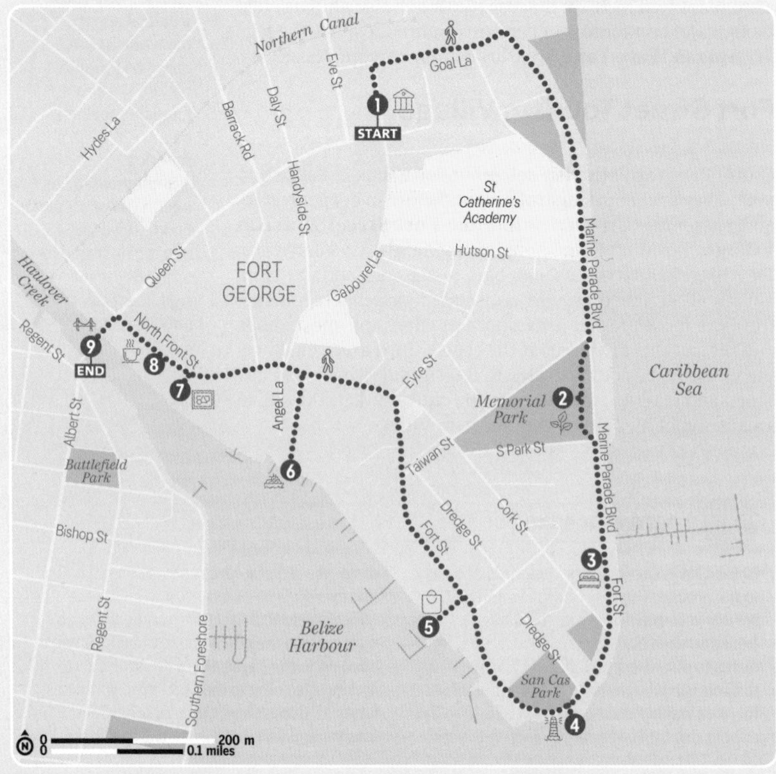

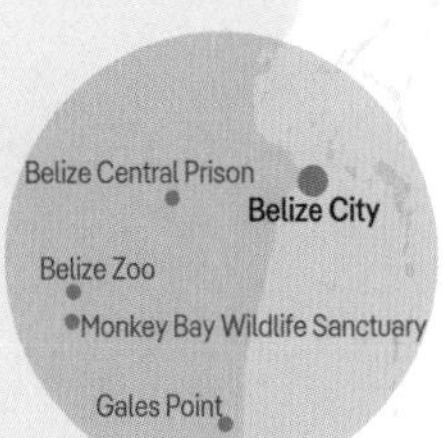

Beyond Belize City

You don't have to head far west of Belize City to leave urban life behind and find some surprising wildlife-watching encounters.

Formerly called the Western Hwy, the George Price Hwy stretches from Belize City through the village of Hattieville, and on to Belmopan and Cayo District. This part of Belize District is mostly agricultural, offering wide vistas of farmland with glimpses of the Mountain Pine Ridge in the distance. The main attractions here, both just off the highway, are the Belize Zoo, and birdlife and canoeing on the Sibun River at Monkey Bay Wildlife Sanctuary. The main reason to venture down the newly sealed Coastal Rd – other than heading to Southern Belize – is for manatee-spotting experiences at the remote Creole village of Gales Point.

TOP TIP

Since 2023 the Coastal Rd is sealed all the way from George Price Hwy to the Southern Hwy so is now the main route to Dangriga, Hopkins and Placencia.

***Cabañas*, Monkey Bay Wildlife Sanctuary (p57)**

HIGHWAY NAMES

The main highway out of Belize City towards Belmopan and San Ignacio was originally known as the Western Hwy, and to many locals it still is. In 2012 it was renamed as the George Price Hwy to honor the late George Price, the nation's first prime minister after independence. He is still widely regarded as 'Father of the Nation'.

Likewise, the Northern Hwy heading towards Orange Walk was also renamed in 2012 as the Philip Goldson Hwy after politician and activist Philip Goldson who served as a minister in both of Belize's major political parties (PUP and UDP). He was awarded the Order of Belize and, posthumously, the Order of the National Hero, Belize's highest honor.

PAUL HARDING/LONELY PLANET ©

Belize Central Prison

Prison Souvenirs

CRAFTS BY CONS

The 'Hattieville Ramada' (as it's called on the streets) is the only prison in Belize but it's hardly a high-security Supermax – it almost looks like the inmates could walk right out the front door or pole vault over the fence. Breakouts are not common but in 2020, 28 prisoners absconded after taking prison guards hostage. Still, **Belize Central Prison**, 18 miles (29km) west of Belize City, is a low-key affair surrounded by farmland where the inmates regularly work and it's renowned for its prisoner-education programs and the attached gift shop that stocks handicrafts made by the inmates.

The **Prison Gift Shop** is filled with items from the reformatory's renowned wood workshop, including hand-carved walking sticks, traditional masks and Belizean birds and animals crafted by the prisoners from locally grown woods, such as mahogany, teak and sandalwood. The shop is attended by one of the prisoners – in jail-issue orange overalls – between 8am and 3pm.

WHERE TO STAY BEYOND BELIZE CITY

Belize Zoo Lodge
The Tropical Education Center, run by Belize Zoo, has three large guesthouses and dorm-style private rooms. **$**

Monkey Bay Ecolodge
At the wildlife sanctuary, accommodations include private *cabañas* (cabins), rustic bunkhouses and camping. **$**

Cheers
Cheers Restaurant, on the highway near Monkey Bay, has three simple but spacious *cabañas*. **$$**

Take a Dip at Monkey Bay

CRUISE THE SIBUN RIVER

The **Monkey Bay Wildlife Sanctuary**, 34 miles (54.7km) southwest of Belize City, stretches from the George Price Hwy to the Sibun River, encompassing tropical forest, savanna and riparian ecosystems while providing an important link in the biological corridor between coastal and inland Belize. Across the river is the remote Monkey Bay National Park, which together with the sanctuary creates a sizable forest corridor in the Sibun River Valley. The park and the sanctuary get their name from a bend in the river – called a 'bay' in Belize.

A natural, privately protected area just off one of the country's main highways, this 1070-acre wildlife sanctuary and environmental education center hosts visiting tour and school groups but also offers accommodations and activities for casual travelers. A well-stocked library provides plenty of reference and reading matter on natural history and the country.

Activities focus on the Sibun River, where there's a popular swimming hole and beach about 2 miles (3.2km) south of the accommodations base. Guided jungle hikes can be arranged from the lodge to the river and other activities include canoeing and trips to nearby **Tiger Cave**.

Around 250 bird species have been identified at the sanctuary. Larger wildlife, such as pumas, tapirs and coatimundi, have been spotted on the 2-mile track running down beside the sanctuary to the river.

The rustic lodge here looks out to the sanctuary and is great value with *cabañas,* bunkhouse rooms, camping, a large dining area and hammocks swinging beneath *palapas*.

STORY OF THE ZOO

The story of the Belize Zoo began with filmmaker Richard Foster, who shot a wildlife documentary entitled *Path of the Raingods in Belize* in the early 1980s. Sharon Matola, a Baltimore-born biologist, was hired to take care of the animals. By the time filming was complete, the animals had become partly tame so Matola founded the Belize Zoo.

From these beginnings, the zoo has grown to provide homes for animals endemic to the region that have been injured, orphaned at a young age or bred in captivity and donated from other zoos. Sharon Matola sadly passed in 2021 but the zoo and the Tropical Education Center continue her conservation work.

Belize Zoo

WILDLIFE HALFWAY HOUSE

If most zoos are maximum-security wildlife prisons, then the **Belize Zoo**, 30 miles (48.2km) southwest of Belize City, is more like a halfway house for wild animals that can't make it on the outside. It's a good opportunity to see animals you're unlikely to see elsewhere – several tapirs (a Belizean relative of the rhino), gibnuts, jaguars, a number of coatimundi (they look like a cross between a raccoon and a monkey), scarlet macaws, white-lipped peccaries, pumas and many others.

But what really sets Belize Zoo apart is that the zoo itself – and in some cases, even the enclosures of

WHERE TO EAT BEYOND BELIZE CITY

Harpy Cafe
The cafe at Belize Zoo serves light meals for breakfast and lunch as well as snacks and drinks. **$**

Cheers
Popular roadside diner near Monkey Bay serving American and Belizean dishes and all-day breakfasts. **$$**

Amigos
Roadside *palapa* that's part-bar part-restaurant serving barbecue pork ribs and Belizean staples. **$$**

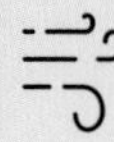

HURRICANE WATCH

Hurricane Lisa, the latest Category 1 hurricane to hit Belize, blew through Belize City and across Belize District in early November 2022. The winds did some damage to buildings and flattened parts of the Belize Zoo, but there were no fatalities.

Hurricanes and tropical storms are an ever-present danger for Belize during the wet season. The worst in history were: Hurricane Five (1931), which killed 2500 people; Hurricane Hattie (1961), which killed 275 people and destroyed much of Belize City; Hurricane Iris (2001), which killed 20 and left 10,000 homeless; and Hurricane Earl (2016), which caused US$100 million in damages.

individual animals – are relatively porous. This means that the wildlife you'll see inside enclosures are outnumbered by creatures who have come in from the surrounding jungle to hang out and forage. Among the animals you'll see wandering the grounds (aka 'free runners') are Central American agoutis (also called bush rabbits), huge iguanas, snakes, raccoons, squirrels and jungle birds of all sorts.

Avoid the hot afternoon hours and visit early (from 8:30am) or late afternoon (from 3pm), or book a night tour (many of the animals are nocturnal), though this must be arranged in advance.

Chasing Manatees

HANG OUT AT MANATEE HOLE

Remote **Gales Point**, 56 miles (90km) by road south of Belize City but around 30 miles (48.2km; 1½ to two hours) by boat, is a fascinating Creole village founded around 1800 by runaway slaves from Belize City. The traditional enclave sits on a narrow peninsula that juts out about 3 miles (4.8km) into the Southern Lagoon, one of a series of interconnected lakes and waterways between Belize City and Dangriga.

These lagoons are home to the highest concentration of West Indian manatees in the Caribbean, and the nearby beaches are Belize's primary breeding ground for hawksbill turtles, while the 14-sq-mile (36.2-sq-km) Gales Point Wildlife Sanctuary offers some amazing birdwatching opportunities.

Nature tours bring most visitors to Gales Point, and for the majority of these you'll need to hire a guide with a boat; the few accommodations here can set you up with one or you may be approached by a guide or a boat owner when entering the village.

The main accommodations here, at the very northern tip of Gales Point, is **Manatee Lodge**. The owners can arrange boat tours as well as kayaks for self-exploration on the lagoon. To the east of the village and lagoon on the Caribbean coast are a couple more ecolodges, including the recommended **Leaning Palms Resort** (leaningpalmresort.com), which can be reached by boat from Belize City or by car along a rugged unpaved road.

Manatees graze on sea grass in the shallow, brackish Southern Lagoon, hanging out around the **Manatee Hole**, a depression in the lagoon floor near its east side that is fed by a warm freshwater spring. The manatees rise about every 20 minutes for air, allowing spectators views of their heads

WHERE TO STAY & EAT IN GALES POINT

Manatee Lodge
Popular lodge at Gales Point overlooking the lagoon; eight spacious rooms, veranda and free kayaks. **$$**

Leaning Palms Resort
Beachfront resort and restaurant east of Gales Point village, best reached by boat from Belize City. **$$$**

Gentle's Cool Spot
South of the tip of Gales Point, village store and three small basic rooms with cold-water showers. **$**

Gales Point

and sometimes their backs and tails. A 1½-hour manatee-watching boat trip costs around BZ$150 per person. Around 100 protected hawksbill turtles, as well as loggerheads, lay their eggs on the 21-mile (33.8km) beach that straddles the mouth of the Bar River. For both species, this is one of the main nesting sites in the country.

Although the Coastal Rd has now been sealed all the way, the road into Gales Point is still unpaved, potholed and can be rough going in the wet. A high clearance vehicle is useful. Alternatively, you can arrange a boat for the two-hour trip from Belize City through Manatee Lodge for around BZ$500.

MANATEES

Belonging to a unique group of sea mammals comprising only four species worldwide, manatees are thought to be distantly related to elephants.

Manatees are herbivores and require huge amounts of vegetation each day, and graze on a wide variety of aquatic plants.A large adult can process as much as 110lb every 24 hours, producing a prodigious amount of waste in the process.

The best places for a chance to observe manatees are around 'blowing holes' or *sopladeros* (deep hollows where manatees congregate to wait for the high tide). In Belize you can observe them (but not interact with them in the water) at Gales Point and around Swallow Caye.

GETTING AROUND

The region is easily (and best) explored by car, though you might need a high-clearance vehicle to get right into Gales Point village (ask the rental company). The Coastal Rd is newly sealed.

Regular buses between Belize City and Belmopan run on the George Price Hwy and can drop you at Hattieville and the entrance to Belize Zoo and Monkey Bay Wildlife Sanctuary.

NORTHERN BELIZE DISTRICT

Northern Belize District
BELMOPAN

The region north and northwest of Belize City is home to two unique community-based wildlife reserves and the Maya ruins of Altun Ha. Other than a few small villages, the Belize River and two very nice jungle lodges there's not much else here, so plan your time around these three attractions with an overnight stay at Crooked Tree or Bermudian Landing. The Philip Goldson Hwy (aka Northern Hwy) stretches from Belize City into Orange Walk District, passing by the community of Ladyville. Turn west off the highway to reach Burrell Boom and the Community Baboon Sanctuary, detour onto the Old Northern Hwy to the jungle ruins of Altun Ha and, back on the main highway, take the turnoff to Crooked Tree for the bird sanctuary.

TOP TIP

The Old Northern Hwy is sealed only as far as Altun Ha, while the causeway road to Crooked Tree is unpaved but in good condition. Public transportation to either place is near nonexistent. The road is sealed to Bermudian Landing via Burrell Boom.

Little Blue Heron, Crooked Tree Wildlife Sanctuary (p64)

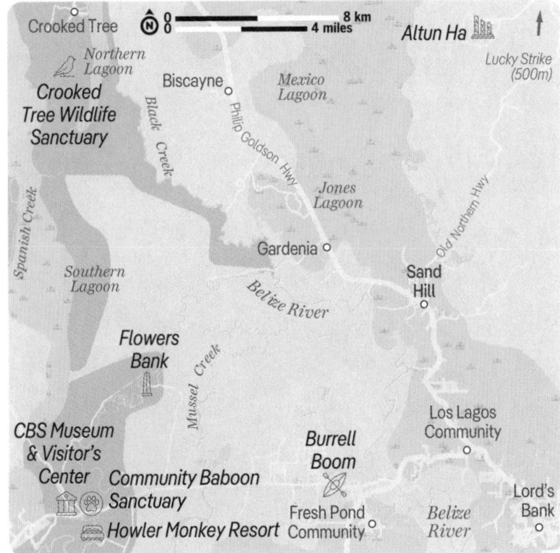

Boom Town

QUIET TOWN ON THE BELIZE RIVER

Ok, so it's not a 'boom town' these days but **Burrell Boom**, 19 miles (30.5km) northwest of Belize City, is a tranquil village with some nice riverside boat landings north of the center. It takes its name from the iron chains ('booms') that loggers extended across the river to trap the mahogany logs that were sent from further upriver. You can see the old boom and anchors on display in Elton Gillett Park in the village center.

The river setting is ideal for canoeing, birding and croc-spotting, though it's easier to organize these activities up the road at Bermudian Landing, where most travelers are headed for the Community Baboon Sanctuary. Locals take advantage of the lush fruit trees and distill a huge variety of fruit wines, especially sweet berry and cashew wines.

Burrell Boom is close to the Belize River and annually celebrates the passing of the **La Ruta Maya River Challenge** in March. Another tiny community along the river is **Flowers Bank**, about 10 miles (16.1km) northwest of Burrell Boom. A memorial here commemorates a group of local freed slaves who cast the deciding votes in favor of defending Belize City from the invading Spanish in the 1798 Battle of St George's Caye, a pivotal moment in the nation's history.

BLACK ORCHID RESORT

The only truly upmarket jungle resort on the west side of the highway, Black Orchid Resort occupies a serene spot on the Belize River just east of Burrell Boom. Spacious rooms feature big mahogany beds and private balconies provide the perfect place to sip your morning coffee while listening to the birdlife.

The verdant flower-filled grounds stretch down to the river, where canoes, kayaks and paddle boats are available for guests' use. Or just relax in the garden pool or day spa. Naturally, there's an inhouse restaurant and bar, and free international-airport transfers.

Scan this QR code for details about bookings and prices.

WHERE TO GET MORE INFORMATION

Community Baboon Sanctuary Visitor Center
Open 8am to 5pm. Admission and a nature walk costs BZ$20 (howlermonkey.org).

Crooked Tree Wildlife Sanctuary Visitor Center
Visitor center is open 8am to 5pm. Admission BZ$8 (belizeaudubon.org/ctws).

Altun Ha
Admission to the site and museum costs BZ$10. Open 8am to 5pm.

MONKEYS THAT ROAR

You will hear a howler monkey before you see one.

The howl peaks at around 128 decibels, which is louder than a lion's roar, an elephant's trumpet or even a chainsaw. This makes the howler the loudest of all land animals. A hollowed-out bone in the throat gives the primate the anatomical ability to crank up the volume.

The male monkeys make all the noise as a territorial message. Howler troops, that number about a dozen members, are matriarchal. The females only need one or two mature males around to defend their preferred patch of rainforest from hungry rivals.

So early in the morning and late in the afternoon the dominant male makes his booming broadcast from the treetops: stay away!

Howler monkey, Community Baboon Sanctuary

Howlers in the Jungle

HOWLS IN THE NIGHT

There are no real baboons in Belize, but locals use the name for the Yucatán black howler monkey (Alouatta pigra), an endangered species that exists only in Belize, northern Guatemala and southern Mexico and is one of the largest monkeys in the Americas. The **Community Baboon Sanctuary** (CBS), 27 miles (43.5km) northwest of Belize City, is a community-run, grassroots conservation operation that has engineered an impressive increase in the primate's local population.

CBS occupies about 20 sq miles (51.8 sq km), spread over a number of Creole villages in the Belize River valley. Since 1985, more than 200 landowners in seven villages have signed pledges to preserve the monkey's habitat by protecting forested areas along the river and in corridors that run along the borders of their properties. The black howlers have made an amazing comeback here, and the monkeys now roam freely all around the surrounding area. The sanctuary is home not just to monkeys, but diverse plant and animals species

WHERE TO STAY NEAR THE COMMUNITY BABOON SANCTUARY

Howler Monkey Resort
Riverside jungle lodge with eight rustic cabins, meals, boat tours and a bat sanctuary. **$$**

Nature Resort
Next to the CBS visitor center, comfortable good-value rooms and *cabañas;* meals available. **$**

El Chiclero Inn
Motel-style place in Burrell Boom village with air-con rooms and restaurant. **$$**

that are native to the Belize River valley. The conservation project also educates the community, supports research and promotes rural tourism.

The small **CBS Museum & Visitors Center**, on the main road in Bermudian Landing, about 12 miles (19.3km) west of Burrell Boom, has some displays on the black howler, other Belizean wildlife and the history of the sanctuary. Book here for a guided 45-minute nature walk (BZ$20) between 8am and 3:30pm on which you're likely to get a close introduction to a resident troop of black howlers. Along the way the trained local guides also impart their knowledge of the many medicinal plants. The walk is an easy stroll and starts across the road from the visitor center.

The center also offers canoe trips (BZ$120), horseback riding (book a day in advance) and rents bicycles. Since COVID-19, village tours and the local homestay program have been suspended but they might restart in the future. Night hikes and croc-spotting trips can be arranged if you ask earlier in the day. There are a couple of excellent rustic resorts next to the center so it's worth considering an overnight stop – **Howler Monkey Resort** has river frontage.

Altun Ha

WELL-PRESERVED MAYA RUINS

The Maya ruins that have inspired Belikin beer labels and Belizean banknotes, **Altun Ha** stands majestically 31 miles (49.9km) north of Belize City, off the Old Northern Hwy. While smaller and less imposing than some other Maya sites in the country, Altun Ha, with its immaculate central plaza, is still spectacular and well worth the short detour to get here. The original site covered 1500 acres, but what visitors see today is the central ceremonial precinct of two plazas surrounded by temples. The ruins were originally excavated in the 1960s and now look squeaky clean following a stabilization and conservation program from 2000.

Altun Ha was a rich and important Maya trading and agricultural town with a population of 8000 to 10,000. It existed by at least 200 BCE, perhaps even several centuries earlier, and flourished until the mysterious collapse of Classic Maya civilization around 900 CE. Most of the temples date from around 550 to 650 CE, though, like many Maya temples, most of them are composed of several layers, having been built over periodically in a series of renewals.

In Plaza A, structure A-1 is sometimes called the **Temple of the Green Tomb**. Deep within it was discovered the tomb of

JADE HEAD

The jade head of Maya sun god Kinich Ahau, the largest well-carved jade object ever recovered from a Maya archaeological site, was unearthed at Altun Ha in 1968, discovered in the Temple of the Masonry Altars aka Temple of the Sun God.

The size and status of the jade carving likely indicated that Altun Ha was a wealthy Maya civilization and that the person it was buried with held a position of great importance.

Today, the original priceless head is usually kept securely in the vault of the Central Bank, though there's a replica on display in a glass case in the museum at Altun Ha.

WHERE TO STAY & EAT AT CROOKED TREE

Bird's Eye View Lodge
Largest resort in Crooked Tree on the lagoon with 25 rooms and a host of activities. $$

Carrie's Kitchen
Reliable kitchen south of the bridge where Carrie serves local faves into the evening. $

Village Stores
There are two village stores stocking groceries, snacks and drinks, including alcohol. $

BELIZE BOUTIQUE RESORT & SPA

Located in splendid isolation, Belize Boutique Resort takes the jungle-lodge-and-spa concept to extremes of expensive pampering. There are luxurious amenities and a slew of health and rejuvenation treatments.

Lush tropical grounds harbor individually designed rooms in a variety of African, Creole, Maya and even Gaudíesque styles – including honeymoon and 'fertility' suites and a jungle tree house.

There are two pools and a stylish open-air restaurant. The resort is located 2 miles (3.2km) north of Maskall village and 13 miles (20.9km) from Altun Ha.

a priest-king dating from around 600 CE. Many riches were found intact: shell necklaces, pottery, pearls, stingray spines used in bloodletting rites, ceremonial flints and the nearly 300 jade objects that gave rise to the name Green Tomb.

The largest and most important temple is the **Temple of the Masonry Altars** (B-4), also known as the Temple of the Sun God. The restored structure dates from the first half of the 7th century CE and takes its name from altars on which copal was burned and beautifully carved jade pieces were smashed in sacrifice. This is the Maya temple depicted (in somewhat stylized form) on Belikin beer labels.

Excavation of the structure in 1968 revealed several priestly tombs. Most had been destroyed or desecrated, but one, tomb B-4/7, contained the remains of an elderly personage accompanied by numerous jade objects, including a unique and priceless 6in-tall carved head of Kinich Ahau, the Maya sun god – a national treasure. An illustration of the carving appears on the top-left corner of Belizean banknotes.

A path heading south from structure B-6 leads 600yd (549m) through the jungle to a broad pond that was the main reservoir of the ancient town.

At the site entrance there is a small **museum** with informative displays covering the history of Altun Ha and a full-scale model of the Kinich Ahau carving. You can find licensed guides (BZ$20 per visitor) outside the museum building. While you don't need a guide to find your way around the site, they can show you details you might otherwise miss. Toilets, souvenir stands and food and drink stalls are near the ticket office, and the site has good wheelchair access.

Crooked Tree

BIRDWATCHING BY THE LAGOON

Reached via a causeway spanning the Northern Lagoon from the Philip Goldson Hwy, **Crooked Tree**, 35 miles (56.3km) northwest of Belize City, is a small secluded village surrounded by sublime lagoons, wetlands and the expansive wildlife and bird sanctuary of the same name. Between November and April, migrating birds flock to the lagoons, rivers and swamps of the huge **Crooked Tree Wildlife Sanctuary**. The best birdwatching is in April and May, when the low level of the lagoon draws thousands of birds into the open to seek food in the shallows, but at any time between December and May birdwatchers will be in heaven. Boat-billed and bare-throated tiger herons, Muscovy and black-bellied whistling ducks, snail kites, ospreys, black vultures, black-collared hawks and all of

WHERE TO STAY AT CROOKED TREE

Jacana Inn
Facing the lagoon, this budget hotel is well placed and great value. $

Beck's Bed & Breakfast
Set well back from the lagoon, this three-room home is one of Crooked Tree's best choices. $$

Tillet's Village Lodge
Long-running guesthouse north of the bridge with comfortable budget rooms. $

Crooked Tree Wildlife Sanctuary

Belize's five species of kingfisher are among some 300 species recorded here. Jabiru storks, the largest flying bird in the Americas, congregate here year-round.

At the village entrance, just off the causeway, stop by the **CTWS Visitor Center** to browse the interesting displays and pay your one-off admission fee, which is valid for as long as you stay in the village. The helpful, knowledgeable staff will provide a village and trail map for self-guided exploration, as well as information on local bird guides.

Founded in the early 18th century, Crooked Tree – 33 miles (53.1km) from Belize City – may be the oldest non-indigenous village in Belize. Early logwood cutters boated up Belize River and Black Creek to a giant lagoon marked by a tree that seemingly grew in every direction. These 'crooked trees' (logwood trees, in fact) still grow in abundance around the lagoon. Until the 3.5-mile (5.6km) causeway from the highway was built in 1984, the only way to get here was by boat. These days there are half a dozen lodges for overnight stays. Most can arrange lagoon **boat tours**, though the main operator is **Bird's Eye View Lodge**, which runs tours and has kayaks for rent. A series of walking trails and boardwalks weave along the lakeshore and through and beyond the village.

CROOKED TREE TOURS

While you can find local birding guides around Crooked Tree village, a good bet for joining boat tours is Bird's Eye View Lodge (birdseyeviewbelize.com) on the lagoon south of the causeway.

Tours include a two- to three-hour birding boat cruise, sunset cruise,and croc-spotting night safari, as well as guided nature walks. The lodge also offers canoe and kayak rental, bicycle rental and horseback riding.

Scan this QR code for more details and pricing.

GETTING AROUND

Most places in the region are connected to Belize City by infrequent bus services that usually leave the villages early in the morning and return in the late afternoon. There are no bus connections between villages on different side roads so travelers must either backtrack to Belize City or make their way out to the Philip Goldson Hwy and try to flag down a passing service. Renting a vehicle is the best way to fully explore the region.

Street signs, Caye Caulker (p89)

NORTHERN CAYES

ISLAND LIFE AND THE DEEP BLUE

Speckling the Caribbean Sea and straddling the barrier reef, this is the Belize of postcards and dreams.

BELMOPAN

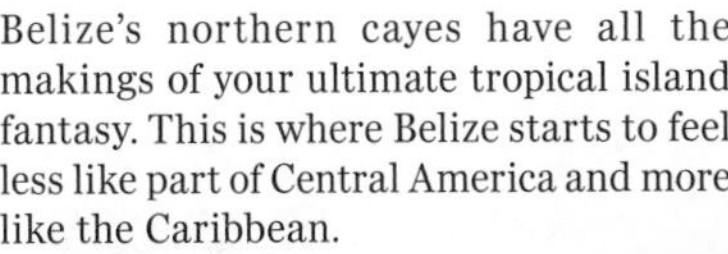

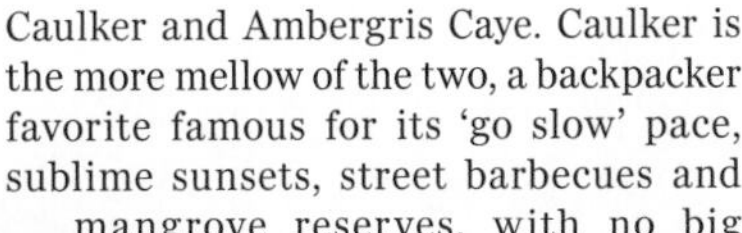

Belize's northern cayes have all the makings of your ultimate tropical island fantasy. This is where Belize starts to feel less like part of Central America and more like the Caribbean.

For holidaymakers lounging on Caye Caulker (pictured) or Ambergris Caye it might be hard to conceive but there are more than 200 coral cayes and islands scattered around this region off the coast of North Belize, along with the world's second-longest barrier reef and two world-class atolls in Lighthouse Reef and Turneffe Atoll. The Blue Hole is the most famous dive site here and an enduring symbol of Belize.

Regular water taxis from Belize City (and from Corozal and Chetumal) ferry travelers to the main islands of Caye Caulker and Ambergris Caye. Caulker is the more mellow of the two, a backpacker favorite famous for its 'go slow' pace, sublime sunsets, street barbecues and mangrove reserves, with no big resort developments. San Pedro, capital of Ambergris Caye, is more upbeat and touristy, full of golf carts, fabulous eateries, expats and beach bars, but still moving to an easy island pace.

These islands are the main population and tourist centers but they're only the beginning: just a few miles offshore, the Belize Barrier Reef flourishes for 190 awe-inspiring miles (306km), offering unparalleled opportunities to explore canyons and coral, snorkel with nurse sharks and stingrays, and to dive among schools of fish painted every color of the palette.

THE MAIN AREAS

AMBERGRIS CAYE
The 'Big Island' and party central.
p70

CAYE CAULKER
Laid-back island paradise.
p89

Find Your Way

Most travelers stay in San Pedro or on Caye Caulker so getting around is a breeze with regular water taxis shuttling between Belize City and the main islands and tour operators taking care of transportation to dive sites. Scheduled passenger boats also connect San Pedro with Corozal, Sarteneja and Chetumal (Mexico), and there are direct flights from Belize City to both islands.

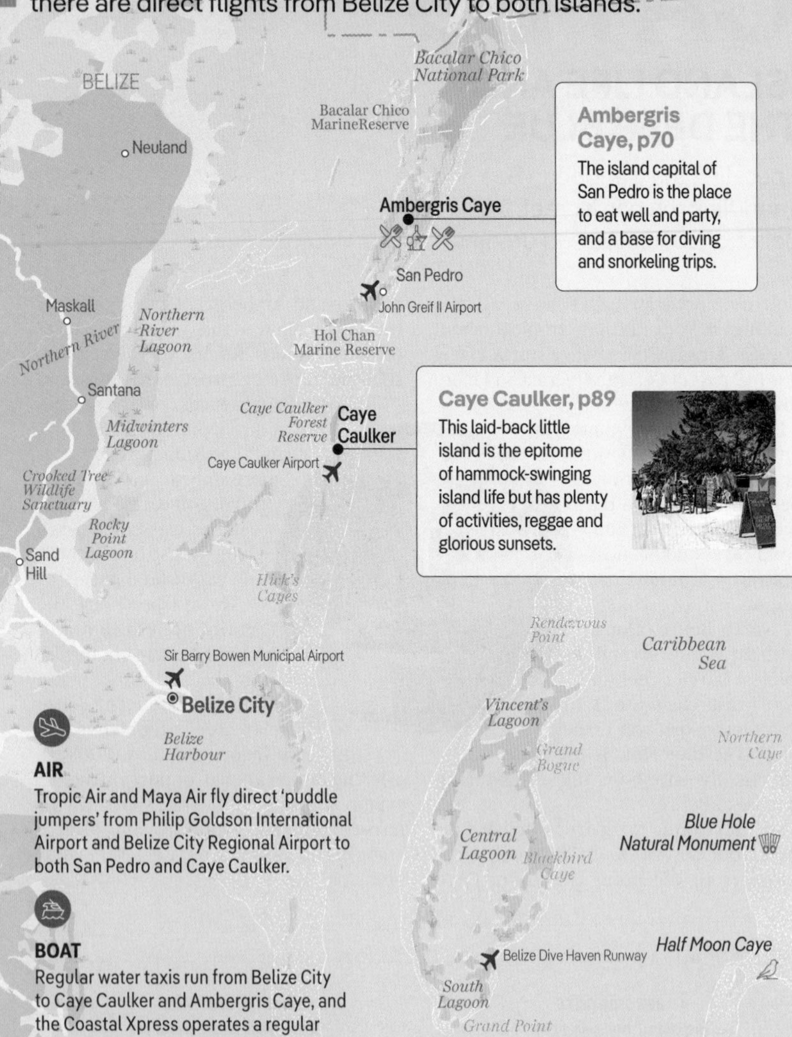

Ambergris Caye, **p70**

The island capital of San Pedro is the place to eat well and party, and a base for diving and snorkeling trips.

Caye Caulker, **p89**

This laid-back little island is the epitome of hammock-swinging island life but has plenty of activities, reggae and glorious sunsets.

AIR

Tropic Air and Maya Air fly direct 'puddle jumpers' from Philip Goldson International Airport and Belize City Regional Airport to both San Pedro and Caye Caulker.

BOAT

Regular water taxis run from Belize City to Caye Caulker and Ambergris Caye, and the Coastal Xpress operates a regular passenger boat service between San Pedro and the resorts on the North Island.

Central Park, San Pedro (p71)

Plan Your Time

Exploring the northern cayes isn't so much about traveling from place to place as it is about settling into an island location and then taking trips to the reef and atolls. Most spend time on both Ambergris Caye and Caye Caulker.

Ambergris Caye

Most travelers stay in San Pedro but with a bicycle or golf cart you can explore further afield. Enjoy swimming and sun at **Secret Beach** (p71). Take a day trip by boat to **Bacalar Chico National Park** (p76) or a dive and snorkel site, including **Lighthouse Reef** (p86) and **Turneffe Atoll** (p85). Or try **spa treatments** (p79), **food tours** (p80) and **watersports** (p78) in San Pedro or North Island resorts.

Caye Caulker

Caye Caulker can be explored easily on foot or by bicycle. Spend a day north of the Split visiting **Caye Caulker Forest Reserve** (p93) and **Northside Beach** (p92) and swimming at the Split itself. Take a snorkeling trip to **Shark Ray Alley** (p76) or **Caye Caulker Marine Reserve** (p93) and a **sunset sailing cruise** (p82). Caulker is more laid-back than San Pedro and tends to be a bit cheaper.

Seasonal Highlights

DECEMBER TO APRIL

Dry season means sunny days and mostly calm sea conditions, though winds pick up prior to Easter celebrations in April.

FEBRUARY

The weekend before Lent is a big party in San Pedro. Parades and costumes are replaced with body-painting and flour-fighting.

JUNE

The reopening of the lobster season is a time to celebrate everything lobster-related in San Pedro and Caye Caulker.

AUGUST

San Pedro's **Costa Maya Festival** has Maya music, parades, dancing and drinking, and the crowning of a festival queen.

AMBERGRIS CAYE

Ambergris Caye

BELMOPAN

'La Isla Bonita' (the beautiful island) is the star of Belize's tourism industry, striking a balance between resort development and laid-back island lifestyle. This is the prime base for diving and snorkeling trips to the reef and beyond, the best place to dine and dance in Belize and the kind of island where you can easily find your own slice of tropical paradise.

It can get busy around San Pedro in high season, when a procession of golf carts clog the streets, but explore south and north of the main town and you'll find it's not really crowded at all. The south has a distinctly local feel, while the North Island has a string of evermore remote resorts and condos lining the eastern seafront. Days can be consumed with simple pleasures like riding a bike along a windswept beach path, watching the sunset with a rum punch, swimming at Secret Beach or sampling myriad island cuisines.

TOP TIP

The island is long and thin, measuring 25 miles (40.2km) long and 5 miles (8km) across at its widest point. Get around by bike or golf cart. Otherwise, a regular water shuttle runs between Amigos Dock and the North Island resorts.

Hammocks, Ambergris Caye

Sunny San Pedro

DREAMING OF SAN PEDRO

When Madonna sang of her dreams of **San Pedro** ('Last night I dreamt of San Pedro...'), some say she was referring to the captivating main town on Ambergris Caye, though Madonna herself said that San Pedro could be any tropical hideaway. Still, locals have adopted the song title 'La Isla Bonita' as a nickname for their island paradise, and who can blame them?

For many people Ambergris Caye *is* San Pedro and that's what most call the island. But technically the name refers to the town that sprawls around the southern part of the caye, between the airstrip and the bridge leading to the North Island.

Once a laid-back little village dotted with colorful Caribbean houses, San Pedro is now a busy tourist town, lined with souvenir shops and beach bars, restaurants and taco stands. Water taxis dock in the town center and golf carts clog the streets at varying times of day or night. Still, there's an infectious vibe, some fabulous local restaurants, waterfront bars and a few hidden attractions.

The central plaza is a meeting place on the waterfront with the San Pedro sign and the clocktower as obvious landmarks. Many dive trips and sailing tours leave from near here and the central area is eminently walkable so you can save on the golf cart for a day or two and explore the backstreets and waterfront, mingling with the many tourists, expats, locals and layabouts that give San Pedro its Belizean island charm.

Secret Beach

THE NOT-SO-SECRET BEACH

The island's worst-kept secret is a pretty stretch of seaweed-free soft white sand on the western shoreline of Ambergris, known as **Secret Beach**. Where the road ends there are beach bars and restaurants such as **Pirates**, wooden docks jutting out into the clear turquoise water, sunbeds, umbrellas and thumping reggae. Further north, **Secret Beach Water Park** has floating *cabañas* (cabins), floating volleyball and all sorts of giant inflatable toys. You can rent paddleboards, kayaks and canoes. It's touristy but still a lot of fun and local families come here to relax on weekends. To the left of the main entrance, **Secret Beach Cabanas** (secretbeachcabanas.com) is the place to stay. The restaurant-bar does good fish tacos, or grab some takeaway and cheap beer at **Aurora's** food shack.

WHY I LOVE AMBERGRIS CAYE

Paul Harding, writer

'It's hard to think of a reason not to love Ambergris Caye and San Pedro. Even without the diving and snorkeling opportunities of the barrier reef and outer atolls, the island offers so much energy.

Locals love to share their island's riches and the food offerings alone can fill your time as you graze at local taco and fry-jack restaurants or dig in to seafood at overwater *palapa* restaurants. I love the hole-in-the-wall restaurants, rum tastings, late afternoon happy hours, sunsets and evening music. I even enjoy getting around in a golf cart.'

WHERE TO DRINK ON AMBERGRIS CAYE

Palapa Bar
San Pedro's most famous overwater bar where you can float in rubber rings with a beer or cocktail.

Sandy Toes
A short walk north of Palapa, Sandy Toes does great food and morphs into a popular local music bar later.

303 Belize
One of the newer overwater *palapa* bars north of the bridge; live music, DJs, ladies nights and good food.

ACTIVITIES, COURSES & TOURS
1 Ak'bol Yoga
2 Belize Chocolate Company
3 Belize Food Tours
4 Boca del Rio
5 Cork & Cooperage
6 Eco Iguana Corner
7 El Pescador
8 Esmeralda
9 Go Fish Belize
10 Island Dream Tour
11 Just Relax Massage
12 Massage by the Reef
13 Oasis Spa
14 Ocean Essence
15 Ramon's Village Pier
16 Seaduced by Belize
17 Searious Adventures
18 Secret Beach Water Park
19 Tackle Box Canyons
20 Tiburon Rum
21 Travellers Liquor
22 Tres Cocos
23 Tres Pescados Fly Shop
24 Xsite Belize Sailing

SLEEPING
25 Secret Beach Cabanas

EATING
26 Aurora's Bar & Grill
27 Blue Bayou
28 Caye Custard
29 Pirates
30 Truck Stop

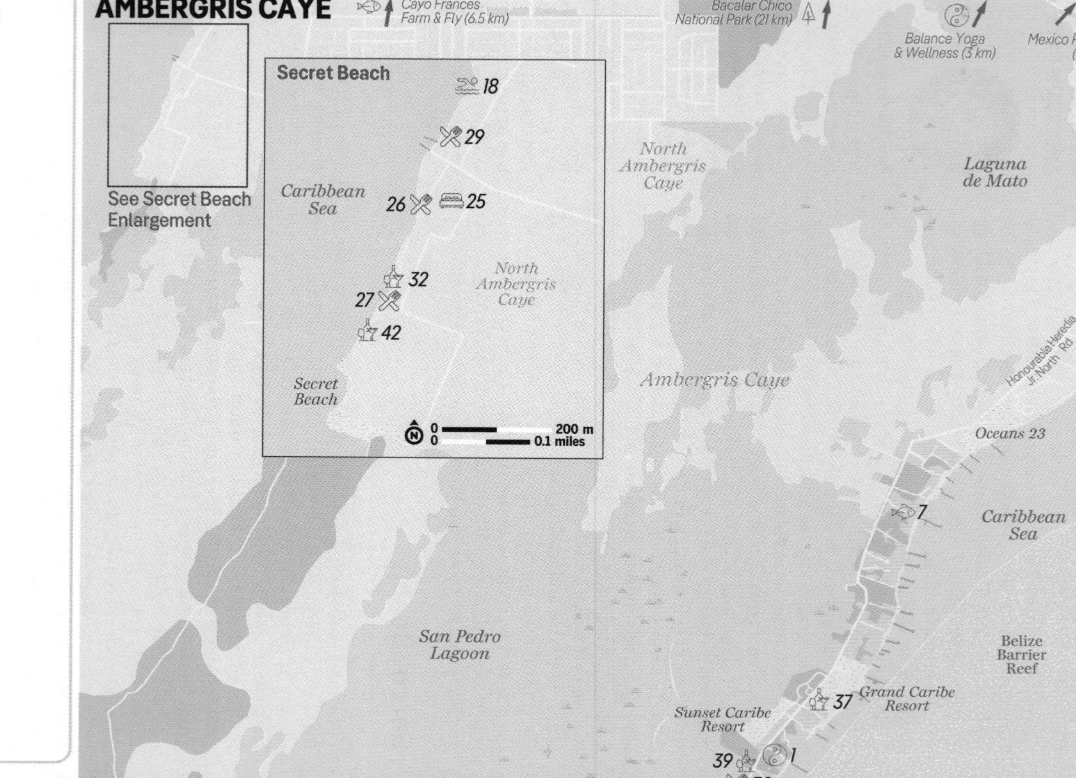

DRINKING & NIGHTLIFE
31 303 Belize
32 Bamboo Fence Restaurant & Swing Bar
33 Crocs Sunset Sports Bar
34 Losers Bar
35 Nauti Crab
36 Palapa Bar
37 Rain Restaurant
38 Saul's Cigar & Coffee House
39 Stella's Sunset Wine Bar
40 Wahoo's Lounge
41 Wayo's Beernet
42 Wet N'Wild

TRANSPORT
43 Breeze E Bike Rentals

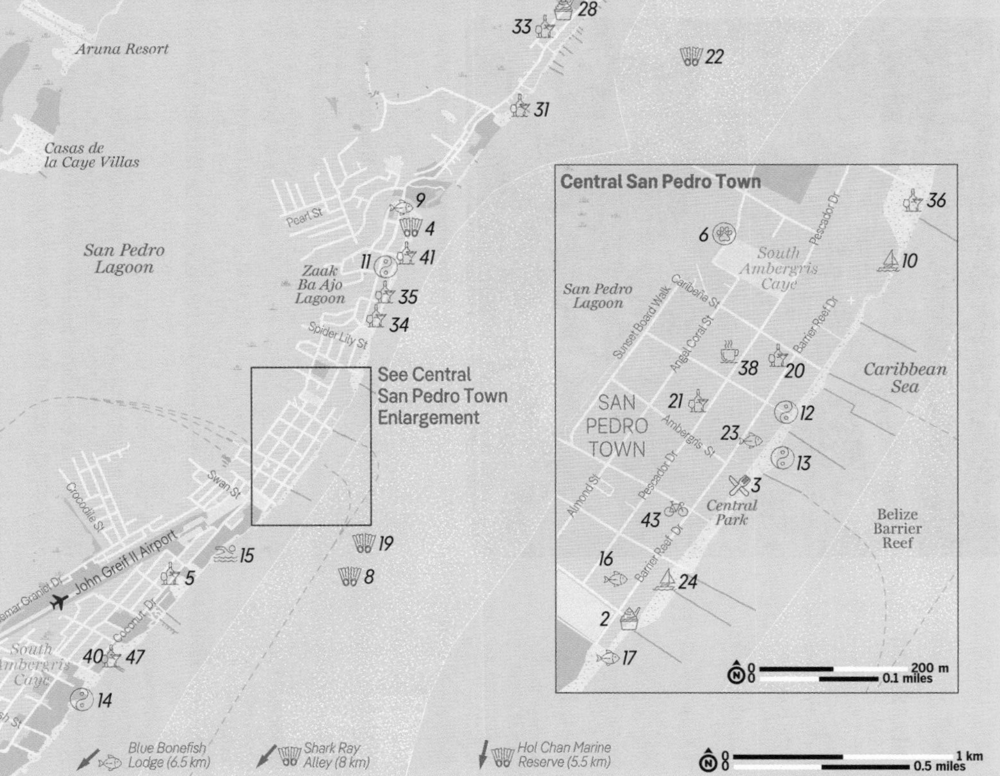

CHEAP SLEEPS IN SAN PEDRO

Sandbar Hostel
San Pedro's best hostel is on the beachfront opposite Palapa Bar. Book ahead. $

Pedro's Backpackers Inn
South of the airport, this cheapie and party place gets mixed reviews. $

Ambergris Sunset Hotel
Small guesthouse on the lagoon side with rooms around a tiny pool. A great deal for private en suite rooms. $

Sun & Reef
Modern, affordable multistorey hotel in the middle of town; large comfy beds and secure entry. $

La Casa de Paz Hotel
Close to the waterfront and center; reasonable option for price and amenities. $

PAUL HARDING/LONELY PLANET ©

Green iguana, Eco Iguana Corner

You need to take another road to reach a small group of more sophisticated beach bars favored by locals: **Bamboo Fence Swing Bar** and **Blue Bayou** each have semi-submerged picnic tables or *palapas* where you can sit in the water with a bucket of Belikin. Blue Bayou is recommended for its food too. A little way further south again, **Wet N' Wild** is far enough from the main road that it's rarely crowded.

Most people get here by golf cart. It's about 8 miles (12.8km) or 45 minutes from San Pedro with the last third on an unpaved and sometimes rough road. It crosses the flat middle of the North Island, passing steamy lagoons and mangrove swamps where locals fish and crocodiles lurk. A lot of land is up for sale so it might not be long before development creeps this way. The **Coconut Shuttle** runs a twice-daily boat from San Pedro to Secret Beach for BZ$50 return.

Island Wildlife Encounters

IGUANAS & WILDLIFE REHAB

Most wildlife around the cayes is underwater, but you don't have to look far from San Pedro to see land-based creatures.

WHERE TO STAY IN SAN PEDRO

Blue Tang Inn
Beachfront retreat with large suites with kitchenettes, sea views and a fine rooftop area. **$$$**

Ramon's Village
Large seafront resort with tropical gardens, faux Maya jungle setting and thatch-roofed *cabañas*. **$$$**

Mahogany Bay Village
South of San Pedro, this is one of the largest resorts on the island with pool, beach club and luxury cottages. **$$$**

On the lagoon side of town, just north of Caribena gas station, local Calvin Young has established the unique **Eco Iguana Corner** sanctuary in a patch of mangrove, complete with bamboo boardwalks so visitors can walk through and observe these giant lizards. The sanctuary is a haven for dozens of green and black iguanas, native to the island but suffering a population decline due to human encroachment and loss of habitat. It's free to visit (donations welcome) and the iguanas are harmless and not too shy.

Another organization rescuing and rehabilitating island wildlife, especially crocodiles, is **ACES** (American Crocodile Education Sanctuary; aceswildliferescue.org). The volunteers rescue sick, injured or orphaned crocs, turtles, birds and iguanas and care for them at their rehabilitation sanctuary on the North Island. You can visit the center with advance reservation but this is not a zoo and guided visits (by donation) focus on education and the conservation work. In general the animals you will see are residents that cannot be released back into the wild, such as a dwarf crocodile.

Golf Carts & Bikes

ISLAND TRANSPORTATION

Where can you find a thousand golf carts but no golf course? Ambergris Caye, of course! Traffic jams are not unusual in San Pedro due to the glut of golf carts cruising the streets. Some streets are one-way for golf carts; obey stop signs or give way to the right and use hand-turning signals. Some golf carts are battery-powered and others run on gas – a couple of gallons (BZ$14 a gallon) should keep you going for a few days. Carts are available to rent everywhere (BZ$100 to BZ$160 for 24 hours). In low season you can negotiate a sizable discount. You need a driver's license and credit-card imprint as security. Carts are handy for exploring the North Island, Secret Beach and the far south but you don't need one to get around San Pedro.

The North Island is a cool place for beach cycling and a bike is a convenient way to get around San Pedro and the south. You'll see locals on single-gear rattlers but there's nowhere to rent these. Ask at your hotel or resort as they might have bikes available for guest use (often for free). Otherwise, **Breeze E Bike Rentals** (breezebikerentals.com) has good-quality cruiser bikes for rent (BZ$50 a day) and heavy-duty e-bikes (BZ$80 a day), an interesting two-wheel alternative to golf-cart travel.

CULTURAL DINING

Black & White
Garifuna culture is celebrated with drumming, cultural shows and specialties like *hudut* (whole fish and mashed plantain cooked in coconut milk and spices) and cassava. $$

Pupuseria Salvadoreno
Cheap and filling Salvadoran *pupusas* (filled maize pancakes) cooked on a hot plate on the street then served inside. $

Robin's Kitchen
This simple roadside place does Jamaican fish BBQ and superb jerk chicken. $$

Jambel Jerk Pit
Popular waterfront Caribbean place. Live reggae, tasty food and all-you-can-eat buffet on Wednesday and Saturday nights. $$

El Fogon
Belizean Creole cuisine with Mexican influences like fish empanadas and *salbutes* (mini tortillas, usually stuffed with chicken) cooked on a fire hearth in the traditional way. $$

Caye Casa
Sweet colonial-style *casitas* (small cottages) and villas with thatched-roof porches and sea views. **$$$**

Hotel del Rio
Small lodge on a quiet stretch of beach close to town with thatched-roof *cabañas*. **$$**

Conch Shell Inn
Lovely beachfront hotel with 10 bright and spacious rooms on two levels. **$$**

DIVE OUTFITS

Ambergris Divers
Experienced operator with a San Pedro shop.

Amigos del Mar
The island's largest dive operator. Daily local trips plus Blue Hole and Turneffe trips.

Belize Pro Dive Center
Highly regarded with daily Hol Chan trips.

Chuck & Robbie's
Popular dive shop with personalized attention.

Ecologic Divers
High-end dive shop. Solid environmental credentials and small group dives.

Elite Diving Adventures
PADI courses and day trips to Lighthouse Reef and Turneffe Atoll.

Neptune's Cove
Top-notch dive and snorkel shop at Corona de Mar dock.

Searious Adventures
Snorkeling and sailing.

Bacalar Chico National Park

WORLD HERITAGE SNORKELING

At the northern tip of Ambergris Caye, **Bacalar Chico National Park** is a Unesco World Heritage Site made up of 41 sq miles (106.2 sq km) of protected land and sea, accessible only via an hour-long boat ride from San Pedro. At the San Juan ranger station there's a small museum showcasing Maya artifacts and 11 miles (17.7km) of nature trails. Although sightings are infrequent, the area is home to crocodiles, white-tail deer, ocelots, pumas and jaguars.

Back on the water, tour boats make snorkeling stops and motor through the ancient channel that was dug by seafaring Maya about 1500 years ago and now separates Ambergris Caye from the Mexican mainland. The coral is extra colorful around the reserve, as there's less damage from boats and tourists. Besides the bountiful fish, you might see manatees, as well as green and loggerhead turtles. If waters are calm, some tour boats go to Rocky Point, notable as one of the only places in the world where land meets reef.

The return trip hugs the east side of the island, and some boats make a final snorkeling stop at Mexico Rocks. Not all tour operators run trips to Bacalar Chico, due to the long travel distance, but **Seaduced by Belize** and **Searious Adventures** are two reliable options with day trips for around BZ$210 including lunch.

Diving & Snorkeling from San Pedro

CAYE DIVE SITES

San Pedro is a great base for diving and snorkeling as many of the premier reef sites are a short boat-ride away from Ambergris Caye and the islands' many operators run regular trips. Some of the larger hotels and resorts have their own dive shops that rent equipment, provide instruction and organize diving excursions. There are lots of independent dive operators around town, and many also run snorkeling, sailing, fishing and even mainland tours. Prices are similar but quality varies; diving is a big investment so it's worth shopping around and spending a little extra if necessary to go with a crew you're comfortable with.

Among the closest and most popular dive sites are **Hol Chan Marine Reserve**, south of the island, and **Esmeralda** in front of the school, while top snorkeling trips include **Hol Chan** and **Shark Ray Alley** or **Mexico Rocks** and **Tres Cocos**. A local single dive costs from BZ$120 and two dives

WHERE TO EAT IN SAN PEDRO

Lily's Treasure Chest
Beachfront restaurant serving traditional Belizean food and seafood and the island's best ceviche. **$$**

Blue Water Grill
Super popular beachfront restaurant with an international menu leaning toward Asian and Caribbean flavors. **$$$**

Anglers Seafood Restaurant
Backstreet family restaurant serving the freshest seafood and Belizean dishes prepared with love. **$$**

Dive boats, San Pedro

from BZ$180 but most outfits charge extra for equipment hire. Quoted prices sometimes don't include admission to the marine reserves, which is BZ$20 for Hol Chan, BZ$20 for Half Moon Caye and BZ$60 for the Blue Hole. Many companies also quote prices without including equipment hire so make sure you confirm what is included.

Day trips further afield to the Blue Hole and Lighthouse Reef (three dives) excluding park fees and gear rental cost around BZ$650 while Turneffe trips (three dives) cost from BZ$500.

There are a number of local dive sites. **Mexico Rocks**, declared a marine park in 2015, is a snorkeling site 15 minutes from San Pedro with a maximum depth of just 8ft (2.5m). It's a unique patch of reef toward the northern end of the island.

A half-mile northeast of San Pedro, **Boca del Rio** has spur-and-groove terrain featuring rolling coral hills and sandy channels. This is one of the few sites with healthy staghorn coral as well as plate corals.

Deeper than most dive sites around San Pedro, **Tres Cocos** has coral heads rising up to 50ft (15m) and a wall with spurs that spill out from 90ft to 120ft (27–36m), but there's also a shallow snorkeling area nearby. It's renowned for shoals of schooling fish, including snapper, horse-eye jack and spotted eagle rays.

A mile offshore from downtown San Pedro, **Tackle Box Canyons** has big, steep coral grooves and swim-throughs in

STINKY SEAWEED

The foul stench you'll notice near the shoreline of Ambergris Caye and other islands is due to large blooms of noxious sargassum seaweed. When the seaweed is washed ashore it begins to rot and emits hydrogen sulphide gas, producing an overwhelming rotten egg odor.

Since 2014, an unusually hefty bloom of sargassum seaweed has plagued the coast of Belize's northern cayes, choking shorelines and causing tourists to gag over their breakfast.

Scientists believe warming ocean temperatures and agricultural runoff in South America are to blame, as they create ideal conditions for these thick mats of seaweed to proliferate.

Beachfront hotels, restaurants and bars work hard at raking the seaweed out of the water where it dries and ceases to smell. It can then be used as fertilizer.

Elvi's Kitchen
San Pedro institution serving local specialties such as shrimp creole, fried chicken and conch ceviche. **$$**

Caramba
Fresh fish and seafood is displayed out front daily at this fabulous, atmospheric local restaurant. **$$**

Estel's Dine by the Sea
Right on the water, long-running all-day breakfast favorite for its Maya eggs and brekky burritos. **$$**

CHEAP EATS IN SAN PEDRO

Fry Jacks
Popular breakfast spot that does only one thing: fry-jacks, stuffed with eggs, bacon, chicken, sausage or, in season, lobster. $

Neri's Tacos
Cheap and tasty local joint with tacos, burritos, fry-jacks and tostadas served at communal tables. $

Pupuseria Salvadoreno
Pupusas are a great budget meal. Efficient and convivial atmosphere. $

My Secret Deli
Family-run eatery serving filling Belize favorites like stewed chicken, steak and rice. $

Big Taste
Hole-in-the-wall place with authentic *pibil* (pulled pork with onions and beans) and *birria* (meat stew) tacos and Argentinian *parrilladas* (BBQ meats). $.

Shark Ray Alley

many places along the drop-off on the way to the outer reef.

Four miles (6.4km) south of San Pedro is **Hol Chan Canyons**, part of the Hol Chan Marine Reserve. It's famous for its dramatic canyons and ample sea life, including eagle rays, stingrays and shoaling schools of fish.

Shark Ray Alley is known for the big southern stingrays and nurse sharks that come right up to the boat. Only snorkeling is allowed at this perennially popular spot, which is in a shallow part of the Hol Chan Marine Reserve.

Fun on the Water

SWIM, SAIL, FISH AND FUN

Diving and snorkeling aren't the only watery pursuits on and around Ambergris Caye. San Pedro is awash with tour companies and individuals organizing kayaking, windsurfing, sailing, kitesurfing, stand-up paddleboarding and fishing trips.

Swimming is not great from beaches around San Pedro because of seaweed at the water line, so you'll mostly be swimming from docks in waters protected by the reef. Watch out for boats: you often can't see or hear if a boat is coming

WHERE TO STAY SOUTH OF SAN PEDRO

Victoria House
An island original, this upmarket beach resort has gardens, pools and luxury villas. **$$$**

Coral Bay Villas
Colonial-style hotel set back from the ocean well south of San Pedro. Five deluxe condos with full kitchens. **$$$**

Xanadu Island Resort
Surrounded by lush tropical gardens this beachfront resort exudes rustic luxury in its rooms and *cabañas*. **$$$**

your way. **Ramon's Village Pier** is the best spot in town and the further north or south you go on the island, the fewer people there are on the piers. Secret Beach (p71) is a great place to swim, usually combined with lunch and a few drinks.

San Pedro draws **fly-fishing** enthusiasts who are anxious for a crack at Belize's 200-sq-mile (518-sq-km) classic tarpon flats. The ultimate angling accomplishment is the Grand Slam: catching bonefish, permit (best from March to May) and tarpon (best from May to September) all in one day. On the reef, fishers get bites from barracuda, snapper, jacks and grouper. As well as fishing tours with **Go Fish Belize** and **Tres Pescados Fly Shop**, there are several dedicated fly-fishing lodges on Ambergris Caye including **Blue Bonefish Lodge**, **El Pescador** and remote **Cayo Frances Farm & Fly**.

Sailing is the ultimate way to cruise around the island aboard a yacht or catamaran. Outfits such as **Xsite Belize Sailing** (xsitebelizesailing.com), **Island Dream Tours** (islanddreamtours.com), **Seaduced by Belize** (seaducedbybelize.com) and **Searious Adventures** (seariousadventuresbelize.com) all run full- and half-day trips and sunset booze cruises.

Island Pampering

MASSAGE BY THE SEA

If you have come to Ambergris Caye for a bit of rest and relaxation it's easy to schedule a massage at one of the waterside spas, or get active with a yoga session. Well-run **Oasis Spa** is good for massages, manicures, body wraps, body scrubs, ear candling and facials at Fido's dock. **Ocean Essence**, on a seaside dock in front of Caribbean Villas, is a tiny place that wins the award for its overwater location. For a beachfront day spa out of a lovely cloth tent, try **Just Relax Massage**. **Massage by the Reef** offers a massage with a view above the Amigos del Mar dive shop. **Ak'Bol Yoga** has open thatch-roof yoga studios with daily walk-in classes and week-long yoga retreats. Popular yoga studio **Balance Yoga & Wellness** is at Mangata Villas on the North Island.

Truck Stop Belize

ISLAND ENTERTAINMENT

The oh-so-cool lagoon-side **Truck Shop**, about a mile north of the San Pedro bridge, is a roadside food park built from shipping containers, but so much more. The colorfully painted

BOAT TO MEXICO

Many travelers choose to exit the cayes by sea to Mexico using Water Jets International (sanpedrowatertaxi.com), which offers a fairly efficient ferry service four times weekly between Caye Caulker, San Pedro and Chetumal (Mexico).

Boats leave Caye Caulker at 12.45pm on Monday, Wednesday, Friday and Saturday, stopping in San Pedro to pick up passengers and clear immigration. Boats depart San Pedro at 2.30pm, arriving in Chetumal at 5pm. There's a BZ$40 exit fee, and the fare is BZ$150.

Scan this QR code to find out about boats to Mexico.

WHERE TO EAT SOUTH OF SAN PEDRO

Black Orchid
Way down south, burgers and light meals by day, international fine dining by night. **$$$**

Hidden Treasure
Gorgeous open-air bamboo-accented restaurant hidden away but known for its fine Caribbean cuisine. **$$$**

Frenchy's
Fine dining where French and Mediterranean meets Caribbean cuisine from escargot to filet Oscar. **$$$**

BEST FOR COFFEE

Farmhouse Market & Cafe
Fantastic roadside artisan market and cafe, 500m north of the bridge with super espresso.

Lavish Habit Cafe
In San Pedro's center, this may be the best place for espresso and cafe latte. Also good breakfast.

Marbucks
One of the North Island's original coffee shops; uses quality Guatemalan beans.

Saul's Cigar Coffee House
Part shop, part cafe. You can drink coffee and buy beans and Cuban cigars.

Green Espresso
Great coffee and breakfasts, in the heart of backstreet San Pedro.

Caye Coffee Roasting Company
Not a cafe but you can buy freshly roasted beans.

containers feature a bar, ice-cream shop, Latin American and Southeast Asian food and a pizzeria. But look further and there's another lagoon-side bar with beer garden, outdoor movie screen, swimming pool, sunset-view swings and backyard games such as ping pong and cornhole.

In the center of the action is a stage for live music and the entertainment list includes trivia nights, adult spelling bees and more. It's a one-stop entertainment hub that you should definitely schedule in to your time on Ambergris Caye.

Food Tours & Rum Tasting

TASTE YOUR WAY AROUND THE ISLAND

Dining and drinking are as much a part of the Ambergris Caye experience as diving and snorkeling. The good news for food-lovers is that San Pedro has some fabulous little eateries and numerous opportunities for sampling local food and tasting rum, wine and coffee.

The first stop for foodies should be **Belize Food Tours** (belizefoodtours.com). Passionate and informative guides run the three-hour lunch tour, 'Belizean Bites', and dinner tour, 'Savor Belize', both walking tours through San Pedro's mom-n-pop kitchens and hole-in-the-wall eateries that you might not otherwise stumble upon. As well as learning the history and background of the restaurants, you'll sample a wide variety of authentic dishes and drinks hailing from Belize's many cultural influences. Don't eat beforehand!

Belize Chocolate Company (belizechocolatecompany.com) is the place to sample the wonderful Maya-style handmade cacao chocolate. The chocolate-making class, held weekdays at 10:30am (BZ$25), covers the history of cacao in Belize and the chocolate-making process. Sweet little backstreet family-run **Saul's Cigar & Coffee House** (saulscigarandcoffee.com) is part coffee shop and part cigar store, with everything from Cubans to hand-rolled cigars. A bonus is the free rum-cream tasting and it does a good line in Panama hats! Closed weekends. For Caribbean-rum tasting, **Travellers Liquor** (onebarrelrum.com) is another small backstreet store that belies the fact that this is Belize's largest distiller. There are free tastings and all sorts of rum for sale including rum cream, coconut rum and various flavors. **Tiburon Rum** (tiburonrum.com) is a boutique distiller and relative newcomer. At its main-street tasting room you can indulge in tastings of their stock rums as well as some fruit-infused rums (BZ$15 with a souvenir shot glass).

WHERE TO EAT NORTH OF SAN PEDRO

Aji Tapas Bar
Romantic Mediterranean garden hideaway serving tapas, paella and seafood steps from the sea. **$$$**

Garage Seafood & Steakhouse
One of the best places on the island for steak and quirky auto-garage decor. **$$**

Mambo Restaurant
Award-winning Italian and seafood restaurant at the plush Matachica Beach Resort. **$$$**

PAUL HARDING/LONELY PLANET ©

Tiburon Rum

There's no wine produced in Belize's tropical climate but **Cork & Cooperage** (corkandcooperage.com) stocks wines from around the world and offers wine and whiskey tastings in its little San Pedro wine bar.

For sweets you can't beat sampling the flavors of the island's famous frozen custard at **Caye Custard** in San Pedro. The high-quality ice cream is made with eggs for extra richness, then churned as it freezes for dense creaminess. Exotic flavors range from cookies and cream to sour-sop and coconut to cheesecake – or just plain vanilla and chocolate.

Island Nightlife

PARTY ON IN SAN PEDRO

San Pedro is the party capital of Belize but it's still pretty laid-back and low-key rather than a debauched spring-break scene. There's live music somewhere on the island every night of the week and most hotels and resorts have their own bars.

Palapa Bar is a popular overwater bar with a swimming deck out back with rubber tubes for relaxing in with a beer. Other good overwater bars include **303 Belize**, **Losers Bar** and **Wayo's Beernet**. On Tuesday nights **Nauti Crab** hosts fun hermit-crab races and has entertainment on other nights from trivia to karaoke. At **Wahoo's Lounge**, Thursday night is the infamous 'chicken drop'. Like bingo with chickens, participants bet on which number the chicken will drop its load. One-stop entertainment venue **Truck Stop** has great food, a beer garden, a pool, an outdoor cinema and games nights.

MAINLAND TOURS

Some island-based travelers don't give much thought to mainland Belize. That's a shame but fortunately local tour outfits organize trips to the best of the mainland experiences, all with a boat trip or flight to Belize City then by road to the attractions.

The closest Maya ruin to the cayes is Altun Ha (p63), reached by boat across the lagoon, then by bus for the final stretch. Wildlife trips should include howler monkeys at the Community Baboon Sanctuary (p62), birdlife at Crooked Tree Wildlife Sanctuary (p64) or rescued wildlife at the Belize Zoo (p57).

Another popular adventure trip is cave-tubing at Nohoch Che'en Caves Branch Archaeological Reserve, which can also include ziplining and ATV touring.

WHERE TO STAY NORTH OF SAN PEDRO

Daydreamin' B&B
Four tidy cabins and a cafe around a small, relaxing pool; charming North Island getaway. **$$**

Ak'Bol Yoga Resort
Long-running yoga retreat with colorful *cabañas* and cheaper private rooms with shared bath. **$$**

Matachica Beach Resort
One of the north's swankiest. Luxury villas have private terraces and hot tubs; good restaurant and day spa. **$$$**

CAYO ESPANTO

The coconut-covered Cayo Espanto is just 3 miles (4.8km) or a seven-minute boat ride from San Pedro, but feels a world away.

As the story goes, the island was christened Cayo Espanto or 'Phantom Caye' by local fishers who claimed it was populated by *duendes* (mischievous Maya pranksters). If fish and rum were left unguarded on this island, the mythical creatures apparently snatched them up.

Today it's a private island resort frequented by the likes of Robert De Niro, Harrison Ford and Tiger Woods.

Leonardo DiCaprio loved it so much that he bought neighboring Blackadore Caye in 2015 with plans to build an eco-resort.

Scan this QR code to find out more about Cayo Espanto.

Secret Beach

Sunsets & Sundowners

ROMANTIC VIEWPOINTS ON AMBERGRIS

As if Ambergris Caye isn't beautiful enough, sunsets on the lagoon side are stunning, and rum punch is the usual drink of choice to accompany it.

In San Pedro head down to the 'back side' where fishing boats bob in the lagoon. On the North Island, several bars and restaurants face the sunset side. Triple-decker **Crocs Sunset Sports Bar** is perfect for a sunset cocktail and popular with locals and expats. Further up, **Truck Stop** (p79) has a jetty over the water where swing chairs provide a perfect viewpoint. Next door, **Stella's Sunset Wine Bar** lives up to its name with a lovely garden facing the lagoon. The rooftop bar at **Rain Restaurant** atop Hotel Gran Caribe is the most stylish spot for a sundowner, with 360-degree views.

Secret Beach faces west and most bars remain open for sunset. A sunset cruise is a great way to combine a sailing trip with sunset drinks. Various two-hour cruises by sailing boat or catamaran usually include snacks and unlimited drinks.

WHERE TO SHOP IN SAN PEDRO

Belizean Arts Gallery
Locally made arts and handicrafts including ceramics, wood carvings, Garifuna drums and antiques.

Belizean Breezes Soap Co
Sells a variety of unique, natural aromatic products from cupcake soaps to whipped shower butters.

12 Belize
Selection of interesting, locally made gifts including handmade soaps, Maya bags and local sauces.

Festive San Pedro

THE REAL ISLAND PARTIES

San Pedro really knows how to party. The biggest event is **El Gran Carnaval**, on the first weekend before Lent. The parades and costumes of more typical carnival celebrations are replaced with body-painting and flour-fighting – great fun to watch and even more fun to participate in.

The reopening of the lobster season on the third week in June is a big reason for celebration and the **San Pedro Lobster Festival** is the biggest in the country. Live music, delicious seafood and the crowning of the Lobsterfest king and queen. Also in June, **San Pedro Day** commemorates St Peter, the patron saint of fishers.

In the first weekend in August the **Costa Maya Festival** (internationalcostamayafestival.com) brings participants from all over Central America to celebrate their shared heritage. The streets of San Pedro are filled with music, parades, dancing and drinking, culminating in the crowning of a festival queen.

September Celebrations are celebrated throughout Belize and San Pedro is no exception. It all starts on September 10, commemorating the Battle of St George's Caye, and continues for two weeks until Independence Day on September 21.

WHAT'S IN A NAME?

Ambergris (gray amber) is a waxy gray substance once used in perfume production that comes from the bile duct in the intestines of sperm whales.

It's thought that whalers in the 17th century probably named the island after the substance, which is secreted by a small percentage of whales, so is considered rare.

According to folklore, British, French and Dutch pirates used the island's many coves as hideouts when ambushing Spanish ships, so they may also be responsible for the title.

GETTING AROUND

Water taxis dock in San Pedro town and the airport is only a five-minute walk south. Minivan taxis ply the streets looking for customers but most people hire a golf cart or bike if they're venturing further than the town center.

Coastal Xpress operates a boat service between San Pedro town and the resorts on the North Island departing from Amigos del Mar pier.

Many resorts and restaurants also offer a water-shuttle service into town for clients. Caribbean Sprinter Water Taxi and San Pedro Belize Water Taxi run regular boats to/from Belize City and via Caye Caulker.

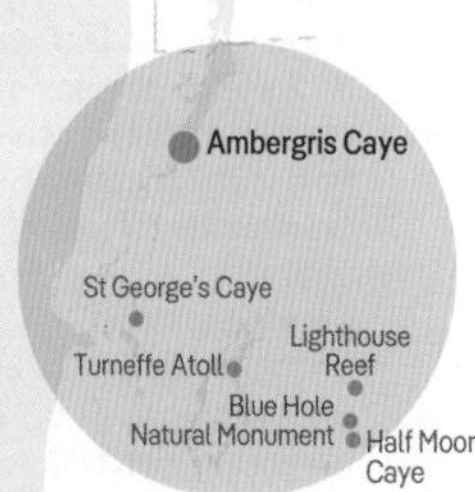

Beyond Ambergris Caye

To the south and east of Ambergris and Caye Caulker lies the barrier reef and the diving meccas of Lighthouse Reef and Turneffe Atoll.

Although there are a handful of upmarket lodges on Turneffe Atoll and Long Caye, most visitors to this part of Belize are divers and snorkelers on day trips but this is unquestionably the most popular destination for serious underwater exploration. Lighthouse Reef is the furthest of the three atolls from the coastline and draws divers to the world-renowned Blue Hole Natural Monument as well as wall-diving and nesting boobies at Half Moon Caye.

Turneffe Atoll, a protected marine area, is alive with coral, fish and large rays, making it a prime destination for diving, snorkeling and catch-and-release sportfishing. All the major dive operators on Ambergris Caye and Caye Caulker can arrange diving trips out to this Caribbean underwater wonderland.

TOP TIP

Boat trips to the reefs and atolls can take up to 2½ hours through sometimes rough open waters. If you suffer from seasickness take precautions such as medication, and try to not drink too much alcohol the night before a diving trip.

Beach shacks

TAYLOR WHITELEY/SHUTTERSTOCK ©

Lobster, Turneffe Atoll

Turneffe Atoll

PROTECTED MARINE AREA

Protected marine reserve **Turneffe Atoll**, about 1½ hours by boat from San Pedro, is the largest and most biologically diverse atoll in the Americas. At 30 miles (48.2km) long and 10 miles (16.1km) wide, the area is alive with coral, fish and large rays, making it a prime spot for diving, snorkeling and catch-and-release sportfishing. In 2012 environmental groups succeeded in protecting the 131,690-hectare (1317 sq km) area now dubbed the Turneffe Atoll Marine Reserve. The atoll is dominated by mangrove islands, the nurseries on which almost all marine life depends to ensure juvenile protection and biological productivity. Although the atoll is best known for its walls, it also has many shallow sea gardens and bright sand flats inside the reef that are excellent sites for novice divers and snorkelers. Fishing enthusiasts are attracted by the flats, which are ideal for saltwater fly-fishing.

Turneffe Elbow was for years the most popular site, until overfishing became an issue in 2014. Now protected, the site is again welcoming big schools of fish and predators in large numbers. Other sites include **Myrtle's Turtle**, named for the resident green turtle that appears annually, and **Triple Anchor**, marked by three anchors remaining from a wreck.

TURNEFFE RESORTS

Turneffe Atoll has four secluded, far-flung resorts offering three-day all-inclusive packages from around US$1500.

Belize Dive Haven Resort (belizedivehaven.com) Large luxury Turneffe Island dive resort with 96 rooms and penthouse suites.

Blackbird Caye Resort (blackbirdresort.com) Secluded and intimate dive resort with just 20 renovated luxury seafront villas.

Turneffe Flats Lodge (tflats.com) Best known as a fishing retreat, this Blackbird Caye resort also offers diving trips and snorkeling ecotours.

Turneffe Island Resort (turnefferesort.com) At the southern tip of the atoll, Turneffe's fanciest resort has luxurious *cabañas* facing the beach

WHERE TO STAY AT A REMOTE ISLAND RESORT

St George's Caye Resort
Luxury resort on remote but inhabited St George's Caye with overwater bungalows and garden villas. **$$$**

Shaka Caye Island Resort
Tiny private island resort near St George's Caye with half a dozen luxury villas. **$$$**

Cayo Espanto
Exclusive private island resort near Ambergris Caye, known to host celebrities. **$$$**

ETHAN DANIELS/SHUTTERSTOCK ©

TOP SIGHT

Lighthouse Reef & Blue Hole Natural Monument

Spectacular Lighthouse Reef is the furthest of the three atolls from the Belize coast (50 miles; 80.5km), but is the most famous and most visited, thanks to the allure of the mysterious Blue Hole Natural Monument. Stunning wall dives, with majestic swim-throughs and clear blue water, make the reef a diving bucket-list favorite.

DON'T MISS

- Diving the Blue Hole
- Half Moon Caye Wall
- Nesting birds on Half Moon Caye
- Snorkeling off Long Caye
- Blue Hole joy flight
- Birdwatching on Long Caye
- Luxury lodges

Blue Hole Natural Monument

At the center of Lighthouse Reef is the world-famous **Blue Hole Natural Monument**, an incomparable natural wonder and unique diving experience – famously seen from the air as a symbol of Belize. It may not involve a lot of visible undersea wildlife, but it remains a recreational diver's best opportunity for a heart-pounding descent into a majestic submarine sinkhole. The chance of spotting circling reef sharks and the occasional hammerhead further sweeten the deal.

In the 1970s, underwater pioneer Jacques Cousteau explored the sinkhole and declared the dive site one of the world's best. Since then the Blue Hole's image – a deep azure pupil with an aquamarine border surrounded by the lighter shades of the reef – has become a logo for tourist publicity. The hole forms a perfect 1000ft (300m)-diameter circle on the surface and is said to be 430ft (131m) deep, but as much as 200ft (61m) of this may now be filled with silt and other natural debris.

Divers drop quickly to 130ft (40m), from where they swim beneath an overhang, observing stalactites above and the odd reef shark. Although the water is clear, light levels are low, so a good dive light will enable further appreciation of the rock formations. Because of the depth, ascent begins after eight minutes; the brevity of the dive may disappoint some divers. The trip is usually combined with other dives at Lighthouse Reef that some divers consider the real highlight.

On day trips, the Blue Hole will be your first dive, which can be nerve-racking if you're unfamiliar with the dive master and the other divers. Most outfits require you to have a logged a dive within the previous six months to at least 80ft (25m) or to do some local dives with your dive masters before setting out cold on a Blue Hole trip. Because of the depth you must have advanced open-water certification.

The trip involves a bit over two hours each way by boat in sometimes rough, open waters. Be prepared if you suffer seasickness.

Half Moon Caye

A nesting ground for the rare red-footed booby bird, the **Half Moon Caye Natural Monument** is the most visited of the Lighthouse Reef islands, and for good reason. Its palm-lined beaches are castaway-cool; its verdant, tropical interior nurtures a stunning array of life; and its crystalline underwater surrounds are ideal for peeking in on coral and sea critters.

Rising less than 10ft (3m) above sea level, the caye's 45 acres hold two distinct ecosystems. To the west is lush vegetation fertilized by the droppings of thousands of seabirds, including some 4000 red-footed boobies (pictured), the magnificent frigate bird and 98 other bird species. The east side has less vegetation but more palms.

The **Wall** at Half Moon Caye is a spectacular dive site with bright corals and schools of barracuda and snapper, as well as rays and turtles. Underwater visibility can extend more than 200ft (61m) here. Loggerhead and hawksbill sea turtles, both endangered, lay their eggs on the island's southern beaches.

WHERE TO STAY

Long Caye is the only place to stay. Upmarket lodges Huracan Diving (huracandiving.com) and Itza (itzalodge.com) at the northern tip have multi-day packages. Idyllic 710-acre Long Caye at Lighthouse Reef (longcayebelize.com) is a private island with a 210-acre nature reserve and plans to develop a resort.

TOP TIPS

- Avoid partying too hard in San Pedro the night before diving the Blue Hole.
- The national park fees for the Blue Hole Natural Monument (BZ$60) and Half Moon Caye Natural Monument (BZ$20) are usually paid separately to the cost of your dive.
- If you don't want to dive the Blue Hole you can take a joy flight over it from San Pedro.

CAYE CHAPEL

Caye Chapel is a private island community south of Caye Caulker with the exclusive Four Seasons resort and the only golf course on the cayes.

The 18-hole course was designed by Australian golf legend Greg Norman and Mexican golfer Lorena Ochoa, former number-one ranked LPGA Tour pro. The layout covers most of the long skinny island, with just enough room for an airstrip at the southern end. Every hole has Caribbean Sea views and there are further water hazards built into the challenging layout.

LEONARD ZHUKOVSKY/SHUTTERSTOCK ©

St George's Caye Resort

Historic St George's Caye

ISLAND GETAWAY WITH A STORY

Lightly populated St George's Caye, 25 miles (40.2km) south of San Pedro, is important to Belizean history. It was from here, on September 10, 1798, that British settlers fought off invading Spaniards in the **Battle of St George's Caye**, now celebrated as a national public holiday. Boat tours don't visit here but you can stay at the luxurious **St George's Caye Resort** (belizeislandparadise.com) or the more low-key six-bedroom **Casa Almar Belize** (casaalmarbelize.com) that sleeps eight to 16 guests. Since there are no regular tours, dive boats or visiting cruise-ship passengers, St George's offers a secluded, intimate and romantic island experience without being super-exclusive like some private islands (the island has a permanent population of around 20). From the resorts you can go diving, snorkeling, fishing or kayaking – or just relax on the sand or by the pool – without the crowds.

St George's Caye is also home to the **Oceanic Society** (oceanicsociety.org) research station, a US-based NGO that runs volunteer and educational programs on reef protection and collection of marine data on turtles, manatees, dolphins and sharks.

GOFF'S CAYE

Tour companies in San Pedro and Caye Caulker occasionally run trips to tiny Goff's Caye and manatee-spotting off Swallow Caye but Goff's is much closer to **Belize City** (p48) so we've covered it there.

GETTING AROUND

Most Lighthouse Reef visitors are either on a one-day dive trip or liveaboard dive excursion from San Pedro or Caye Caulker. Long Caye lodges run scheduled boat trips from Belize City when there's demand.

Turneffe Atoll is closest to the mainland and the most accessible. It's within reach of Caulker, Ambergris and Belize City to the north, and Glover's Reef and Hopkins village to the south, so usually visited by day trip. Even Placencia dive boats occasionally make the trip to Turneffe Elbow, at the southern tip of the islands.

On rough days it's favored by San Pedro dive operators because much of the trip can be made behind the barrier reef, protecting passengers from choppy open seas.

CAYE CAULKER

Caye Caulker
BELMOPAN

Ah, Caye Caulker, the laid-back little sibling to Ambergris Caye, where signs proclaim 'No Shirt, No Shoes...No Problem.' and 'Go Slow'. Nothing is too hurried here but the mellow Caribbean lifestyle is infectious. There are no cars and few golf carts, sandy streets, colorful clapboard houses, bike riders on single-gear clunkers and shimmering blue water all around.

As well as balmy breezes, fresh barbecued seafood and the fantastic barrier reef off the eastern shore, the western side of the island rewards with sublime sunsets while north of the Split the island is largely deserted. The easygoing attitude is due in part to the strong Creole presence on the island, which pulses to a classic reggae beat and is home to a small community of Rastafarians. This has long been a backpacker's mecca, but in recent years tourists of all ages and incomes have come to appreciate the island's unique atmosphere.

TOP TIP

Take care with belongings left in hotel rooms as room robberies are regularly reported. If your room doesn't lock properly, ask for another and make use of the hotel safe if one is available.

Sunset, Caye Caulker

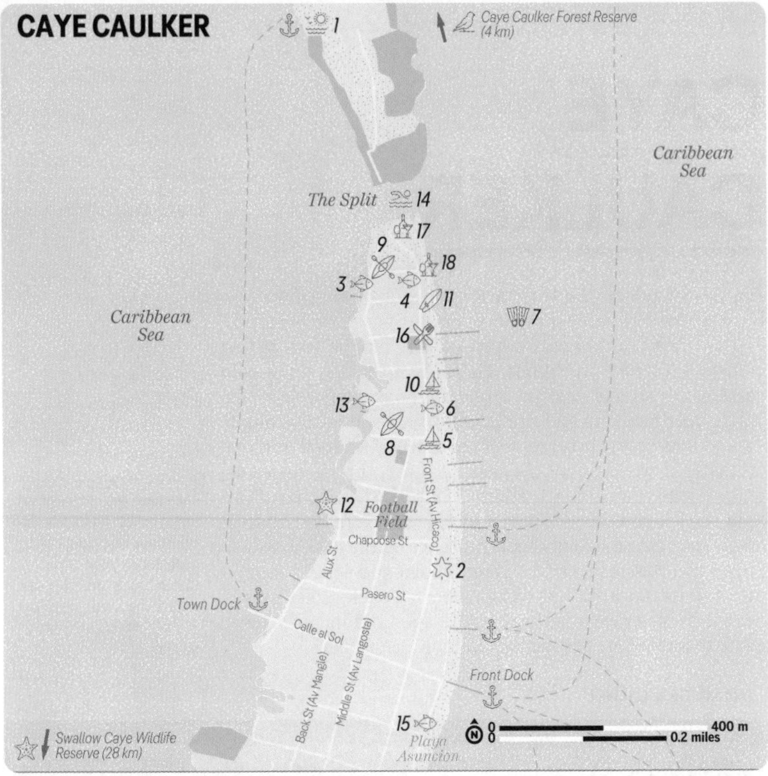

CAYE CAULKER

Caye Caulker Forest Reserve (4 km)
Caribbean Sea
The Split
Caribbean Sea
Football Field
Chapoose St
Front St (Av Hicaco)
Alux St
Pasero St
Town Dock
Calle al Sol
Middle St (Av Langosta)
Back St (Av Mangle)
Front Dock
Swallow Caye Wildlife Reserve (28 km)
Playa Asuncion
0 400 m
0 0.2 miles

HIGHLIGHTS
1 Northside Beach Club

ACTIVITIES, COURSES & TOURS
2 Anda De Wata Tours
3 Anglers Abroad
4 Barefoot Fisherman
5 Blackhawk Sailing Tours
6 Calle La Posa
7 Caye Caulker Marine Reserve
8 Good Vibes Tours
9 Ocean Academy
10 Ragga Sailing Adventures
11 Reef Break Surf Shop
12 Stingray Beach
13 Tarpon Feeding Dock
14 The Split
15 Tsunami Adventures

EATING
16 Beachside Barbecues

DRINKING & NIGHTLIFE
17 Lazy Lizard Bar & Grill
18 Sip N'Dip

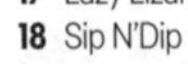

Stand-up paddleboarding, Caye Caulker

WHERE TO STAY ON CAYE CAULKER

Oasi
Four elegant apartments in tropical gardens in a quiet southside location; also Il Baretto and bar. **$$**

Caye Reef
Six apartments with super attention to detail and a rooftop deck with hot tub and fine island views. **$$$**

Island Magic
Great value beachfront place with pool, restaurant and apartments with kitchen and dining areas. **$$**

The Split

The Split

SWIMMING AT THE SPLIT

The narrow channel that splits Caye Caulker in two is the island hot spot, thanks to clean seaweed-free waters for swimming and the **Lazy Lizard Bar & Grill** where everyone gathers for drinks beneath *palapas,* dancing to all-day reggae or swimming in the adjacent seawater pool. There's even a diving platform and the seawall makes this one of the island's safest and best swimming spots.

As well as the main bar and restaurant, there's an upstairs lounge-bar, juice bar, pizzeria, souvenir shops, and kayak and paddleboard rentals. Full-moon parties are a big monthly event. At the entrance, **Sip N'Dip** is an excellent overwater bar with a lovely deck and submerged *palapas*. Ferries to the north of the island leave from the western side on demand (BZ$5 pedestrians, bikes free).

It's said that Hurricane Hattie carved the Split in 1961, though locals finished the job to create a passable boat channel.

BEST BARS

I&I Reggae Bar
The island's most happening spot for sunset and after dark. Its three levels each offer a different scene. The top-floor 'chill-out zone' has hammocks and panoramic views.

Barrier Reef Sport Bar
Popular with locals, expats and tourists, this waterfront beach bar has good international food, Fireball shots, live music and sports on TV.

Lazy Lizard
With prime position on the Split, the Lazy Lizard pumps out reggae by day, attracting travelers for swimming and sunbathing while being plied with booze. The second-story balcony has elevated Split views.

Sea Dreams Hotel
Lovely guesthouse near the Split with swimming dock, rooftop lounge, paddleboards, bikes and canoes. **$$$**

Iguana Reef Inn
Upmarket but informal, beachfront Iguana Roof has a great poolside bar area and fine rooms. **$$$**

Weezie's
Dreamy oceanfront rooms and cottages in a peaceful location with lap pools and spacious interiors. **$$$**

CAULKER CLASSICS

Harry the Caveman, long-time local boat operator and owner of Caveman Snorkeling Tours, shares his tips for the island.

Hol Chan Marine Reserve
This is the best place to start with a snorkeling day trip. Visitors love to snorkel at Shark Ray Alley.

Croc spotting north of the Split
In the mangroves past Northside Beach you can see our local crocs.

Best for food
The street barbecues are the best for cheap snacks and seafood. Il Pelicano is my favorite restaurant on the island. Go to Barrier Sports Bar for a drink with locals.

Barbecued lobster

Beachside Barbecues

SNACK TIME NEAR THE SPLIT

You'll probably smell the wafting aromas and smoking braziers as you wander up toward the Split, where local BBQs fire up from around lunchtime until late afternoon. Jerk chicken, shrimp kebabs, whole fish, grilled lobster and pork chops are all cooked at individual BBQs with names like Betty's, Ester's and Chef Kareem's. Good prices and fun atmosphere. You'll find other BBQs scattered around the island.

Swim on the Northside

KING OF BEACHES

For those looking to kick back on soft white sand and in the docile sea, tropical cocktail in hand, **Northside Beach Club** (formerly Koko King) is worth a visit. On a good day it's a beach party, with bar, restaurant, beach games and water toys – you can easily spend all day here. It's a quick ferry trip from the Split (BZ$5 return) or via self-guided kayaking, paddleboarding or swimming across the Split.

WHERE TO EAT ON CAYE CAULKER

La Cubana
Cuban sandwiches, paella and other Latin American specialties at decent prices. **$$**

Errolyn's House of Fry Jacks
The island's best-value breakfast – delicious filled golden fry-jacks. Cheap and filling. **$**

Happy Lobster
Caye Caulker institution even when lobster is not in season. Good breakfast and there's another at Northside. **$$**

North of the beach, large swathes of natural areas are still untouched by the tourist boom. Particularly rewarding to explore are the remote parts, including a crocodile sanctuary at the island's northern end, within **Caye Caulker Forest Reserve**. Here, a raised, 1-mile (1.6km) boardwalk cuts through the mangrove forest. It's an excellent place to spot crocs and water birds, including rails, stilts and herons, as well as ospreys and mangrove warblers.

Birdlife in the Forest Reserve

EXPLORE THE MANGROVES

The island's northernmost 100 acres constitute the **Caye Caulker Forest Reserve**, declared in 1998. Birdlife is prolific, particularly wading birds such as the tricolored heron, and songbirds, like the mangrove warbler. Somewhat rare species include the white-crowned pigeon, rufus-necked rail and black catbird. Inland lagoons provide habitat for crocodiles and turtles, five species of crab, boa constrictors, scaly tailed iguanas (locally called 'wish willies'), geckos and lizards.

The littoral forest on Caye Caulker is mostly red, white and black mangrove, which grows in the shallow water. The mangroves' roots support an intricate ecosystem, including sponges, gorgonians, anemones and a wide variety of fish. The forest also has buttonwood, gumbo-limbo (the 'tourist tree'), poisonwood, madre de cacao, ficus and ziracote. There's no shortage of non-native coconut palms and Australian pines.

The forest reserve is an excellent but challenging kayaking destination. You may prefer to paddle up the calmer, west side of the island to avoid strong winds and rough seas. **Richard's Adventures** leads guided tours along a 1-mile boardwalk through the crocodile habitat.

Caye Caulker Marine Reserve

SNORKEL WITH TURTLES

Declared a marine reserve in 1998, the 61-sq-mile (158 sq km) **Caye Caulker Marine Reserve** includes the portion of the barrier reef that runs parallel to the island, as well as the turtle-grass lagoon adjacent to Caye Caulker Forest Reserve. It's rich with sea life, including colorful sponges, blue-and-yellow queen angel fish, Christmas tree worms, star coral, redband parrotfish, yellow gorgonians and more. From April to September, snorkelers and divers might even spot a turtle or manatee. All local dive operators lead tours to the reserve.

BEST DAY SPAS

Healing Touch Spa
Manicures and pedicures, Reiki, reflexology, body scrubs, facials, aura cleansing and aromatherapy are all available on the island's original spa.

Namaste Yoga
Above Namaste Cafe, this long-running yoga studio has morning classes (Monday to Friday) by donation.

IxChel Day Spa
Full-service spa near the Split with a full range of massage styles, scrubs, facials and combination packages.

Purple Passion Studio & Spa
Recommended for beauty treatments including hair, nails and facials.

Amor Y Café
One of the most popular breakfast spots on the island for eggs, grilled cheese and brewed coffee. **$**

Caribbean Colors Art Cafe
Local art and a health-conscious menu of smoothies, salads or sandwiches; vegan options. **$$**

Wish Willy
Local institution for Belizean food, tables on the sand, calypso beats and grilled seafood. **$$**

DIVE OUTFITS

Recommended Caye Caulker dive and snorkeling outfits.

Blue Wave Divers
Trips to the outer reef, overnight tours and local reef dives.

Caveman Snorkeling Tours
Popular snorkeling trips in local waters, manatee-watching expeditions and occasional private trips to Goff's Caye and Swallow Caye.

Frenchie's Diving
Well-regarded local operator with dives throughout the region including Caye Caulker Marine Reserve night dives.

Nauti Time Tours
Budget-conscious and ecofriendly snorkeling trips to Hol Chan/ Shark Ray Alley and local sites.

Stressless Eco Friendly Tours
With a focus on sustainability and passionate guides, Stressless stands out in a crowded snorkeling market.

Tarpons & Stingrays

MARINE ENCOUNTERS FROM SHORE

Sportfishers might have heard of the **Atlantic tarpon**, Belize's most prized catch-and-release fish, protected under Belizean law. Tarpons can grow to 8ft (2.5m) long so are coveted among anglers for their size and fight. Down a sandy lane, **Calle La Posa** (opposite the street BBQs), is a small deck where dozens of tarpons gather and swim about, ostensibly waiting for a free feed, though locals say they're mainly attracted to a freshwater spring here. It's an amazing experience (and free) to watch these fish swimming around in the clear waters below the deck. While we don't recommend feeding fish, you can buy a small bucket of sardines for BZ$5 and hand-feed them – hold the fish about 2ft (0.5m) above the water and the tarpon will launch itself up and take it right out of your hand.

Just south, on the beach outside Iguana Reef Inn, is another remarkable marine experience. Daily from 4pm to sunset, dozens of **stingrays** arrive in the shallows and glide around, unfazed by humans in the water. There's no regular public feeding though hotel staff occasionally feed them. You may also see **seahorses** clinging to ropes in the small seahorse reserve.

Diving & Snorkeling

UNDERWATER FUN FROM CAULKER

There aren't as many diving operators on Caye Caulker as in San Pedro, but there's still plenty of opportunity for local diving and snorkeling. Common dives from Caulker include two-tank dives to the **local reef** as well as further afield to Esmeralda off San Pedro and Turneffe Atoll. Trips to Lighthouse Reef and Half Moon Caye can be arranged but these are sometimes subcontracted out to bigger San Pedro operators. You can snorkel around the **Split**, but to really experience life undersea you need to sign up with a tour operator and go out to the reef. Some trips visit a sunken barge near the northern tip of Caulker and, in season, go manatee-spotting in the channel. Half-day snorkeling trips visit **Caye Caulker Marine Reserve** just off the east coast of the island, and include Coral Gardens, the Swash (a stand of coral near an opening in the reef where the current and swells attract a good variety of marine life) and Shark Ray Village (Caulker's own shark and ray habitat).

Most dive-tour operators in town take groups snorkeling, as do the sailing companies. Shop around and find out about group size and what is included before signing up.

WERE TO EAT ON CAYE CAULKER

Hibisca by Habaneros
Brightly painted clapboard house where chefs prepare gourmet international food, including fresh seafood. **$$$**.

Il Pelicano
Wonderful garden Italian restaurant serving home-made pastas and the best pizza on the island. **$$$**

Maggie's Sunset Kitchen
Maggie's is a local favorite for Belizean food, seafood and sunset drinks from the adjacent dock. **$$**

Atlantic tarpon

Sailing & Fishing

BY WIND AND WAVE

Several companies run day sailing trips, with most visiting two or three snorkeling sites – usually around Caye Caulker or Hol Chan marine reserves. It costs the same as a snorkeling tour (around BZ$140), but the journey will be wind-powered so you might spend more time under sail than actually snorkeling. In addition to snorkeling trips, sailing companies also offer sunset cruises and moonlight sailing. Island-hopping trips include overnight excursions to Lighthouse Reef or Turneffe Atoll, and multiday trips to the southern cayes and Placencia.

Just about any skipper will take you fishing in the deep water, flats or reef, and it's generally cheaper from here than from Ambergris Caye. As well as tarpon, permit and bonefish, you often hook snook, barracuda, snapper and shark, usually on a catch-and-release basis. In deeper waters look for wahoo, sailfish, kingfish, snapper, grouper and jacks.

Recommended outfits include locally owned **Blackhawk Sailing Tours**, which also does overnight sailing trips. **Ragga Sailing Adventures** runs sailing and snorkeling tours, including sunset tours. **Anglers Abroad** is a fishing specialist based at Sea Dream Hotel. **Barefoot Fisherman** operates catch-and-release sportfishing trips. **Tsunami Adventures** runs fishing trips and snorkeling trips.

THE ORIGINAL CAYE CAULKER

Caye Caulker was originally a fishing settlement which grew in population with the War of the Castes.

It was purchased in 1870 by Luciano Reyes, whose descendants still live on the island. Reyes parceled the land out to a handful of families, and to this day descendants of those first landowners still live in the general vicinities of those original parcels.

During much of the 20th century, coconut processing, fishing, lobster trapping and boat building formed the backbone of the island's economy.

Today, tourism is an integral part of the island economy.

Suggestion Gourmet
Gourmet French bistro where you make suggestions to the chef as to what to prepare. **$$**.

Namaste Cafe
Fresh and healthy local dishes and good coffee with yoga studio upstairs. **$**

Tropical Cake Wave
Johnny cakes, juices, sweet treats and cocktails at a colorful streetside cafe. **$**

CHEAP SLEEPS ON CAULKER

Bella's Hostel
Backpacker hideaway with good-value dorms, free bikes and kayaks, and a chill vibe. $

Sip N'Dip Guesthouse
Opposite the bar of the same name and right next to the Split. Rooms are super value for the location. $

Traveller's Palm
Bright-yellow backpacker's hostel a few blocks south of the water-taxi terminal. Cheap dorms. $

Barefoot Beach Belize
Candy-colored beachfront cottages at the southern end of the village with kitchenettes and free bikes. Good value. $

Wind & Water

PADDLE THROUGH THE MANGROVES

Kayaking through the calm mangroves in the north of the island, around the Split or along the quieter western side of the island (the sunset side) is a wonderful experience. Kayaks can be hired from many places on the island, including the Split. **Good Vibes Tours** (goodvibestoursbelize.com) rents clear-bottomed kayaks for a better view. At **Ocean Academy** you can book a kayak tour with local high-school students.

With an easterly wind blowing much of the time, and its shallow waters protected by the barrier reef, Caulker has superb conditions for windsurfing and kitesurfing, especially from November to July. **Reef Break Surf Shop** (reefbreaksurfshop.com) is the place for wind-powered sports – kitesurfing, windsurfing, kite-winging, stand-up paddleboarding and even surfing on the reef are on offer, with equipment rental, lessons and tours. **Anda De Wata Tours** offers sunset boat-and-float tours where you're pulled gently around in rubber rings with a rum punch in hand.

Swallow Caye

SPOTTING MANATEES

About 19 miles (30.5km) southwest of Caye Caulker, the vast **Swallow Caye Wildlife Sanctuary** spans nearly 9000 acres, including Swallow Caye and parts of nearby Drowned Caye. The ocean floor is covered with turtle-grass beds, which support a small population of West Indian manatees.

After tireless efforts of conservationists and guides, a wildlife sanctuary was established in 2002. Swimming with manatees is forbidden by the Belizean authorities, and education programs dissuade boaters from using motors near manatees and from speeding in the area (propeller injuries are a chief cause of manatee deaths). There is a permanent caretaker in these waters, although some complain this is not enough to adequately enforce regulations. Patient visitors are usually rewarded with several sightings of breaching and feeding manatees, often a mother and calf swimming together.

GETTING AROUND

Caulker is so small that most people walk or cycle everywhere. A few golf-cart taxis (recognized by the green plates) hang out around Front St for short trips around town (BZ$5 to BZ$7). You can rent a golf cart, but bicycle rental is far cheaper (free at many accommodations) and just as fast a way to get around.

Maya Island Air and Tropic Air connect Caye Caulker with San Pedro and Belize City. The airline offices are at the island's southern end. Caribbean Sprinter Water Taxi (sprinter.bz) and San Pedro Belize Water Taxi (belizewatertaxi.com) run regular boats to/from Belize City and on to San Pedro.

Beachfront, Caye Caulker

Mask Temple, Lamanai (p108)

NORTHERN BELIZE

MAYA RUINS AND REMOTE SEASIDE COMMUNITIES

One of the least-visited regions in the country has some outstanding Maya sites, a laid-back rural vibe, sparkling coastal waters and no crowds.

Northern Belize, a largely agricultural and sugarcane-farming region bordering Mexico and Guatemala, is essentially made up of two districts: Orange Walk and Corozal, traversed by the Philip Goldson Hwy and each with a namesake town as a focal point. Inland Orange Walk Town is marginally the larger of the two but is still a small community of some 14,000 people, with more coming in from the surrounding villages and Mennonite communities to do business and head to the market. On the coast just 9 miles (14.5km) south of the Mexico border, Corozal Town (pictured) has a unique tropical feel without the crowds of the northern cayes and with a direct daily boat to and from San Pedro. Further east, Sarteneja is a dreamy fishing and ship-building village with easy access to the Shipstern Nature Reserve.

Northern Belize lies on the east fringe of the ancient Maya heartland and the real star of this region is Lamanai, a stunning jungle-shrouded Maya site best reached by a boat ride down the New River from Orange Walk to Belize's largest freshwater lagoon, which in itself is a wonderful nature tour. Taking up the entire western part of this region is the remote Río Bravo Conservation and Management Area, teeming with birds and animals, including the largest concentration of jaguars in Central America.

Many travelers save on the cost of getting to Belize by flying into Cancun on Mexico's Yucatàn Peninsula and bussing or driving down to Belize. It may be tempting to continue straight through to Belize City or the cayes but you'll risk missing out on a unique and untouristed part of the country.

THE MAIN AREAS

ORANGE WALK TOWN
Riverside market town.
p102

COROZAL TOWN
Coastal bliss near the border.
p111

Find Your Way

The Philip Goldson Hwy runs straight through the populated eastern half of Northern Belize, via the main towns of Orange Walk and Corozal. Both towns have small airstrips with direct air links to San Pedro, and Corozal has boats to the cayes.

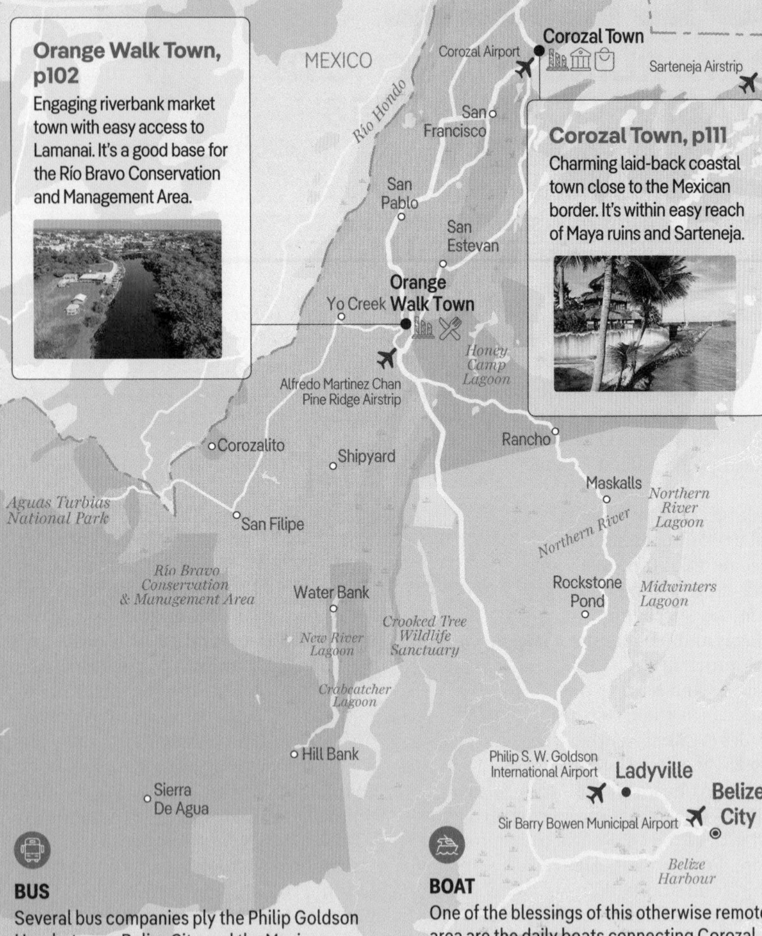

Orange Walk Town, p102

Engaging riverbank market town with easy access to Lamanai. It's a good base for the Río Bravo Conservation and Management Area.

Corozal Town, p111

Charming laid-back coastal town close to the Mexican border. It's within easy reach of Maya ruins and Sarteneja.

BUS

Several bus companies ply the Philip Goldson Hwy between Belize City and the Mexican border (some go as far as Chetumal) via Orange Walk Town and Corozal Town. There's a direct bus to Sarteneja via Orange Walk.

BOAT

One of the blessings of this otherwise remote area are the daily boats connecting Corozal with San Pedro on Ambergris Caye. Between them, Thunderbolt and Belize Sea Shuttle run daily between Corozal and San Pedro, stopping at Sarteneja on request.

Structure 5, Cerros Maya (p115)

Plan Your Time

Northern Belize covers a relatively large inland and coastal area but most visitors stick to the Philip Goldson Hwy and the main towns of Orange Walk and Corozal – backcountry detours are plentiful though!

Orange Walk Exploration

Spend two days in **Orange Walk Town** (p102) mingling with locals at the market, visiting the museum and dining at a riverside restaurant. Book a journey down the New River to **Lamanai** (p108) and spend a day exploring this extraordinary Maya site. If you have a car, drive west to the Maya site **La Milpa** (p107) and for birdwatching at **Río Bravo** (p107).

Corozal & the Coast

Spend a day in pretty Corozal Town, visiting the **House of Culture** (p103) and **Santa Rita ruins** (p113). Drive east to Copper Bank and the beachfront Maya ruins of **Cerros Maya** (p115). Continue to sleepy fishing town **Sarteneja** (p116). Here you can arrange boat trips and explore the **Shipstern Area** (p117). If you don't have a car, boats link Sarteneja with Corozal and San Pedro.

Seasonal Highlights

FEBRUARY TO APRIL
Prime time for birdwatching at Shipstern lagoon and along the New River. Corozal hosts a **Coconut Festival** in March.

JULY
Dry season ends and humidity kicks in. The village of Progresso celebrates **Pibili Fest**, a feast of Maya cooking.

SEPTEMBER
September celebrations take over Orange Walk and Corozal towns, with costumes, music and the 'road march'.

OCTOBER
Sarteneja gets in on the act with its own seafood festival, celebrating the town's fishing traditions.

ORANGE WALK TOWN

Orange Walk Town is the center of the region's sugarcane industry, a market town, economic hub, Mennonite meeting place and street-food capital of the north. It doesn't feel like a tourist town but this is the base for the river trip to the ruins of Lamanai and excursions into the wilds of northern Belize. The town itself, 57 miles (91.7km) from Belize City, has a decent range of hotels and restaurants and a fine location beside the New River, which meanders lazily along the east side of town.

Orange Walk Town was founded as a logging camp in the 18th century, from where mahogany was floated down the New River to Corozal Bay. It began to develop as a town around 1850, when Mexican refugees from the War of the Castes arrived. These migrants, whose agricultural experience was welcomed by the British colonial authorities, started northern Belize's first sugar boom in the 19th century.

TOP TIP

Because of northern Belize's proximity to Mexico and Guatemala's Petén, and the Mexican or Guatemalan origins of many of the people living here, Spanish is the first language of many northerners, but most speak English as well.

Lamanai Landings (p104)

PAUL HARDING/LONELY PLANET ©

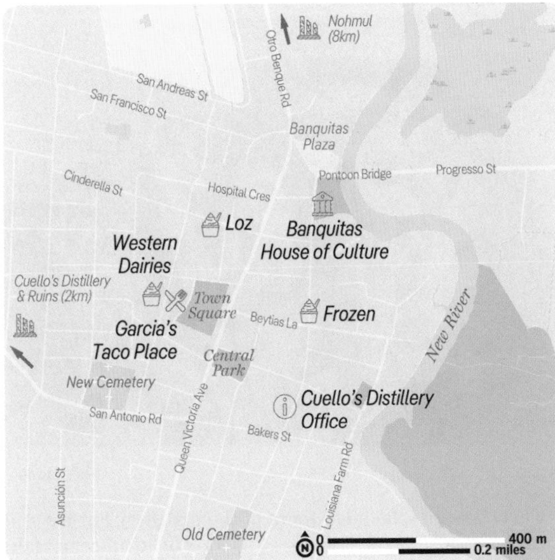

Historic Orange Walk

HOUSE OF CULTURE

The modern air-conditioned **Banquitas House of Culture** displays an easily digested exhibit on Orange Walk's history, from prehistory to its beginnings as a logging camp to the development of the sugarcane industry. It's especially good on the local ancient Maya sites, and has artifacts, maps and illustrations, as well as exhibits that change monthly. It's set beside a pleasant riverside park with an amphitheater. The name Banquitas is derived from the 'little benches' that can be found along the riverfront.

Rum & Ruins

DISCOVER CUELLO'S RUM AND RUINS

Thanks to Orange Walk's sugarcane industry and the production of molasses at the local sugar factory, the region is also one of the major producers of Caribbean rum in Belize. **Cuello's Distillery** (cuellosdistilleryltd.bz), about 4 miles (6.5km) west of Orange Walk Town on the road to Yo Creek, is the largest producer of rum in the region and the second-largest in Belize after Travellers Liquor.

ORANGE WALK TIPS

Luis Ruiz (aka Coconut Pete), legendary boat captain and Lamanai guide, gives tips on his hometown.

Best experience
I'm biased but the boat trip to Lamanai is a favorite, where visitors can see wildlife, crocs, birds and ancient temples in one day.

Best local food
Anyone from Belize will tell you the best tacos are in Orange Walk, made with a soft corn tortilla, chicken or pork, shredded cabbage, onion and hot peppers. Belizean *salbutes* (mini tortillas, usually stuffed with chicken) are a real treat from local street vendors. I also like rice and beans, *escabeche* (spicy chicken with lime and onions) and *chirmole* (stew with chicken and a chilli-chocolate sauce).

Best for tacos or a Belikin
Garcia's is my favorite taco stand. Go to Palm Island Bar for a Belikin or rum cocktail with locals.

WHERE TO STAY IN ORANGE WALK TOWN

Casa Ricky's
Backpacker-friendly guesthouse with kitchen facilities, bikes and a relaxing garden. **$**

El Gran Mestizo
South of town on the New River, excellent resort with cosy *cabañas*, larger cabins and a budget dorm. **$$**

Hotel de la Fuente
Family-run central hotel with some of the best-value rooms in town. **$$**

RIVERSIDE SLEEPS

The New River running through Orange Walk offers good riverfront accommodations.

Lamanai Riverside Retreat Locally popular riverside restaurant-bar with three affordable timber cabin-style rooms. You can also camp. $

El Grand Mestizo One of Orange Walk's fanciest riverside resorts, south of town. Excellent Maracas Restaurant, cosy *cabañas*, larger modern cabins and a dorm. $$

Lamanai Landings On an offshoot lagoon of New River, about 4.5 miles (7km) south of Orange Walk, this hotel is well placed for trips to Lamanai. Water-facing rooms have balcony, air-con, bathroom and cable TV. $$

Fish tacos

There are no scheduled tours of the distillery but it's still possible to visit if you register at Cuello's head office in Main St, Orange Walk, at least the day before. Tours are not always available though and depend on staffing at the plant. But a free tour of the distillery and the bottling plant isn't the only reason to venture out here. Behind the distillery, on a private estate, is a centuries-old Maya ruin.

Cuello (kway-yo) is one of the earliest-known settled communities in the Maya world, dating to around 2400 BCE, although there's not much left to show for it today. Archaeologists have found plenty here, but only Structure 350, a nine-tiered pyramid, is of much interest to the nonexpert. The pyramid was constructed around 200 CE to 300 CE, but its lower levels date from before 2000 BCE. A permit to visit the ruin can easily be arranged at Cuello's head office – a tour of the distillery is a bonus. A taxi to Cuello from Orange Walk costs about BZ$25, round trip.

Street Food & Snacks

TACOS AND ICE CREAM

Orange Walk Town is known for its cheap and cheerful street food, with taco stands (**Garcia's** is a local favorite), snack stalls, burger huts, fruit-juice stalls and smoking BBQs (such as Nellie's) arranged around the town plaza and local bus stand. The atmosphere is especially good on Saturday afternoons

WHERE TO EAT & DRINK IN ORANGE WALK TOWN

Nahil Mayab Fun, kitschy Maya-themed place serving Yucatecan-inspired food, such as *pibil* or *poc chuc*. **$$**

Cocina Sabor Fine Belizean and international fare on the highway south of town. **$$**

Lamanai Riverside Retreat Popular riverside restaurant and bar close to the town center. **$$**

but you'll find a stall open somewhere from morning until evening every day.

Orange Walk Town hosts Belize's only **Taco Festival** in November, where the streets come alive with sizzling taco stands and locals and visitors sample all manner of Belizean and Mexican tacos from chicken to *pibil*.

On hot afternoons head to one of the ice-cream shops in town. **Loz**, on Cinderella St, specializes in ice cream, frozen yogurt and slushies. Around the corner **Western Dairies** is the popular Mennonite brand and Belize's largest dairy, serving ice cream, shakes and pizza. On Main St, **Frozen** does a good line in ice cream and coffee.

Search for Nohmul

UNEXCAVATED MAYA RUINS

Budding archaeologists will be interested in a trip to **Nohmul** (noh-mool), a pre-Columbian Maya site that hasn't been excavated or landscaped and so looks much as it would have when early explorers arrived – a series of hills and mounds with some evidence of exposed structures. The ruins made headlines and there was widespread outrage in 2013 when a construction company bulldozed one of the main temples to obtain material for road construction. The company was later convicted under Belize's protection of Maya site laws and fined.

Meaning 'Great Mound' or 'Big Hat' in Maya, Nohmul was thought to be a town of 3000 people during the late Classic Period, overlooking the Río Hondo (now the border between Belize and Mexico). The ruins themselves aren't spectacular but with some imagination and a sense of adventure it is a rewarding place to visit as you scramble up mounds sheltering untold archaeological riches below.

From the northern edge of Orange Walk, drive 9.6 miles (15.5km) north on the Philip Goldson Hwy to the village of San José. Turn west at the north end of the village and drive 1.3 miles (2.1km) west to Nohmul (toward Douglas village). The site is not well marked so you might have to ask for directions through the maze of sugar roads.

LAMANAI BOAT TOURS

—

A boat ride down the New River from Orange Walk is the best way to experience the epic ruins at **Lamanai** (p108).

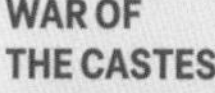

WAR OF THE CASTES

In the mid-19th century, the Caste War in the Yucatán resulted in many Hispanic refugees settling in northern Belize. At the same time tensions arose between the Orange Walk settlers and the local Icaiché Maya.

British loggers had been encroaching on lands that the Icaiché considered their own around the Río Hondo (today's border with Mexico) and, in 1872, the War of the Castes came to Orange Walk when a force of some 150 Icaiché Maya attacked the town's British garrison. After several hours of fierce fighting the Icaiché were repelled, and their leader, Marcos Canul, was fatally wounded.

The attack went down in history as the last significant armed Maya resistance in Belize.

GETTING AROUND

Orange Walk's town center is easily walkable but you'll need a car or taxi to venture further afield off the main highway. This is the major northern Belize hub for buses plying the Corozal–Belize City route, with around 30 buses a day going in each direction. All long-distance buses, including services to Belize City, Corozal, Chetumal and Sarteneja, stop at the Dunn St bus terminal west of the cemetery. Buses to rural destinations around Orange Walk District, such as Copper Bank or Indian Creek, leave from various points around the market square. Schedules are subject to change, so ask in advance around the market or at your hotel.

Beyond Orange Walk Town

Orange Walk District stretches a long way south and west but the star attraction is the jungle-strewn Maya ruins of Lamanai.

TOP TIP

If you're heading to Río Bravo call Programme for Belize (p107) or check the website for detailed directions, advice on road conditions (some can be impassable after heavy rains) or to help arrange transfers from Orange Walk.

Orange Walk is one of the more spread out and thinly populated districts in Belize – most travelers are passing through on the Philip Goldson Hwy or heading to the main town of Orange Walk. Outside this population center, most of the communities and attractions west of the highway are connected by a network of (mostly) unpaved roads linking farming communities.

Further west and to the south, these grid roads disappear entirely, and you're in what Belizeans refer to as 'deep bush,' the backwoods jungle border country that makes up most of Orange Walk District. It's here you'll find the vast Río Bravo Conservation & Management Area. More accessible – particularly via the New River – is the unmissable Maya site of Lamanai.

New River

ERNI/SHUTTERSTOCK ©

Ocelot

Remote Wildlife-Watching

NATURAL RAINFOREST BEAUTY

If you're looking for true, wild tropical rainforest, the 406-sq-mile (1051.5-sq-km) **Río Bravo Conservation & Management Area** (RBCMA) is it. This vast corner takes up 4% of Belize's total land area and is managed by Belizean nonprofit organization **Programme for Belize** (PFB; pfbelize.org). RBCMA harbors astonishing biological diversity – 392 bird species, 200 tree species and 70 mammal species, including all five of Belize's cats (jaguar, puma, ocelot, jaguarundi and margay). Río Bravo is said to have the largest concentration of jaguars in all of Central America.

The beauty is that there are two remote (and far apart) field stations, providing affordable accommodations for visiting naturalists and tourists, and the outstanding, upmarket **Chan Chich Lodge** for a serious Belize bush adventure.

Parts of the territory of the RBCMA were logged for mahogany and other woods from the 18th century until the 1980s, but distance and inaccessibility helped to ensure the survival of the forest as a whole and much of the land was bought and donated as a wildlife reserve in the 1980s and 1990s.

Río Bravo is one of the country's prime birding areas. In 2005 the RBCMA was selected as the release site for the restoration of the majestic and globally threatened harpy eagle; other large avian species include the ocellated turkey, the crested guan and the ornate hawk eagle. The open area around La Milpa Lodge attracts fly-catchers, mannekins, redstarts, orioles, tanagers, trogons and hummingbirds.

CHAN CHICH LODGE

One of Belize's original, most isolated and most rewarding ecolodges, Chan Chich is as remote as it gets in the middle of a 200-sq-mile (518-sq-km) private reserve in the far western corner of Orange Walk District.

The supremely comfortable thatched *cabañas* are built from local hardwoods around the partly excavated ruins of an ancient Maya plaza and feature wooden slat walls that open up to the sounds of nature.

The remote setting and pristine environs make Chan Chich a destination in and of itself: many bird and wildlife enthusiasts arrive via charter flight from Belize City and spend their Belize visit right here.

Scan this QR code to book a stay at Chan Chich Lodge.

WHERE TO STAY IN ORANGE WALK DISTRICT

Lamanai Outpost Lodge
Close to the ruins, this classy upmarket lodge with 17 thatched bungalows is a sweet jungle retreat. **$$$**

La Milpa Lodge
Four comfortable *cabañas* and budget dorm-style room in the northwest corner of the RBCMA. **$$**

Hillbank Field Station
In the southeast corner of Río Bravo and accessible via Burrell Boom; *cabañas* (cabins) and dormitory. **$$**

NATURE'S CHARM/SHUTTERSTOCK ©

Admission costs BZ$10

Boat tours (including admission and lunch) BZ$120

Open 8am to 5pm

TOP SIGHT

Lamanai

Renowned for its impressive architecture and marvelous jungle setting overlooking the New River Lagoon, Lamanai ('submerged crocodile' in Maya) is one of the largest, oldest and most completely excavated Maya sites in northern Belize. It lies 24 miles (38.6km) south of Orange Walk Town upstream on the New River.

DON'T MISS

- Mask Temple
- Jaguar Temple
- High Temple
- Stela 9
- Lamanai Museum
- Boat trip down the New River
- Spotting (and hearing) resident howler monkeys

Lamanai Museum

In the main administrative building where you pay your entrance fee, this small but well-presented museum features photographs and artifacts unearthed throughout the Lamanai complex, including the original Stela 9.

Jaguar Temple

The first site you reach is the **Jaguar Temple** (pictured; Structure N10-9). Fronting a 100yd-wide plaza it was built in the 6th century CE and modified several times up to at least the 15th century. The stone patterning on the lowest level depicts two cleverly designed jaguar faces, dating from the initial 6th-century construction. On the opposite (north) side of the plaza is a set of buildings that were used as residences for Lamanai's royal elite.

Stela 9

This temple was the original site of the intricately carved standing stone erected in 625 CE to commemorate the accession of Lord Smoking Shell in 608 CE that is now on display in the site museum. A faithful replica has been placed in front of the temple in the original position.

The stone shows the leader in ceremonial regalia, wearing a rattlesnake headdress with quetzal feathers at the back, and holding a double-headed serpent bar diagonally across his body, with a deity emerging from the serpent's jaw at the top.

Ballcourt

Not far west of Stela 9 is Lamanai's ballcourt, one of the smallest in the Maya world – but with the largest ballcourt marker found yet! A ceremonial vessel containing liquid mercury, probably from Guatemala, was found beneath the marker.

High Temple

The **High Temple** is the highest structure at Lamanai, rising 125ft (38m) above the jungle canopy. Few large buildings in the Maya world were built as early as this one, which was initially constructed around 100 BCE. The 360-degree view from the top is amazing but tourists are presently not permitted to climb this temple for safety reasons.

Mask Temple

The famous **Mask Temple** (Structure N9-56) was begun around 200 BCE and modified several times up to 1300 CE. It has two 13ft (4m) stylized masks of a man in a crocodile headdress emblazoned on its west face to the north and south of the main stairs. Dating from about 400 CE, these are considered some of the finest big masks in the Maya world.

What you actually see are fiberglass replicas that have been crafted in front of the original limestone masks to protect them. Deep within this building archaeologists found the tombs of a man adorned with shell and jade jewelry, and a woman from almost the same date. The pair are thought to be a succession of leaders – perhaps husband and wife, or brother and sister.

BOAT TOURS

Most boats depart from Tower Hill Bridge or Bats Landing, with Orange Walk Town pickups.

Lamanai Eco Adventures Tower Hill Bridge.

Lamanai Eco Tours Bats Landing. Also runs birding and fishing tours.

Lamanai River Tours El Gran Mestizo in Orange Walk Town.

TOP TIPS

- Bring plenty of bug spray – the jungle surrounding the ruins can be home to vicious mosquitoes.
- A tour of the ruins takes a minimum of one hour, but can be done more comfortably in two or three hours if you're not on a tour.
- You can drive to Lamanai on unpaved roads from Orange Walk Town via Shipyard in about one hour.
- Boat tours down the New River take about two hours to New River Lagoon, Belize's largest freshwater lake.
- Not on tour? You can overnight at nearby Indian Creek village or Lamanai Outpost Lodge.

LA MILPA

In the northwestern corner of the RBCMA, **La Milpa** is the third-largest Maya site in Belize, believed to have had a population of 46,000 at its peak between 750 CE and 850 CE.

Its 5-acre Great Plaza, one of the biggest of all Maya plazas, is surrounded by four pyramids up to 80ft (24m) high.

Today, the structures are all covered with jungle and inhabited with howler monkeys, evoking the mystery and history of the ancient ruins.

Guides from the field station at La Milpa Lodge can accompany your hike to shed light on the function of the various structures, and to point out the stelae and other moss-covered artifacts that still remain in the area.

Horse and buggy, Shipyard

Shipyard Mennonites

INDUSTRIOUS COMMUNITIES

There are two main Mennonite communities in northern Belize: the Old Order Mennonites of **Little Belize** (p117) near Progresso, and the more progressive (but still conservative compared with those at Spanish Lookout) Mennonites of **Shipyard**, southwest of Orange Walk Town.

Shipyard is a wide-ranging, industrious community of farmers, carpenters and builders around 20 miles (32.2km) southwest of Orange Walk and with your own transportation or taxi it's an easy drive through farmland on dusty roads via Guinea Grass. Another option is to arrange a boat trip on the New River from Tower Hill, which passes by the eastern side of the community.

Although this is not a tourist attraction and there are no organized activities, it's an interesting trip to drive around the farming community, passing local Mennonite families in their horse-drawn buggies or stopping by one of the village stores where you'll likely meet some locals. The Mennonites speak *Plautdietsch* (Low German) among themselves, but some also speak English and Spanish.

GETTING AROUND

Orange Walk District is well connected by buses to the rest of Belize with frequent services running north into Corozal District and south into Belize District.

There is an airfield near Orange Walk Town but it only receives a couple of flights a day from San Pedro.

The main highway is sealed but most roads west of this highway towards Río Bravo and south to Shipyard are still unpaved.

COROZAL TOWN

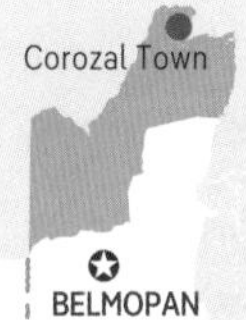

Corozal sits charmingly on the soapy-blue waters of Corozal Bay and has a vibe different from any other town in Belize, thanks in part to its obvious Mexican influence. Most of the town's prosperity comes from its position as a commercial and farming center and trade with Mexico, rather than from tourism. Still, a trickle of cross-border tourists and travelers coming to or from San Pedro by boat stop here, and Corozal remains a fine place to hang out as it completely escapes the holiday-ville atmosphere of the northern cayes. With ocean breezes, affordable (cheap by San Pedro standards) hotels, fine food and easy access to the rest of the district, Corozal and the surrounding region is worth a stop on the way to or from Mexico or as a detour from your Belizean itinerary.

TOP TIP

Corozal House of Culture is an informal tourist office and can help with local information, including a self-guided historical walking tour. The Immigration Office in town provides 30-day visa extensions for most nationalities.

Corozal beachfront

BEST CHEAP SLEEPS & EATS IN COROZAL

Hotel Maya
Budget favorite guesthouse. Clean, homey rooms and apartments available long-term. $

Hok'ol K'in Guest House
Unassuming waterfront hotel with spacious, excellent-value rooms on two floors. $

Mirador Hotel
Landmark multistorey corner hotel on the beach road. Outstanding value. $

Mexican Taste
Standout tacos and Mexican dishes in an open-fronted restaurant. $

RD's Diner
Local legend for Belizean food such as *gibnut* stew or more typical Mexican and continental fare. $

Wood House Bistro
Chinese-meets-Caribbean restaurant and bar with dumplings, wontons, noodles and more. $$

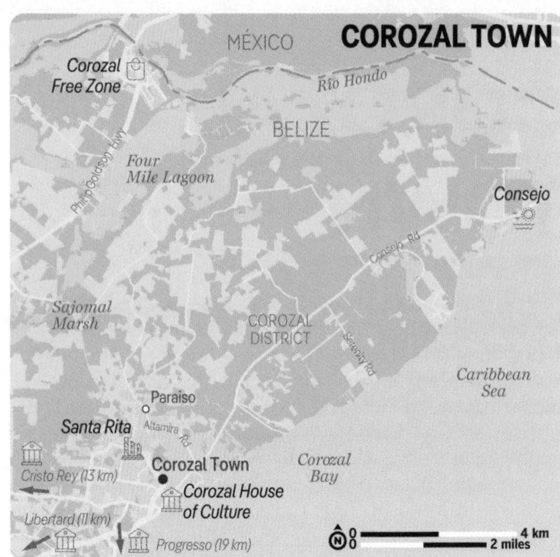

Corozal History & Culture

HOUSE OF CULTURE

Modern Corozal dates from 1849, when it was founded by Mexicans fleeing the War of the Castes. The refugees named their town Corozal after the Spanish word for cohune palm, a strong symbol of fertility. In 1955 Hurricane Janet blew away many of the thatched-roof buildings, so much of Corozal's present-day wood-and-concrete architecture dates from the late 1950s.

Built in 1886, **Corozal House of Culture** is in a fine old Spanish colonial building that once housed a bustling market beside the old customs house. Today, the historic building houses a cultural center and museum with exhibits of local artifacts. About a half-mile south of town on the Philip Goldson Hwy in **Ranchito**, the **Window into the Past Museum** focuses on the experience of the East Indian population who arrived in around 1838 as indentured servants working on sugar plantations. Other small cultural community museums are in villages surrounding Corozal: Yucatec Maya Museum in **Cristo Rey**; Darina Museum covering Garifuna culture in **Libertad**; and Malate Creole Museum in **Progresso**. Contact the Corozal House of Culture first for directions and to check if they're open.

WHERE TO STAY & EAT IN COROZAL TOWN

Almond Tree Resort
Gorgeous 10-room seafront resort with lush grounds, swimming pool and home-cooked meals. **$$**

Tony's Inn & Beach Resort
Large southside beach resort with spacious well-equipped rooms and Cielo's Restaurant. **$$**

Corozo Blue's
Waterfront restaurant and day resort with woodfired pizzas and a sunset bar. **$$**

Chill Out in Consejo

BEACHY FISHING VILLAGE

About 7 miles (11.3km) north of Corozal, small fishing village **Consejo** is set on Chetumal Bay, offering little more than a few patches of pristine beach, sea views and a small expat population. The expat community has created Consejo Shores residential development and one of Belize's few golf courses. If you have time it's worth an afternoon drive from Corozal or a stay at waterfront **Casa Blanca by the Sea**. There aren't many tourist amenities, though the convivial **Buccaneer Palapa** and **2020 Cafe** are both worth a stop. There's a small public beach and **Tamay Park** is a lovely spot with beach access, though signs warn it's for 'residents and guests only'.

Corozal Free Zone

DUTY FREE AT THE BORDER

At the Belize–Mexico border, 9 miles (14.5km) north of Corozal Town, **Corozal Free Zone** (belizecorozalfreezone.com) is essentially a tax-free shopping district designed to boost the economy of northern Belize by attracting Mexican shoppers and providing jobs for Belizeans. It's bigger than most Belizean towns, with streets, gas stations, banks, cafes, casinos and, of course, lots of shops selling knock-off brand-name gear, cheap alcohol and jewelry. The catch, of course, is that you need to exit (or enter) Belize in order to shop for a bargain.

Santa Rita Hill

HIDDEN MAYA SITE

Santa Rita was an ancient Maya coastal town that once occupied the same strategic trading position as present-day Corozal Town, namely the spot between two rivers – Río Hondo (which now forms the Belize–Mexico border) and New River (which enters Corozal Bay south of town). Much of Santa Rita is unexcavated, but it's worth the short excursion north of town to view and climb the partially restored pyramid.

ART IN THE PARK

On one Saturday evening of every month, downtown Corozal hosts an outdoor art exhibition and mini music festival, known as Art in the Park.

Artists congregate in Central Park to display their wares, with paintings, photography, woodwork and more. Music is performed live or piped in over the loud speakers and the whole town comes out to socialize.

It's usually the second Saturday of the month but ask at the House of Culture (p103) for the latest schedule.

For more local art, check out the lobby of the town hall, where a colorful and graphic mural by Belizean-Mexican artist Manual Villamor Reyes enlivens the wall.

GETTING AROUND

Corozal's main bus terminal is a key stop for bus lines that ply the Philip Goldson Hwy to Orange Walk and Belize City and north to the border. *Colectivos* (shared taxis) to the Mexican border depart for the Belizean immigration post from outside the main bus terminal. Once you complete border formalities, Mexican *colectivos* and private taxis run into Chetumal. If you're in a hurry, these minivans run private transfers for BZ$25 to the border post or BZ$60 to the ADO intercity bus terminal in Chetumal.

Corozal is connected to Sarteneja (30 minutes) and San Pedro (two hours) by boat.

Corozal Town
Cerros Maya Ruins
Sarteneja
Shipstern Conservation & Management Area
Little Belize

Beyond Corozal Town

The far-northern coast features exotic Maya ruins, the sleepy fishing village of Sarteneja and a bird-filled lagoon at Shipstern.

The country's northernmost district, Corozal is wedged between Orange Walk District, the Mexican border and the sea. Its proximity to Mexico lends it a certain Spanish charm, and offers easy access to travelers coming from Cancún or Chetumal. In recent years, Corozal has been 'discovered' by outsiders, who are racing to buy up the affordable seaside property and build retirement homes on their little plots of paradise. However, this district is still relatively unknown to Belize-bound tourists, who don't often venture off the Philip Goldson Hwy.

Spread around Corozal Bay, this region is prettier and more compact than Orange Walk District, and most of the sights are well within striking distance – by boat or road – of Corozal Town itself.

TOP TIP

Roads toward Sarteneja are gradually being sealed and the old hand-cranked ferries (p115) are being replaced by bridges.

Seafront, Sarteneja (p116)

Structure 5, Cerros Maya

Explore Cerros Maya Ruins

BEACHFRONT MAYA SITE

Belize's only seafront Maya site, **Cerros Maya** (BZ$10) is a fascinating, partially excavated ruin, across the bay from Corozal Town. Composed of a series of temples built from about 50 BCE, the site is mostly a mass of grass-covered mounds but the center has been cleared and two important structures are visible. There's a **museum** and interpretive center at the site entrance which will give you an understanding of the layout.

In late Preclassic times, its proximity to the mouth of the New River gave Cerros Maya a key position on the trade route between the Yucatán coast and the Petén region. The temples are larger and more ornate than others found in the area, and archaeologists believe Cerros Maya may have been taken over by an outside power at this time, quite possibly Lamanai.

CRANKING FERRIES

Driving through the back bush of Corozal District you might wind up fording two rivers in a distinctly Belizean way – via hand-cranked ferries that run along thick cables strung from riverbank to riverbank.

In the past, too few vehicles made building a bridge not worth the cost and the low-tech, human-powered cable ferry was a way to ensure that cars, bikes, motorcycles and people could get across, while providing work for the ferry operators.

But time moves on and, as of 2023, bridges were under construction to replace both historic ferries: the one north of Copper Bank will be completed by the time you read this and the one on the Corozal–Progresso Rd, sadly, won't be far behind.

WHERE TO STAY AROUND COROZAL DISTRICT

Shipstern Nature Reserve Bungalows
Bungalows at the nature reserve, 3 miles (4.8km) southwest of Sarteneja. **$$**

Cerros Beach Resort
Rustic beachfront property north of Copper Bank with four eco *cabañas*. **$$**

Orchid Bay Resort
Thatched *cabañas* in a remote but upmarket, full-service beachfront holiday resort near Copper Bank. **$$$**

BOATS FROM SARTENEJA

If Sarteneja seems a bit remote by road, never fear! Two water taxis between Corozal and San Pedro stop here on request.

Thunderbolt (501-628-8590) offers daily pick up and drop off in Sarteneja with advance reservation. Heading to San Pedro the boat departs Sarteneja at 7:30am; on the return to Corozal it picks up at 4:30pm.One-way tickets cost BZ$59 to/from San Pedro and BZ$31 to/from Corozal.

Belize Sea Shuttle (belizeseashuttle.com) runs a similar service – except on Tuesday and Thursday. The boat to San Pedro departs at 3pm and to Corozal it's 8:15pm. Tickets are BZ$100 to San Pedro and BZ$50 to Corozal.

Climbing Structure 4 (a funerary temple more than 65ft (20m) high) offers panoramic views of the ocean and Corozal Town. Structure 5, with its back to the sea, was the first temple to be built. Large stucco masks flanking its central staircase have been covered with modern replicas for protection. Southwest of Structure 5, a third structure remains unexcavated, protected by an army of mosquitoes. Be warned: Cerros Maya can get very buggy, especially during the rainy season; cover up and don't skimp on the bug spray!

Get here by car or taxi from Corozal or Sarteneja (via the village of Copper Bank), or charter a boat directly from Corozal across the bay. **Our Island Tour** in Corozal runs boat trips (BZ$50, minimum three people) with advance notice.

Sarteneja by the Sea

DREAMY COASTAL LIVING

If you came to Belize in search of sparkling blue waters, fresh seafood, Caribbean sunsets, fauna-rich forests, village lifestyle and affordable accommodations, **Sarteneja** (sar-ten-eh-ha) may just be your place. This unassuming fishing and shipbuilding village, facing Chetumal Bay on the northeastern tip of the Belizean mainland, is a charming base from which to explore both the nautical and jungle treasures of the region.

The village spreads just a few blocks back from its long, grassy seafront. It's a sweet place to chill out for a few days, with a small but enthusiastic expat population bringing extra life to a scattering of atmospheric local bars and restaurants such as **Crabby's**, **Marteneja** and **Loco-Nuts Social House**. Ask around town or at Fernando's about fishing trips, kayak rental and horseback riding (from Horse Cottage). From this lovely seaside setting, visitors can also head out to the **Shipstern Conservation & Management Area** and take birding and wildlife-watching trips along the fabulous northern Belize coast, including to **Bacalar Chico National Park & Marine Reserve** (p76), on the northern tip of Ambergris Caye.

About 2 miles (3.2km) southeast of Sarteneja, on the shore of the Shipstern Lagoon, **Wildtracks** (wildtracksusa.org) is an established wildlife rescue and rehabilitation center doing great work with sick, injured and orphaned manatees and black howler monkeys. Although they don't currently accept casual visitors or tourists at the centers, they do have an impressive volunteer program with a minimum one-month stay. Find out more and apply at their website.

WHERE TO STAY & EAT IN SARTENEJA

Horse Cottage
Rural property close to town with rustic rooms, *cabañas* and horses. **$**

Fernando's Seaside Guesthouse
Good-value central family hotel with midrange rooms at a budget price. **$**

Crabby's
Welcoming waterfront open-sided restaurant specializing in local seafood. **$$**

PASCAL VOSICKI/SHUTTERSTOCK ©

Roseate spoonbill

Hike & Stay at Shipstern

WETLANDS AND WILDLIFE

Shipstern Conservation & Management Area protects 43 sq miles (111.3 sq km) of semideciduous hardwood forests, wetlands, lagoons and coastal mangrove belts, with its headquarters easily accessible 3.5 miles (5.6km) southwest of Sarteneja on the road to Orange Walk. Lying in a transition zone between Central America's tropical forests and a drier Yucatán-type ecosystem, the reserve's mosaic of habitats is rare in Belize. It's run by the **Corozal Sustainable Initiative Fund** (csfi.bz) which operates comfy forest bungalows, and birdwatching and lagoon tours. All five of Belize's wildcats and scores of other mammals can be found here, and its 250 bird species include ospreys, roseate spoonbills, white ibis and a colony of 300 pairs of American woodstorks, one of this bird's few breeding colonies in Belize.

There's a small museum and butterfly house at the headquarters, and a short botanical trail that leads to an observation tower. The best way to see the lagoon and its birdlife is via a guided mangrove walk and kayaking tour (BZ$150), which can be organized at the headquarters.

Accommodations at the park headquarters include two bungalows sleeping up to eight people each in single and double rooms. Call ahead (501-6320939) to check on road conditions, accommodations and to book tours.

LITTLE BELIZE

Located on the eastern shore of Progresso Lagoon, Little Belize is an Old Order Mennonite community of approximately 2000 residents.

Among the more traditional Mennonite groups, these folks look as though they've come straight from the prairie, driving around in horse-drawn carriages, with men wearing broad-brimmed hats and denim overalls and women in long dresses and bonnets

Like most Mennonite villages, Little Belize is an industrious place, with an economy thriving on farming. One of the largest employers in the village is Little Belize Exporters Ltd, which grows papayas for export to North America.

GETTING AROUND

Corozal District is the first taste of Belize for many travelers crossing the border with Mexico at Santa Elena.

Most roads east of the highway are unpaved, though the road to Sarteneja is being sealed. Check conditions before heading out.

Local buses and minivans connect the border with Corozal Town. The main bus route between Corozal District and the rest of Belize is along the Philip Goldson Hwy, connecting Corozal Town with Belize City via Orange Walk Town.

Another major bus line connects Belize City and Sarteneja via Orange Walk Town.

An airport south of Corozal Town has flights to/from San Pedro but most travelers use daily water taxis between Corozal Town and San Pedro via Sarteneja.

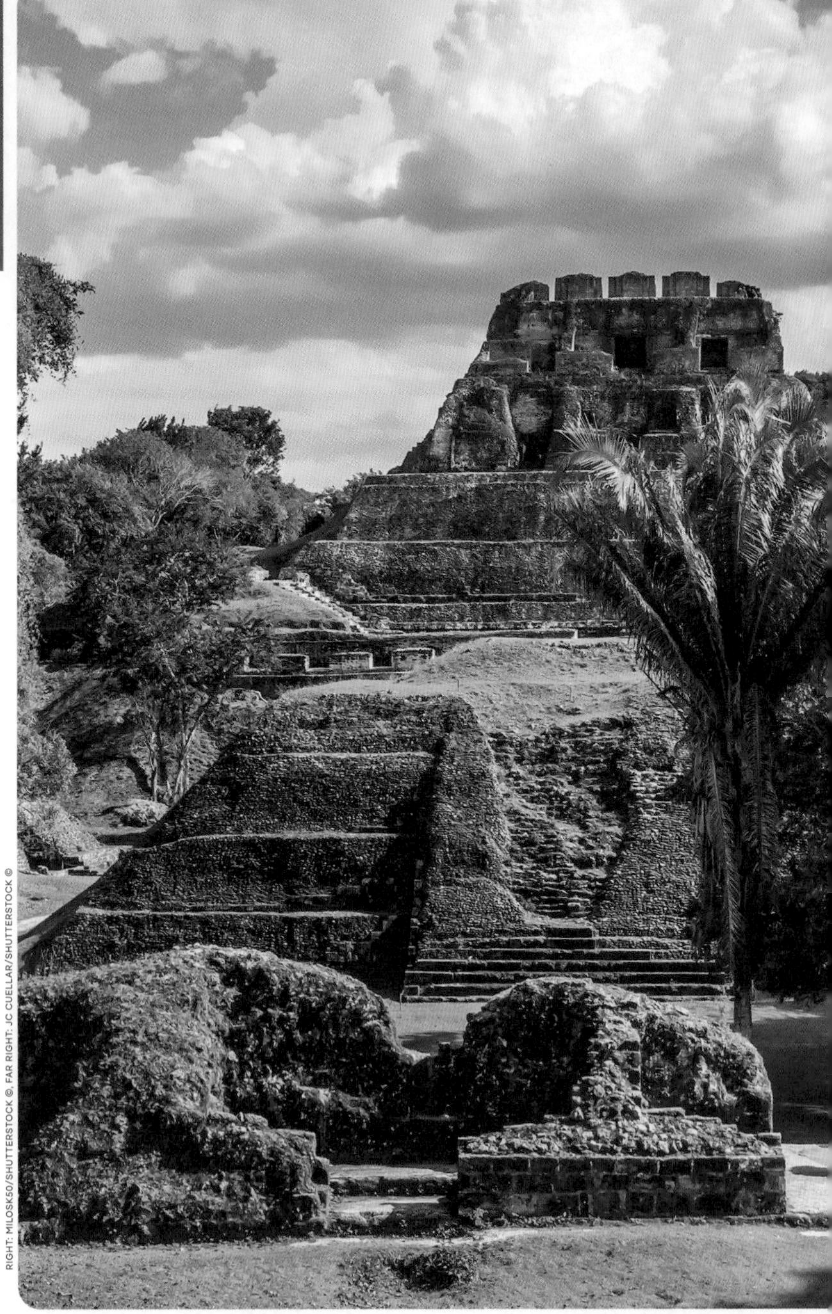

RIGHT: MILOSK50/SHUTTERSTOCK ©, FAR RIGHT: JC CUELLAR/SHUTTERSTOCK ©

Xunantunich (p129)

CAYO DISTRICT

GATEWAY TO ADVENTURE AND MAYA HISTORY

BELMOPAN

Where tropical savanna gives way to vast jungles and forests filled with bountiful wildlife, Maya ruins and cowboy culture: welcome to western Belize.

The Cayo District in western Belize is the country's land-based adventure hub, with lush jungles crisscrossed by winding rivers, cascading waterfalls and shockingly blue cenotes, and magnificent Maya temples. Cahal Pech, Xunantunich, El Pilar, and the mother of all Belizean Maya sites – Caracol – are all in Cayo. There is a nearly endless network of underground caves here, once thought to be the entrance to Xibalba, or the Maya underworld. Spelunkers of all skill levels have no shortage of options from which to choose.

Travelers leave the coast and head west all the way to the border of Guatemala along the George Price Hwy to tube through river caves, zipline over the jungle canopy or horseback ride through the Maya Mountains. From a base at San Ignacio or Belmopan – or one of the numerous outstanding jungle lodges nearby – tour operators can easily get your adventure started. This region teems with nature, from botanic gardens and butterfly houses to primeval jungles and rainforests, where the only thing coming between you and the wildlife is a pair of binoculars.

Cayo is rich with culture as well, from the cattle-raising cowboys to traditionally minded Maya communities. And because of the proximity to the western border, Spanish is widely spoken here, though English and Kriol reign supreme. Shopping for artisan crafts and sampling some of Belize's finest fare is all on the menu in this abundant region.

THE MAIN AREAS

Find Your Way

Cayo's top to-dos are widely dispersed throughout the district, making cars the best way to get around independently. Local bus operators and taxis can fill in the gaps of resort transfers and tour-operator pickups.

BUS

Cayo has frequent bus service. Most buses heading south and west stop in Belmopan. While sticking to a schedule isn't their forte, buses are an inexpensive way to travel the country, and will do drop-offs and pickups at non-designated highway stops.

CAR

Car rentals are readily available at the international airport, but can also be acquired in Belmopan and San Ignacio. Most resorts offer airport transfer services and shuttles to and from town, while independent shuttle companies can customize trips.

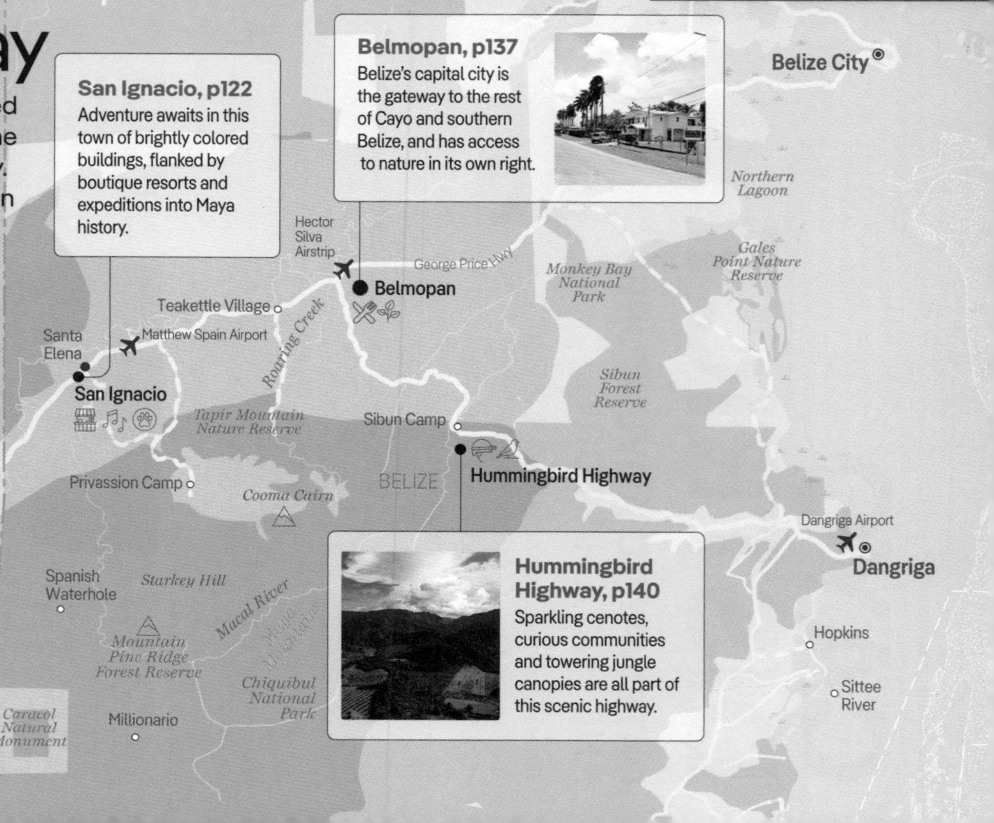

San Ignacio, p122
Adventure awaits in this town of brightly colored buildings, flanked by boutique resorts and expeditions into Maya history.

Belmopan, p137
Belize's capital city is the gateway to the rest of Cayo and southern Belize, and has access to nature in its own right.

Hummingbird Highway, p140
Sparkling cenotes, curious communities and towering jungle canopies are all part of this scenic highway.

FROM LEFT: JC CUELLAR/SHUTTERSTOCK ©, TARAVELWORLD1971/SHUTTERSTOCK ©

Río On Pools (p132)

Plan Your Time

Climb into a cave and scramble over Maya ruins, but take the opportunity to explore San Ignacio and the surrounding area. Go into the pine forests and jungles that await just beyond the beaten path.

Three Days to Explore

Use a jungle lodge near San Ignacio as your base and enjoy the surrounding wildlife. Head into town for a self-guided tour of **San Ignacio Market** (p123). Book a tour either to the **ATM Cave** (p128), or a **cave tubing tour** (p129) at Nohoch Che'en. Make the long drive through the Mountain Pine Ridge to the Maya ruins of **Caracol** (p129). Stop at **Río On Pools** (p132) for a dip on the way back.

More Time To Spare

Drive along the Hummingbird Hwy. Stop to explore caves and swim at **St Herman's Blue Hole National Park** (p141). Belmopan has shopping, restaurants and **Guanacaste National Park** (p139) to enjoy. See everything Mountain Pine Ridge has to offer, from birdwatching to **Big Rock Falls** (p129). Go beyond the pine forest into the towering **Chiquibul National Forest** (p134), where jaguars and tapir roam.

Seasonal Highlights

JANUARY TO MARCH
Manageable temps, peak crowds and prices in January. February brings Carnival and March has **La Ruta Maya**.

APRIL TO AUGUST
High temps, low rainfall, low crowds. Hotels can cost 50% less than peak season. June is hurricane and lobster season.

SEPTEMBER
Happy birthday Belize! Celebrations abound in September, and while tourism is slow, there's plenty of fun to be found.

NOVEMBER & DECEMBER
Crowds begin again as temperatures start to cool off. It's the perfect time for outdoor adventures.

SAN IGNACIO

San Ignacio is the heart and soul of the Cayo District, a vibrant traveler center from where all roads and activities fan out. Together with twin town Santa Elena, on the east bank of the Macal River, this is the main population center of Cayo, with lots of good budget accommodations, decent restaurants and frequent transportation.

But as much as it is geared to travelers, San Ignacio is no inland San Pedro, existing only for tourism. It has a very positive and infectious vibe, with a market and a steady influx of immigrants, mainly from nearby Guatemala. Residents are mestizos, Maya and Garifuna, as well as free-spirited expats from Europe and North America.

Most travelers come to San Ignacio as a base for the adventures of Cayo or as a stepping stone to or from Guatemala; but with welcoming locals and plenty to do, many stay longer than they expected.

TOP TIP

Don't be afraid to branch out with accommodations. Most hotels and adventure activities are beyond the bounds of San Ignacio. Tour operators, shuttle services, hotel transfers and car rentals are all available to get you where you need to go.

Burns Ave, San Ignacio

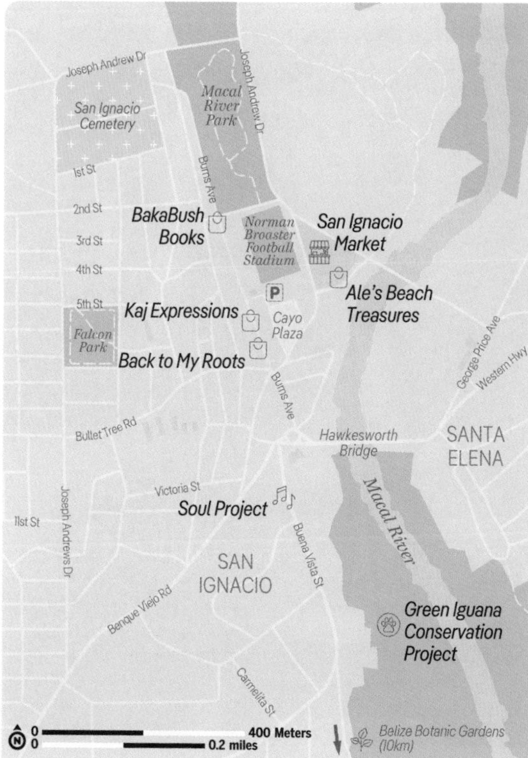

A Taste of Life in Cayo

EXPLORE SAN IGNACIO'S SATURDAY MARKET

In the heart of San Ignacio, between the Welcome Center and the Macal River, is the bustling **San Ignacio Market**, where a diverse collection of Belize's farmers and traders gather every Saturday to sell their goods. Maya, Mennonites, Creole and Mestizo Belizeans intermingle at the stalls, a variety of languages serving as the backdrop for this unique foray into the culture of the country. The market operates daily, but there's a marked uptick in activity on Saturday, when the whole of Cayo seems to be in attendance. Every stall is filled with products from fresh fruit and vegetables to colorful, handmade souvenirs to makeshift thrift shops filled

WHY I LOVE SAN IGNACIO

Ali Wunderman, Writer

'San Ignacio is where I've lived and where I choose to return because every morning begins with birdcalls from swooping toucans and curious mot-mots, and jungle mist rising off the trees as the sun comes out.

As the day progresses, there's a sense of adventure and possibility as everyone cools off in rivers and waterfalls, farmers fill their roadside stands with fresh produce, and tour operators enthusiastically share their passion for inland Belize atop Maya ruins or inside echoing caves.

That desire to enjoy the beauty and bounty of the wilderness is pervasive in San Ignacio, and it's hard not to feel present and alive when in its midst.'

WHERE TO EAT IN SAN IGNACIO

Guava Limb Café
This date-worthy spot is known for delicious, organic food including wood-fired pizza and wildly creative cocktails. **$$**

Booze & Branches
This beautiful bar beneath the branching limbs of a giant tree serves delectable bites in an upbeat environment. **$**

Hode's Place
A casual spot with an expansive menu including Belizean classics and comfort food favorites. **$**

SPACE FOR LOCAL ARTISTS

Daniel Velasquez owns and operates Soul Project. He has lived in Belize for 24 years.

How has Soul Project impacted the community?
As an independent community art space, Soul Project has incubated local artistic expression and welcomed international cultural exchange.

Why do Cayo artists need to have a space to create?
Consumer pop culture is heavily promoted in Belize. This space changes things by promoting original art and diversity.

What kind of music is played at Soul Project?
We've always had a world-music play list, and play a large amount of Belizean music. Even the world-famous Garifuna Collective comes by to play.

Belize Botanic Gardens

with interesting finds. Other products like medicinal herbs, soaps and handmade clothing make for excellent reminders of time spent in Belize. There are also restaurants peppered among the stalls, serving hot, local food like *pupusas* (filled maize pancakes), and rice and beans.

While picking up cooking ingredients may be unnecessary for a visitor, exploring the Saturday market is still an incredible opportunity to experience the life of Belizeans in Cayo. The people-watching is superb, with gossip and information exchanged in numerous languages and across various cultures, but it's also a chance to engage directly with hospitable locals. Bring a camera, cash and a friendly attitude to make the most of the singular experience.

WHERE TO STAY IN SAN IGNACIO

San Ignacio Resort Hotel
A charming, Belizean-owned hotel with an excellent pool and high level of service and amenities. **$$$**

Cocopele Inn
This Santa Elena hotel is ideal for the midrange traveler with a range of room types available. **$$**

Old House Hostel
Belizean-owned spot at the center of the action. Clean, fun and friendly: everything a great hostel should be. **$**

San Ignacio's Wild Side

NATURE EXPERIENCES CLOSE TO HOME

There is endless nature to explore around San Ignacio, but leaving town isn't required to enjoy Belize's plants and animals. Two experiences in particular offer a connection with the wilderness as close to San Ignacio as it gets.

Conservation is big in Belize, and the impact of this mindset can be experienced at the San Ignacio Resort Hotel's **Green Iguana Conservation Project**. Since 1996 the hotel has played host to the successful breeding and release of Belize's endangered green iguana (pictured), sharing every stage of the project with visitors on guided tours. Guests can get up close and personal with the charismatic animals, from their juvenile stage to just before they're old enough to be released. This educational experience explains their role in the ecosystem while allowing visitors the opportunity to take photos with the animals. Everyone is welcome to explore the 'San Iggy Hotel,' which has tours operating on the hour throughout the day. Just head to the front desk to book and pay.

To be immersed in the country's flora without stepping all the way into the jungle, head to the **Belize Botanic Gardens**, just outside town. This 45-acre Eden has a medicinal trail, fruit orchard and rainforest trail chock-full of native plants. Numerous birds can be found here too. The beauty and serenity makes it hard to believe that San Ignacio is so close. Guided tours are offered, but guests are free to roam.

WHERE ELSE TO SEE WILDLIFE IN SAN IGNACIO

San Ignacio Resort Hotel
You know about the iguanas, but this hotel is also home to tons of other species, like collared aracari, keel-billed toucans and all sorts of other critters.

Cahal Pech
This Maya ruin at the top of the hill in San Ignacio is a quiet respite from the bustle of town, and animals love it. Parrots, monkeys, butterflies; it's possible to spot all of the local wildlife here.

The Sounds of San Ignacio's Soul

A SPACE FOR CREATIVITY AND MUSIC

San Ignacio's nightlife might not compare with that found in towns along the coast, but the unique brand of after-dark fun here is worth checking out. Of particular note is twice-weekly **Soul Project** where the bar beneath the Old House Hostel is opened to the community for live-music performances. Every Wednesday and Friday from 6pm until 11pm, locals, hostel guests and others attracted by the sounds of reggae and rock 'n' roll gather to play music and sing for the crowd.

There's a tremendous amount of musical talent in Cayo that comes on display when Soul Project opens its doors. Other artistic talent can be witnessed as well, including paintings and sculptures decorating the space. Visitors are encouraged to

---

Cahal Pech Village Resort
A Belizean-owned hotel with the best view in town, and a wide selection of onsite dining options. $$

Midas Belize
Right in town, this hotel has a supersized pool for beating the heat. $$

Hi-Et Guesthouse
Basic accommodations for a good price, and a name filled with Belizean humor. $

THE HISTORY OF THE TAMALE

Belize's blend of Caribbean and Central American cultures makes the country's cuisine unique, and the tamale is part of that rich tapestry.

Often affiliated with Mexico, the tamale originated in Mesoamerica between 10,000 and 7000 years ago.

Maya tamales were originally steamed, not boiled, or cooked like a tortilla on a comal. Today tamales are a staple food in Belize, typically made with sweet corn and sometimes called *dukunus* due to the Garifuna influence. They are usually vegetarian but can be filled with meat too.

TIME FOR TAMALES

Hungry for the best tamales in Belize? Take a trip down the Hummingbird Hwy and stop at **Miss Bertha's** (p143) for a culinary classic.

sit at the piano or pick up a guitar and jam with whoever else has elected to go on stage. For those who are more comfortable in the audience, there are plenty of places to sit and take it all in, including a few swing chairs hanging from the ceiling. The bar, one of few in town, serves Belikin beers and the owner's homemade wine derived from local seasonal fruits like sorrel and *tambran*. Food is served on occasion, most often homemade dumplings with teriyaki sauce.

Overall, Soul Project is a great place to enjoy San Ignacio's nightlife, and a great opportunity to meet locals and even form friendships in a fun, casual environment.

Buy Local

SHOP AT THE SOURCE

Creativity abounds in Belize, and the country's penchant for artisanship is a delight to explore, especially when hunting for unique souvenirs. San Ignacio's shopping is mostly located along the pedestrian road at the town center, Burns Ave, where a range of stores can be found. Of particular note is **Kaj Expressions**, the jewelry store of a local designer gifted in hand-making accessories. Kaj uses beads, wire and even lionfish to create beautiful, ever-changing pieces that can't be found anywhere else in the world. Nearby gift shop **Back to My Roots** is run by the hospitable Barbara and Carlton Flowers. Between special souvenirs like drums and handicrafts, they also sell medicinal products derived from the surrounding jungle to help with ailments like bug bites and sunburn. Inside the restaurant Ko-Ox Han Nah, the colorful art of Walter Castillo decorates the walls. His paintings depict Belizean beach and jungle scenes, and can be bought right here.

Further in town, **Bakabush Books** offers used titles hand-selected by the literary-loving owner. This is one of the only dedicated bookstores in the country, and a great place to find unique copies of beloved stories. During the **San Ignacio Market** (p123), other local artisans set up stalls to peruse. **Ale's Beach Treasures** has a lovely collection of beach-inspired jewelry. If you're lucky, the beautiful stained-glass creations of Leisa Beliza will be available as well.

GETTING AROUND

Walking is easy, albeit hilly, with most shopping and tours based on pedestrian-only Burns Ave.

For Santa Elena, Bullet Tree Falls, Spanish Lookout, or destinations beyond town, a car is best. Self-driving is somewhat confusing, with poorly marked one-way streets, liberties taken by drivers when encountering obstacles, and confusion about the town's one streetlight (it's new).

Parking is generally free and easy to find, except near the market.

Taxis have green license plates and often wait near Cayo Welcome Center or Court's at the Burns Ave roundabout. A 'gringo tax' is likely if you look the part.

Buses stop at the Welcome Center, sometimes on schedule. There are shuttles to other parts of Cayo too. Locals mostly use them, but tourists are welcome to take them.

Beyond San Ignacio

San Ignacio is at the center of the action in Cayo, so adventure can be found any direction you go.

West to the Maya site of Xunantunich and the border of Guatemala, south into Mountain Pine Ridge and the jungles beyond, northeast past the Mennonite town of Spanish Lookout and back to Belmopan, and north into the fast-developing Bullet Tree Falls: this is why San Ignacio makes such a good base camp for exploring the region.

Most visitors take adventures in multiple directions over the course of their visit, particularly the cave experiences to the east and Mountain Pine Ridge to the south. Tours into these areas take advantage of the region's natural proclivity for adventure. Even with so much well-documented tourism activity, there's plenty left to discover.

TOP TIP

A car is essential for exploring the wide reaches beyond San Ignacio, with a 4WD being the best option in many cases.

Mopan River, Bullet Tree Falls (p128)

BULLET TREE FALLS

Bullet Tree Falls is a quickly growing village just beyond San Ignacio, particularly popular among ex-patriates thanks to ample land-purchasing opportunities. The culture of the place is developing as well, with restaurants, bars and activities to explore.

In addition to the El Pilar Maya archaeological site, visitors enjoy tubing down the Mopan River, along which the village is based.

There are a few hotels in town, including Vanilla Hills Lodge, but the village is easily accessible by bus, taxi, or car. There are any number of street-food and fast-food places to check out, each as delicious as the next.

MICHELE WESTMORLAND/GETTY IMAGES ©

Cave tubing

Descend into the Maya Underworld

A CAVE FOR EVERY SPELUNKER

It's said that the entrance to **Xibalba**, or the Maya underworld, is found in Belize. The extensive cave network found in Cayo was of great importance to the various generations that comprised the ancient Maya, with evidence of their use still visible today. There is much left to be mapped and documented, but those that have been make for incredible exploration opportunities today.

One of the most popular activities in all of Belize is the **Actun Tunichil Muknal**, or ATM, cave tour. Meaning 'Cave of the Crystal Sepulcher,' the ATM is one of the most exciting and rewarding caves to visit. A baseline of physical capability and a sense of adventure is required, as the ATM is not for every spelunker. It begins with a 45-minute hike, including three relatively shallow river crossings, before reaching the cave entrance. Over the next few hours, guests

CONTINUE TO TIKAL

The ancient Maya world did not have today's political boundaries. Cross into Guatemala to see **Tikal** (p184) to fully grasp how expansive Maya history extends.

WHERE TO EXPLORE OTHER CAVES

Crystal Cave
The incredible rock formations are worth the strenuous effort of hiking, rappelling and traversing slippery rock.

Barton Creek Cave
Serene canoe ride into the mouth of a cave in the heart of the jungle – one of Cayo's most intriguing cave experiences.

Rio Frio Cave
This 65ft (20m)-high cave in the Mountain Pine Ridge has pools, stalactites and a quarter mile of cave to walk through.

swim, scramble and squeeze through waist-high water and narrow passageways. Cameras aren't allowed to protect the 14 skeletons and pottery shards hiding within this cave system.

A more relaxing alternative is **cave tubing** through the **Nohoch Che'en Caves Branch Archaeological Reserve**. You can float lazily downriver through several dark caves and under the jungle canopy. There are opportunities to 'disembark' and check out some cool archaeological and geologic sites along the way too.

Both caving experiences require a licensed tour guide to enjoy, which can be arranged either directly with tour operators or through hotels. Wearing shoes that are sturdy but can get wet is highly recommended.

A LOCAL'S FOOD HIGHLIGHTS

Belizean-born **Davina Bedran**, owner of the Old House Hostel, shares where she sends guests when they're hungry.

Ko-ox Han-nah
This popular spot has an extensive menu. Of particular note is their spin on rice and beans: coconut rice with beans served separately. Order with stewed chicken for an excellent meal.

Pop's Restaurant
The best fry-jacks in Cayo are found at Pop's Restaurant, an air-conditioned eatery best visited for breakfast.

Cenaida's
A homey spot for reliably delicious Belizean food, with great service at a reasonable price.

The Past Revealed

EXPLORE THESE MAYA RUINS

Maya history is found throughout Belize, but Cayo is the place to go for a concentrated look into ruins that remain.

Xunantunich, pronounced something like shoe-nan-too-nitch, is a well-excavated site overlooking San Ignacio from its island vantage point. Located in the village of Benque Viejo, about a 15-minute drive toward the border, Xunantunich requires a delightful hand-crank ferry to be accessed. At any time the ferry might be loaded with cars, motorcycles, pedestrians, and even horses.

After another short drive, visitors reach the 'Maiden of the Rocks,' an impressive collection of stone pyramids around a peaceful grass lawn, the former temple forecourt. The tallest ruin is called El Castillo, rising 128ft (39m) into the sky. It pokes out among the canopy and can be seen from elsewhere in Cayo. Spider monkeys and birds abound at this site, so be sure to keep an eye out for them while climbing these incredible structures.

Deeper into Cayo is **Caracol**, which remains the tallest human-made structure in Belize. Getting there requires a bumpy, four-hour drive, but it's well worth the journey. This is the largest Maya site in the country, and once supported a population of 150,000 people. Exploring Caracol takes a full day, revealing detailed history about the Maya, modern archaeological endeavors, and most likely a fair amount of wildlife spotting. When combined with a stop at **Big Rock Falls** or **Río On Pools** (p132) on the way back, a trip to Caracol makes for an unforgettable experience.

WHERE TO KEEP EXPLORING MAYA HISTORY

Cahal Pech
Peaceful San Ignacio ruin, perched over the Macal River. The easiest way to explore Maya history with limited time.

El Pilar
Ancient Maya city among 5000 protected acres, combining nature with the awe of history. Access via Bullet Tree Falls.

Chaa Creek
Maya sites and artifacts, including mounds and chultuns (ancient storage systems) in an expansive jungle resort.

I SPY BIRDS

Cameron Boyd, owner of Black Rock Lodge, tells us which of Belize's 590 bird species to look out for in the jungle.

Orange-breasted Falcon
Possibly the rarest falcon in the world, look for it above the forest canopy capturing other birds in flight.

Black-and-white Hawk-Eagle
Sitting at the pinnacle of the food pyramid, this bird is found in remote forests, including at Black Rock Lodge.

Northern Emerald Toucanet
The smallest of Belize's toucans, this stunning green bird is truly a marvel to behold.

Book a Stay in Paradise

JUNGLE LODGES OFFER COMFORT AND NATURE

While the town of San Ignacio is well-situated for jungle exploration, there are several luxury lodges that bring their guests beneath the canopy itself.

One such property is **Black Rock Lodge**, perched on the banks of the Macal River across from Elijio Panti National Park, less than a 30-minute drive from San Ignacio. After exiting the Western Hwy, it's a bumpy but scenic drive past farms and fields into the jungle-covered limestone cliffs surrounding this property. Guests are greeted by a percussive chorus of tropical birds – sometimes even the rare scarlet macaw. Black Rock Lodge is a popular choice among birders, due to the avian-rich location and the high quality of the staff guides. The vaulted dining area gives an incredible vantage over the river and cliffs beyond, and the on-site trails mean jungle exploration is only steps away.

Somewhat closer to town is **Chaa Creek**, a luxury lodge that gives guests the chance to become one with the jungle environment. It offers a wide range of on-site experiences, from night safaris to horseback riding, but also boasts creative cocktails at the bar and exceptional meals in the restaurant. It's common to see Belizean wildlife at Chaa Creek, including many species of birds, ground mammals like tayra and gibnuts, and even howler monkeys. They're especially visible in the morning as their loud hoots greet the day, or when the resort's mango trees are rich with fruit for the hungry animals. Overall, Chaa Creek offers a plush way to enjoy everything the jungle has to offer.

A Pontoon-Boat Adventure

A WATERFALL AND JUNGLE EXPERIENCE

Cruising by boat isn't exclusive to the Belizean coast: it can be experienced deep in the jungles of Cayo too. This inland pontoon-boat adventure has quickly become one of the region's most popular activities, as it's fun, relaxing, and adventurous all in one.

Located on **Vaca Lake** on the upper part of the Macal River Valley, **Jungle Splash Eco-Tours** operates all-day pontoon-boat tours that slowly but surely allow guests to have exciting encounters with the many animals, plants and waterfalls that are found along this 6-mile (9.6km) stretch of water.

CAYO'S NATIONAL PARKS

Elijio Panti National Park
A 12,600-acre park with towering limestone cliffs, dense jungle and Belize's most captivating creatures.

Five Blues Lake National Park
A 10-acre park that few see – the mesmerizing blues of the lake are worth the expedition.

Guanacaste National Park
Located in Belmopan, Guanacaste offers a respite into nature without having to go too far from civilization.

TEGRA STONE NUESS/GETTY IMAGES ©

Cabin, Black Rock Lodge

Tours typically begin early in the day, as the drive from San Ignacio can take around one to two hours, depending on the condition of the road. Once on board, guests can expect a relaxing journey across the placid human-made lake, stopping at various waterfalls and swimming holes throughout the day. **Río Frio Waterfall**, **Twin Falls** and **Sandpaper Falls** (when there's enough water for it to run) are all on the schedule, though impromptu stops can often be expected. Guides are quick to point out the rich wildlife that can be found in this remote rainforest location, including ocelots, tapir and crocodiles. Swimming, tubing and exploring are all encouraged. A Belizean BBQ lunch is cooked and served on board, though stopping to picnic on a sandy spit is typically an option as well.

The Jungle Splash office is in San Ignacio, and tours can be booked there, though hotels and other tour operators can help make arrangements as well. A booking includes transportation, food and the tour.

HOW VACA LAKE CAME TO BE

There are three hydroelectric dams along the Macal River, at the top of which now exists the Vaca Lake Reservoir, where the pontoon-boat tours operate.

Construction began in 2008 and was completed the following year, complementing the Chalillo and Mollejon dams.

The dams were built to reduce Belize's energy reliance on neighboring Guatemala, while also controlling floods along the Macal River.

The project was, and remains, controversial among Belizeans who are suspicious of anything that interferes with the natural workings of the environment.

That said, the creation of Vaca Lake has enabled local innovators and tour operators to bring guests closer to the incredible surrounding environment.

WHERE TO VISIT OTHER NEARBY VILLAGES

San Antonio
A small agricultural village largely home to Yucatac Maya-speaking Belizeans, about 10 to 15 minutes from San Ignacio.

Cristo Rey
Waterfalls and swimming holes are tucked away on the Macal River. Visit the Bluff for food, drinks and entertainment.

San Jose Succotz
Between San Ignacio and the border, this village is home to Xunantunich and a selection of restaurants worth exploring.

DEEPER INTO XIBALBA

Xibalba literally translated means 'place of fear,' and that's what it was to the ancient Maya.

Maya mythology proclaimed it as the realm of the dead, the lowest of the nine underworlds, and it was a place where great suffering occurred.

It was believed that Xibalba could be accessed through every cave and every cenote in their domain, which is why many ceremonial activities took place inside them, the evidence of which can be found today.

The Popol Vuh is a story in which hero twins rescued their father and uncle from the depths of Xibalba by challenging the Lords of Death and succeeding.

The sacred narrative remains foundational in modern Maya cultures across the Yucatán.

Big Rock Falls, Mountain Pine Ridge Forest Reserve

Mountain Pine Ridge's Change of Scenery

TALL TREES AND DEEP POOLS

Among the broadleaf jungles of the Maya Mountains sits a vast expanse of pine forest, an unexpected shift in landscape reflecting the ecological diversity of Belize. The **Mountain Pine Ridge Forest Reserve** is an adventure destination, home to a nearly endless list of things to do and see.

Some of Belize's best waterfalls and swimming holes can be found here, including Thousand Foot Falls, which is great for viewing, and Big Rock Falls, which is a beautiful place to cool off on a hot day. There's also **Río On Pools** (fun fact: 'on' is not a preposition, but the name of the river), which is a series of waterfalls cascading over rocks that are fun to scramble over and sit on. The birding here is similarly incredible, as it's home to the endangered orange-breasted falcon, and some even claim to have witnessed the elusive harpy eagle here. Unfortunately, a pine beetle infestation took hold of the forest some 20 years ago, but there has been rich regrowth since then, thanks to targeted management practices.

WHERE TO STAY IN THE MOUNTAIN PINE RIDGE

Blancaneaux Lodge
Luxe riverside lodge as peaceful as it is beautiful, built from filmmaker Francis Ford Coppola's imagination. **$$$**

Hidden Valley Inn
Intimate resort on a massive estate, countless birds, trails and 12 cottages combining nature and comfort. **$$$**

San Miguel Campgrounds
With tents, beds and supplies provided, it's easy to enjoy a night in the woods. Has its own Big Rock Falls entrance. **$**

The road through the Mountain Pine Ridge – which is the pathway to the Maya ruins of **Caracol** (p129) – was recently paved to just past **San Miguel Campgrounds**, one of the only places in Belize where outdoor camping is possible. The formerly hazardous drive is now quick and easy, with plans for the asphalt to reach Caracol in the works.

Adventure on Horseback

THE WILD WEST IS CALLING

Cayo is cowboy country, making it the best place in Belize for a horseback-riding adventure. Horses can be seen all over, sometimes tied up on the side of the road, or, if your timing is good, in the midst of one of the horse races for which the region is known. Even the many beef ranches in western Belize continue to rely on horses for their daily activities tending to the herd.

Many of the larger resorts around San Ignacio have their own stable full of horses, and tour operators can facilitate riding experiences, but the best place for a true rider to look is **Mountain Equestrian Trails** (MET), located off the road to Mountain Pine Ridge. This secluded spot is dedicated to the equestrian arts, boasting a range of horses and riding experiences, as well as eco-*cabañas* (cabins) for guests who want to get as much riding in as possible.

MET is situated on 300 acres of private jungle, through which guests can ride horses to exclusive and secluded destinations. Tour options include half-day and full-day rides, as well as riding lessons for those who want it. The horses are quite calm and steadfast, given they live in a fairly active and challenging environment, and are excellent for beginner riders. However, experienced equestrians will not be disappointed by their strength and energy.

This family-run operation encapsulates the spirit of the west as it's expressed in Belize, with deep respect for the horses they oversee and a passion for sharing the bounty of the surrounding wilderness.

BEST PLACES TO RIDE HORSES

Chaa Creek
The stables are ideally situated among the resort's jungle acreage. Ride to a vantage point that doubles as a site of Maya history – look for Xunantunich peeking out of the foliage in the distance.

Blancaneaux Lodge
Sightseeing the pine forest via horseback is an iconic cowboy experience for riders of all skill levels, especially when riding to nearby Big Rock Falls.

St Leonard's Tours
At San Lorenzo Farms, St Leonard's offers one of the most interesting riding experiences: to the Xunantunich Maya ruins, including over the hand-crank ferry.

Taste the Flavors of San Ignacio

ALL THE FOOD THAT'S FIT TO EAT

Belize's diverse population is reflected in the food, but because cultural populations aren't the same across the country, neither is the cuisine. In southern Belize, for example, you are likely to encounter Garifuna food, whereas San Ignacio's location

WHERE TO EAT BEYOND SAN IGNACIO

Trey's Barn & Grill
Fine fare in a beautiful outdoor setting just off the Western Hwy in the village of Teakettle. **$$**

Benny's Kitchen
A San Jose Succotz staple serving classic Belizean food. Pairs perfectly with a Xunantunich trip. **$**

Western Dairies
An essential stop for ice cream during a visit to Spanish Lookout, but it serves full meals as well. **$**

CHIQUIBUL NATIONAL FOREST

Deep within the Cayo District is Chiquibul National Forest, a dense jungle along the Guatemala border.

It's a place of pride in Belize, where the country's endangered scarlet macaw population nests every summer, but also a source of concern, as a place where poaching of wildlife, plants and hardwood can go unchecked.

Visiting is a spectacular experience, whether that's listening to the melodic call of the slate-colored solitaire at the Natural Arch, or exploring underground caves at Las Cuevas Research Station. Intrepid guides are eager to show guests this remote part of the country, and it's well worth the effort to get there.

near the border means there's more of a Guatemalan and El Salvadoran flavor, among other influences. Foods from Creole, Mestizo and Maya cultures are frequently encountered, as are ingredients reflecting the landscape. This means plentiful fresh juices, steak dishes locally sourced from nearby beef ranches, and fried street food that has turned tourists into devotees.

From the Mestizo culture comes indulgent corn-based foods, like *salbutes, garnaches,* and *panades* (all variations on the tortilla, beans and cheese theme – *salbutes* usually add chicken, *panades* generally have fish). Each of these is a unique take on fried corn, some filled or topped with meat, beans, cheese, coleslaw, and of course, hot sauce. **Taqueria Tipico Salvadoreño** in Santa Elena is a particularly reliable spot to try these tasty treats, as well as to grab a large glass of fresh fruit juice. **Running W Steakhouse** at the San Ignacio Resort Hotel is the place to go for locally raised beef, which comes from just a few miles outside town.

Although nearly tropical, Belize experiences seasons, meaning not everything is available year-round. Some local fruits like sorrel, *tambran* and avocados come and go annually, so it's worth asking around to see what's growing. Mango season, which typically runs from May through September, is a time when everybody gets excited, so aficionados should set their sights on the summer months.

Meet Modern Maya

KEEPING THE CULTURE ALIVE

Over the centuries Belize's cultural makeup used to skew heavily toward the Maya, but today the country is incredibly diverse. Still, while Maya culture has deep roots, it's nowhere close to gone, and can still be seen among Belizeans today. Multiple experiences give visitors the opportunities to see inside the life of modern Maya communities.

About 15 minutes south of San Ignacio is the village of **San Antonio**, a predominantly Yucatec Maya community made up of 3500 people who practice subsistence agriculture. This is the home of the **San Antonio Women's Cooperative**, established in 2001 to provide the women of the village with an alternative income to farming. Here at the center, women provide demonstrations in the traditional making of masa tortillas on a metate, or stone roller. They also showcase the art of pottery-making, and visitors can try their hand at both. This sustainable tourism experience is a fun and delicious opportunity to see how Belize's Maya live today.

WHERE TO STAY BEYOND SAN IGNACIO

Alma del Rio
Only 10 minutes from San Ignacio, this serene eco-property is on the water in Cristo Rey. **$$**

Crystal Paradise Resort
Clean, comfortable and right in the heart of Cristo Rey. Its cabins are perfect for families or larger groups. **$$**

Mahogany Halls Boutique Resort
A popular Bullet Tree Falls spot with air-conditioned rooms and a swimming pool. **$$**

Chocolate-making

Adrian and Elida, Kekchí Maya from Toledo in the south, bring their chocolate-making expertise to San Ignacio with excellent demonstrations that can be combined with a tour of their small cacao farm. The one-hour tour at **AJAW Chocolate** includes grinding and creating your own chocolate drink and chocolate bar from roasted beans. As Belizean chocolate is gaining recognition worldwide, this tour provides a window into the traditional role of cacao in Maya history, and how the Maya are taking ownership of it today. Walk-ins are generally allowed, but it is better to make a reservation in advance.

INTO THE HEART OF CACAO

Adrian Choco, the Kekchí Maya owner of AJAW Chocolate, shares why chocolate matters.

Why did you start AJAW?
We started AJAW to promote and preserve a well-established cultural tradition.

Why is it important for tourists to experience Maya culture?
It's a must-do because Belize is one of the birthplaces of traditional chocolate. The best part is we home grow and produce our very own cacao.

What is something about chocolate most people don't know?
The Maya are the first decision-makers for chocolate, the first to cultivate and domesticate wild cacao and figure out the complex drinking process.

Spanish Lookout: Another World

THE HOME OF THE MENNONITES

There are three options to choose from at the roundabout in Blackman Eddy: go east to Belmopan, west toward San Ignacio and the Guatemalan border, or north to **Spanish Lookout**, home to a community of Mennonites. Follow the horse-drawn carts and you will find yourself in this unique place that feels entirely distinct from the rest of the Cayo District.

Ka'ana Resort
High-end luxury at this Western Hwy resort: outdoor showers, plunge pools and an extensive wine cellar. **$$$**

Sweet Songs Jungle Lodge
On the river and in the jungle, this intimate lodge encapsulates the beauty of the surrounding wilderness. **$$$**

Lost Compass Cabanas
Well situated between civilization and nature, these artfully crafted *cabañas* are a beautiful midrange option. **$$**

THE END OF THE WORLD

In 2012 the Maya Calendar was making headlines for allegedly predicting the apocalypse. In reality, the long count calendar was simply ending the cycle known as the 13th Baktun, and moving on to the next one.

Rather than fearing the worst, Belizean archaeologists spent the winter solstice on December 21, 2012 celebrating overnight at Caracol. There were history and cultural presentations on the ancient Maya, camping and other forms of merriment that went on undisturbed by the end of the world.

Equinox and solstice tours of Caracol are sometimes hosted by the resort Chaa Creek to commemorate this culturally significant time.

PAULHARDING00/SHUTTERSTOCK ©

Spanish Lookout

Visually, **Spanish Lookout** and its surrounding area appear almost midwestern-American in nature, with most of the jungle cut away for the purpose of agriculture and industry. This is also home to the only commercial oilfield in the entire country. The settlement's welcome sign is in both English and Plautdietsch, the mother tongue for most of its citizens. There is some tension between the Mennonite community and the rest of Belize, largely due to differences in opinion around conservation and land use. Culturally, the Mennonite community dresses in a traditional manner and though some drive cars, many don't, which also makes this area stand out.

Many expats and some locals come to Spanish Lookout for the practical purpose of shopping for home goods at **Farmers Trading Center** and auto parts at **Westrac**, though this is also the place to come for prefabricated wooden homes and wooden furniture, specialties of the Mennonite community. Still, there is plenty for a visitor to do. You should drive through **Western Dairies** (p133) for some of the best ice cream in the country, and pick up a fried-chicken dish as well. **Wingz** is another worthwhile stop in town. Other shopping opportunities are available offering products that can be hard to find elsewhere.

GETTING AROUND

There are no consistent, dedicated forms of transportation that can be taken beyond San Ignacio. Destinations along the highway could be close enough to walk to from a bus, but otherwise it's best to rely on cars to get around western Belize. Whether you hire a taxi service, chartered shuttle, hotel transfer, or self-drive, driving is the way to go.

BELMOPAN

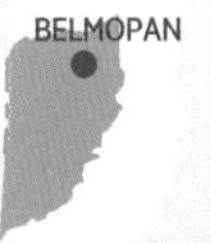

Belize's capital city is predominantly a gateway town, bus stop and government hub, but there is still a lot to explore. When Hurricane Hattie destroyed Belize City in 1961, Belmopan as we know it was created to avoid the problems that come with a coastal capital. Like many purpose-built capital cities around the world, Belmopan can seem a bit dull at first glance. Wide ordered streets, empty urban parklands and drab government buildings conspire to give it a desolate feel. The exception is the vibrant central market area, where cheap food stalls and incoming buses provide some welcome activity.

But this is the national capital, a major transportation hub, a place to extend your visa and an easygoing university city with a decent range of restaurants. More importantly, it's a useful base for exploring nearby caves, national parks, the Hummingbird Hwy and most of the attractions in eastern Cayo.

TOP TIP

Belmopan's main market days are Tuesdays and Fridays. Stallholders from all over the district sell produce, seasonal selections and local crafts. Stalls may sell on other days too but with a smaller selection.

Parliament building

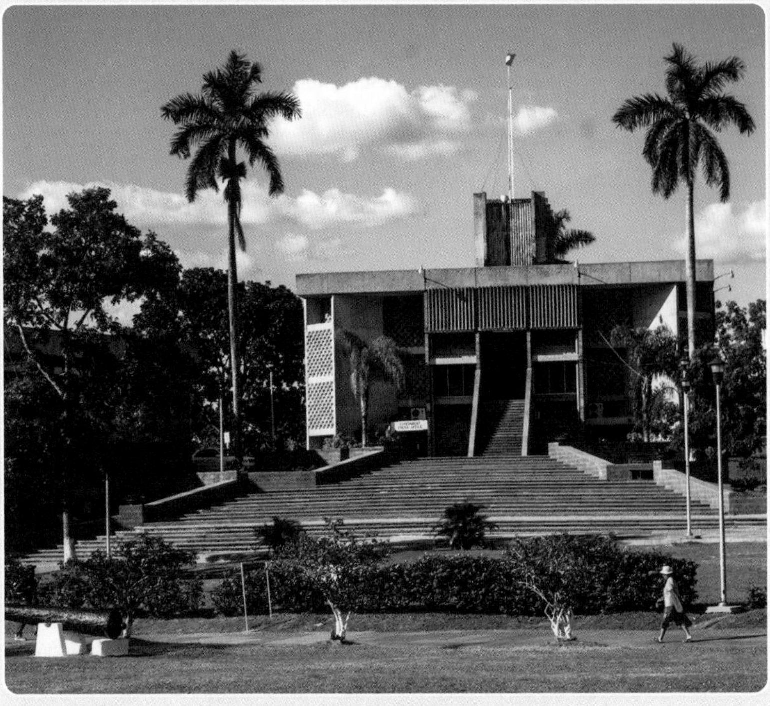

BELIZEDIVERSITY/SHUTTERSTOCK ©

EXTENDING YOUR STAY

Tourists visiting Belize are legally allowed to stay for 30 days, after which they will need to secure an extension at the immigration office in Belmopan.

The cost for 30 more days is BZ$200. The extension can be an all-day ordeal to obtain, so be prepared to settle into a day in the life of Belmopan.

The Ministry of Immigration office is open from 8am to 5pm, but it's recommended to arrive before they open, as a line inevitably forms. You will be given a number and made to sit outside during the wait, so bring water, sun protection and even a portable phone charger.

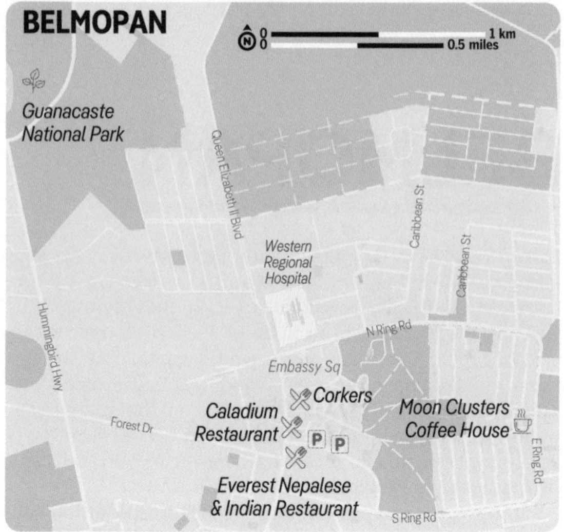

Get into Guanacaste

EXPLORE BELIZE'S SMALLEST NATIONAL PARK

Belmopan is within driving distance of some of Belize's best outdoor experiences, but **Guanacaste National Park**, the country's smallest national park declared in 1990, is the closest to town. It is named after the giant guanacaste tree on its southwestern edge, which survived the axes of canoe-makers but which has now died naturally, though it still stands in its jungle habitat. The 51-acre park, off the highway at the Belmopan turnoff, is framed by Roaring Creek and the Belize River, with 2 miles (3.2km) of hiking trails that will introduce you to the abundant local trees and colorful birds. Birding is best here in winter, when migrants arrive from North America. The entire park is managed by the Belize Audubon Society, and costs BZ$5 for visitors to enter.

Other tree species, like the mamey sapote and the Brazilian fire tree, can be spotted here, as well as kinkajou (pictured), armadillos and jaguarundi. There can be some noise heard from the nearby highway. The park features an education center and gift shop, as well as over 2 miles of hiking trails. On the short Guanacaste Trail there's a timber deck leading down to the river where you can swim in a deep waterhole. Don't leave bags or valuables unattended here while swimming.

BEST THINGS TO DO IN BELMOPAN

Shop at Art Box
A one-stop shop for everything arts and crafts, plus a cute cafe serving homemade ice cream.

Visit the Agricultural Showgrounds
If there's a show on, this is the best way to see Cayo's Wild West persona in action.

Support Belize Bird Rescue
Belize's first line of defense for sick and injured birds isn't running tours, but donating helps them do essential work.

Shrimp tacos

A Taste of Belmopan

WHERE CUISINES COME TOGETHER

Most of what Belmopan has to offer is centered around the bus terminal: the hospital, various embassies and the Market Sq. This is where you'll encounter a concentration of eating options, most of them at extremely affordable prices. The food stalls here serve quick-fire Latin American snacks such as burritos and *salbutes*, as well as Belizean standards such as rice and beans or cow-foot soup. For breakfast, omelets and fry-jacks are typical.

Opposite the market is a collection of shack restaurants, among which is a blue shack serving Belmopan's (and probably Belize's) only Nepalese cuisine. Here at **Everest Nepalese & Indian Restaurant** you can get authentic mutton, chicken and vegetarian curries and biryanis, as well as Indian specialties such as masala tea. There are proper standalone restaurants beyond this concentration, including the Brit-pub-like **Corkers**, which serves a wide range of cuisines, and **Caladium Restaurant**, generally regarded as the best eatery in town. Burgers, BBQ and Belizean favorites can be found here alongside seasonal treats like a lobster creole.

Coffee fans won't be disappointed by the menu at **Moon Clusters Coffee House**, a little old-school place run by the Aguilar family. They know the value of a good espresso, but can make magic happen with shakes and smoothies as well.

BEST PLACES TO SPEND THE NIGHT

Banana Bank Lodge
Old-school lodge just north of Belmopan on the banks of the Belize River with an equestrian center, beautiful *cabañas* and an orchid garden. Climb the observation tower to spot birds. $$

Hibiscus Hotel
Comfortable motel-style spot in Belmopan. It's big on birding and birders, so ecotravelers will feel at home. $$

Belize Jungle Dome
An architectural oddity, this Roaring Creek retreat has a dome which allows sunlight to filter in on the mahogany interior. A treetop cafe makes for a well-rounded stay. $$

GETTING AROUND

Belmopan is a compact city, and most places of note are accessible on foot from the center of town and the bus station. Taxis mill around the bus station and the central market if you want to go beyond the downtown area. The bus station is a hub for traveling to and from destinations around the country.

There are currently no commercial flights to or from the local airstrip, but that could change if it reopens.

HUMMINGBIRD HIGHWAY

The lyrically named Hummingbird Hwy makes for one of the prettiest drives in Belize, winding its way through emerald jungle and rows of citrus orchards, and impossibly small villages with puzzling names, as it skirts the northern edges of the Maya mountain range between Belmopan and Dangriga. There are other ways to get south, but none quite as scenic as this.

Passing caves and jungle adventures, on a clear day the road affords plenty of postcard-perfect vistas. There are even iconic food stops and unsolved mysteries to explore along the way. It's easy enough to drive the 53-mile (85km) length of it in two hours, but taking it slow and steady is the best way to make the most of the excellent ecolodges and budget accommodations that are practically begging for an overnight stay.

TOP TIP

If you have the time, drive the Hummingbird Hwy from both directions. While the stops won't change, the vantage points will, and who knows what you will discover with a fresh perspective.

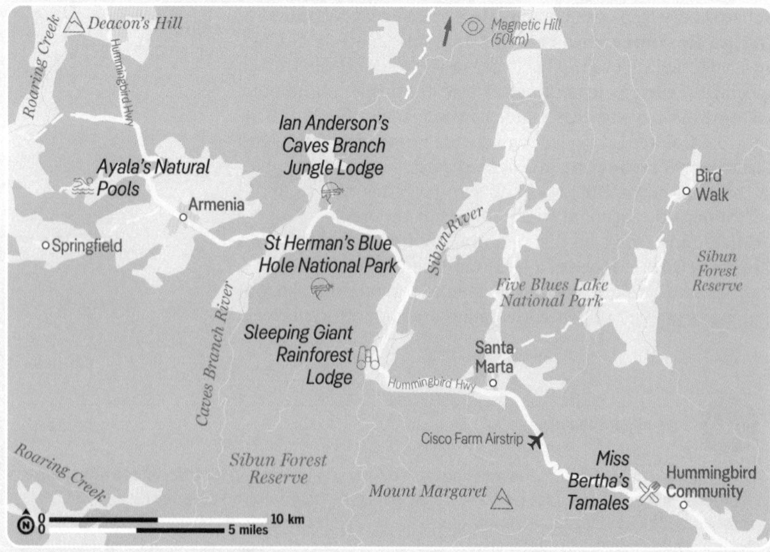

Cave tubing, St Herman's Cave

St Herman's Blue Hole National Park

EXPLORE THE OTHER BLUE HOLE

The 575-acre **St Herman's Blue Hole National Park** contains St Herman's Cave, one of the few caves in Belize that you can visit without a guide. The visitors center (where flashlights can be rented) is 11 miles (17.7km) along the Hummingbird Hwy from Belmopan. From here, a 500yd (450m) trail leads to St Herman's Cave. A path leads 200yd (180m) into the cave alongside an underground river – to go any further you'll need a guide. Return via the Highland Trail, steep in places but with rope guides, for some nice views. Carry a strong flashlight and good insect repellent. If you're keen on a longer hike, there's a three-hour trail from here via Crystal Cave.

The other notable feature of the park is the Blue Hole, a 25ft (26m)-deep sapphire-blue cenote that's quite popular as a swimming hole, and rivals the better-known Blue Hole that exists off Belize's coast. It is about a mile further along the highway, and has its own parking lot. The cenote can be accessed by descending a set of stairs, at the bottom of which there is a cement landing area where clothes and belongings can be left. Take caution when leaving your things, although theft is uncommon here.

BEST TOUR OPERATORS

Caves Branch Adventures
At Ian Anderson's, the signature adventures include jungle treks, river cave and waterfall cave expeditions, and the Black Hole Drop.

Belize Inland Tours
Based just out of Belmopan in Armenia, Belize Inland Tours runs cave-tubing trips, guided tours of St Herman's Blue Hole National Park and tours all over the Cayo District.

M&S Adventures & Archaeology
Tour guide Mario Castellanos is a Belize native with tremendous experience bringing tourists to Belize's best sites. He is known for entertaining as much as he educates.

A BEVY OF BIRDS

As the name of the highway suggests, Belize is full of amazing birdwatching opportunities. To learn more read **Birdwatching in Belize** (p232).

BEST EATS ON THE HUMMINGBIRD HIGHWAY

Country Barn
This Mennonite dairy farm serves frozen treats directly from the source. Grab a scoop or two to beat the heat. **$**

Roadside Fruit Stand
Fruit stands pepper the highway, especially in the valley where fruit is grown, with some of the best pineapple. **$**

Cafe Casita del Amor
This charming little spot makes for the perfect pit stop after exploring nearby Billy Barquedier National Park. **$**

BELIZE AUDUBON SOCIETY

Belize loves its birds, and the Belize Audubon Society (BAS) was formed in 1969 to help protect them.

The BAS manages many of the country's most beautiful natural sites, including St Herman's Blue Hole National Park on the Hummingbird Hwy. While the name of the highway comes from the undulating road's similarity to the swooping pattern of a hummingbird, it's also a great spot to go to see the beautiful birds (among other species).

The BAS plays an integral role in protecting the wilderness along the highway so travelers can see hummingbirds for years to come.

Scan this QR code to find out more about the Belize Audubon Society.

NATURE'S CHARM/SHUTTERSTOCK ©

Hummingbird

The park is operated by the **Belize Audubon Society**, thus the entire place is rich with birdlife to explore: at least 200 species have been spotted. Drive there, or take the 45-minute jungle trek from the visitors center. Admission is with the same ticket as St Herman's Cave. Any bus along the Hummingbird Hwy will drop you at the visitors center or the entrance to St Herman's Blue Hole National Park.

Adventures With Ian Anderson

AN ICONIC JUNGLE HOTEL

Driving the Hummingbird Hwy only takes a few hours, but there's a reason why this region is one of the fastest-growing in the country: it's beautiful! **Ian Anderson's Caves Branch Jungle Lodge** was one of the first to recognize how special the Hummingbird Hwy is, establishing themselves decades ago as a family-oriented adventure destination. The charismatic owner, Ian Anderson, built this rustically charming spot to take advantage of the bounty that surrounds the 90-acre property, and maintains a reputation as a leader in ecotourism.

Hidden away in dense jungle off the Hummingbird Hwy, the estate acts as a base for a variety of exclusive jungle activities on the property, including horseback riding, a waterfall cave expedition and a full-day trek through the jungle. It is also

WHERE TO STAY ON THE HUMMINGBIRD HIGHWAY

Sleeping Giant Rainforest Lodge
A hotel experience with incredible views overlooking the valley and 10,000 acres. **$$**

Ian Anderson's Caves Branch
The roots of Belize's adventure tourism are here. Explore all day, sleep comfortably and enjoy the ride. **$$**

Jaguar Creek
An ecolodge with nine peaceful *cabañas*, Jaguar Creek is close to it all – including the jungle. **$$**

adept at offsite tours to Maya ruins and overnight caving expeditions, which are difficult to find through other operators.

Accommodations are superb, and guests can indulge themselves in the beautiful riverside pool and hot tub, and enjoy meals and cocktails at the family-style restaurant overlooking the river. Most exclusive of the accommodations are the canopy tree houses overlooking the **Caves Branch River**, featuring beautifully carved four-poster beds, screened-in decks, outdoor tropical showers and views to die for. More humble but no less lovely are the wooden *cabañas* closer to the river, and there's a varying range of lodge rooms in between. The lodge also has an onsite artisanal cheese factory and organic soap-making facilities. Most guests to the lodge book multi-day packages, including tours, accommodations, meals and more.

BEST STOPS ON THE HIGHWAY

Ayala's Natural Pools
It doesn't get more photogenic than this oasis under the jungle canopy. You can relax in the pools or zipline over them – the choice is yours.

Sleeping Giant Rainforest Lodge
This swanky property, with its lush grounds and unbeatable views, is worth a pit stop to see the Hummingbird Hwy from above.

Magnetic Hill
Pull over safely at Mile 29 to experience an unexplained phenomenon: your car will roll backwards, uphill!

Stop for a Snack

MISS BERTHA'S TAMALES ARE ESSENTIAL

Tell any Belizean you're planning to drive the Hummingbird Hwy and they'll make sure you make time to stop at **Miss Bertha's Tamales**. The place is simply iconic. The little white and red shack is easy to miss if you're not paying attention, especially with minimal signage, so it's generally easiest to look at where an abundance of cars have gathered.

Before passing away, Miss Bertha Lisbey had been making perfectly spiced, gooey chicken and corn tamales for generations, grinding corn into masa herself every morning. The hot sauce that accompanies the tamales is a family recipe as well. The recipes and the restaurant are now under the purview of Miss Bertha's daughter, Aurora, who carries the family legacy forward along with her own seven children.

These tamales became a national treasure after Sir Barry Bowen, a hometown treasure whose name can be found on businesses throughout the country, was so impressed by Miss Bertha's fare that he had no choice but to invest. Today, locals and tourists alike patiently wait their turn in the typically hot sun until their tamales are ready, sitting to eat either at the provided seats in the shade or wherever they can find a spot along the road.

Whichever direction you drive the Hummingbird Hwy, do not miss the opportunity to indulge in one of the best meals to be found in Belize. Miss Bertha's is open every day and takes cash.

GETTING AROUND

As a scenic drive, wheels are going to be your best bet for traversing the Hummingbird Hwy. Renting a car is the best way for traveling at your own pace, though tour operators will happily customize a trip for you.

Buses also use the highway, and after one drops you off, another one will eventually come by that can pick you up – just make sure they're still running. Due to the many blind curves, it is not recommended to walk or bike this route.

Garifuna Settlement Day (p153), Hopkins

SOUTHERN BELIZE

COASTAL TOWNS, JUNGLE ADVENTURE AND DIVING

Laid-back coastal towns, diving off pristine cayes and reefs, adventures in untamed jungle and a kaleidoscope of cultures await in Belize's south.

Even in a country as rich in natural beauty as Belize, the south of the country bags the top prize. Take the Hummingbird Hwy south from the main highway, and its ribbons lead you alternately through flat plains, dotted with citrus groves, and lush, hilly terrain covered in a riot of jungle vegetation, occasionally punctuated by small agricultural villages. There's a strong Afro-Caribbean flavor to the Stann Creek District coastal settlements of Hopkins and Dangriga that move to the addictive rhythms of traditional drumming and call-and-response song, rooted in West African languages. Determined efforts are made by passionate locals to keep the language and culture alive.

Inland, some of Central America's most intact rainforest in Cockscomb Basin and Mayflower-Bocawina national parks provides a refuge to the country's surviving population of jaguar, tapir, puma and other jungle denizens, while further south, the compact village of Placencia is south Belize's only hint at mass tourism, complete with golf carts, rum bars and excellent restaurants.

Further south still, the Toledo District and its languid capital, Punta Gorda, are fine examples of Belize's absorbing cultural melting pot. Here you'll find hills covered in virgin rainforest, off-the-grid, traditional Maya villages, a wealth of caves and Maya ruins, and old-colony Mennonite villages, as well as Belize's least-visited, pristine cayes and reefs. Together with Punta Gorda, Hopkins and Placencia make terrific jumping-off points with world-class diving and snorkeling.

THE MAIN AREAS

HOPKINS
Garifuna culture & outdoor adventure.
p148

PLACENCIA
Beach life, reefs & excellent dining.
p159

PUNTA GORDA
Low-key charm & Maya hinterland.
p166

Find Your Way

The south is the most culturally diverse, least-developed area of Belize, comprising jungle, reefs and atolls, and coastal settlements. Its attractions are many and we've picked the places that best capture the region's unique historic heritage and natural wonders.

BUS & CAR

There is dependable bus service between Belize City, Dangriga, Hopkins, Placencia, and Punta Gorda; elsewhere service is spotty and schedules are rare. Self-driving gives maximum flexibility; some attractions off the Hummingbird Hwy require a 4WD.

BOAT

A public boat connects Dangriga to Tobacco Caye. Cayes are reachable via charter boat from Dangriga, Hopkins, Placencia and Punta Gorda. Water taxis connect Dangriga, Placencia and Puerto Cortes in Honduras, and Punta Gorda with Puerto Barrios in Guatemala.

Sittee River

Cockscomb Basin Wildlife Sanctuary (Jaguar Reserve)

Hopkins, p148

Friendly and low-key, this coastal village combines Garifuna culture with easy access to offshore cayes and two spectacular national parks.

Red Bank

Mango Creek

Indepence Airport

Placencia Airport

South Water Caye Marine Reserve

Savannah Forest Reserve

Placencia

Columbia Forest Reserve

BELIZE

Placencia, p159

Diving at cayes, excellent restaurants and beach resorts await at this up-and-coming beach destination with its tranquil lanes and barefoot vibe.

Monkey River

Paynes Creek National Park

Punta Gorda, p166

The jumping-off point for Maya villages and ruins, caves, rivers, untamed jungle and Belize's least-developed cayes in the Deep South.

Port Honduras Marine Reserve

Sapodilla Cayes

Gulf of Honduras

Hunting Caye

Punta Gorda

0 20 km
0 10 miles

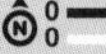

Laughing Bird Caye (p161)

Plan Your Time

A terrific all-rounder, Belize's south has it all: jungle trekking, waterfalls, jaguar-spotting, river tubing, Maya ruins, vibrant Maya and Garifuna culture, terrific coastal gastronomy and world-class diving and snorkeling.

If You Visit One Place

Spend the weekend in **Placencia** (p159), exploring some of Belize's most striking underwater topography. Spend a day at fabled **Glover's Reef** (p164), snorkel at **Laughing Bird Caye** (p161) or **Ranguana Caye** (p161), and work up an appetite for **Dawn's Galley** (p161) and **Rumfish & Vino** (p160). In the evenings, chill with locals and expats at **Barefoot Beach Bar** (p161), **Tipsy Tuna** (p162), or **Little Wine Bar** (p162).

A Week's Adventuring

Look for armadillos, cougars, peccaries and jaguars in **Cockscomb Basin National Park** (p155). From **Punta Gorda** (p166), explore **Tiger Cave** (p177) and **Blue Creek Cave** (p177). Marvel at ancient Maya architecture at **Nim Li Punit** (p174) and **Lubaantun** (p175). Learn Garifuna rhythms at **Warasa Garifuna Drum School** (p167), then delve into Garifuna culture on **Kalipuna Island** (p149) in **Hopkins** (p148).

Seasonal Highlights

SPRING

Dry, sunny weather. Whale sharks appear at Gladden Spit and Punta Gorda hosts Toledo's **Chocolate Festival**.

SUMMER

June marks the start of hurricane season as well as lobster season, and the weather turns wetter, stormier and sultrier.

FALL

Carnival parades, **Independence Day** and Garifuna Settlement Day – the latter with drumming, dancing and drinking.

WINTER

Rain abates as dry season approaches. Nights are cooler, accommodations prices rise, lobster season closes.

HOPKINS

Home to some 2000 people, slightly scruffy 1.5-mile (2.5km) long Hopkins jives to the beat of its mahogany drums and the staccato sounds of *shakas* (calabash gourd shakers). With its Garifuna culture more accessible than in neighboring Dangriga, and its brightly painted seafront houses buffeted by sea breezes, Hopkins is a terrific base for exploring the cayes, reefs and atolls to the east, and the jungle, waterfalls and mountains of nearby national parks. Drumming lessons and village sights will take up a day at most, but you're likely to linger longer on the khaki-colored beaches, just like the growing North American expat community, drawn here by Hopkins' growing popularity, excellent dining and laid-back vibe.

Hopkins was founded in 1942 by people from Newtown, a nearby Garifuna settlement that was destroyed by a hurricane. The village is named for Frederick Charles Hopkins, a Catholic priest who drowned here in 1923.

TOP TIP

Walkable Hopkins is divided by the sealed Hopkins Rd from the Southern Hwy into North and South Side. Accommodations have bikes for guests. Around 2km south is Sittee Point with high-end resorts. Buses connect Hopkins to Dangriga, Belize City and Placencia.

Beachfront, Hopkins

M_AA/SHUTTERSTOCK ©

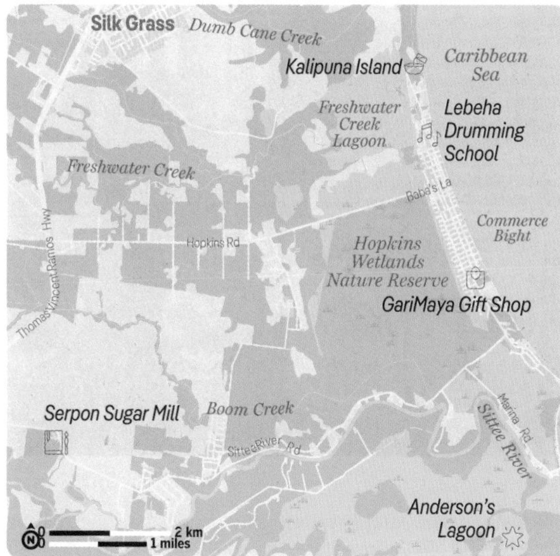

Garifuna for a Day on Kalipuna Island

IMMERSE YOURSELF IN GARIFUNA CULTURE

Picked up by canoe from the beach at Hopkins' north end, you're paddled across the river to **Kalipuna Island** by Uwahnie, a passionate advocate for Garifuna culture, and met by a gaggle of friendly cats and dogs.

The Martinez family walks you around the jungle-fringed **Palmetto Lodge** (palmentogrove.com), teaching jungle survival lore ('this medicinal plant eases your suffering if you walk past that tree that causes your skin to bubble'), and to recognize local fruit, vegetables and herbs, before you help prepare a traditional Garifuna dish. If cooking *hudut* (whole fish and mashed plantain cooked in coconut milk and spices), you'll de-husk a coconut in the traditional kitchen, getting joyfully messy squeezing coconut juice out of the flesh with your bare hands, pounding plantain with a pestle and mortar, and chopping herbs for the broth, while the fish fries on a skillet over an open hearth.

Finally, you sit and enjoy the fruit of your labor with your gregarious hosts, swapping culinary tips, wiping away tears of joy/pain if there's too much homemade hot sauce in your broth, and connecting in that special way people do when they encounter likeminded souls.

BEST PLACES TO STAY IN HOPKINS

All Seasons
Two-bedroom *cabañas* (cabins) and snug air-con guesthouse rooms in south Hopkins, with a patio grill and guest bicycles. $$

Coconut Row
Beachfront rooms, two-bedroom apartments and snug log cabins that are colorful, contemporary and well-equipped, all with air-con. $$

Hopkins Inn
Four stylish and spacious beachside *cabañas*, plus excellent breakfasts of fresh breads, fruit and johnnycakes. $$

Funky Dodo
Colorful maze of rustic rooms and dorms surrounding a leafy garden; perks include kitchen, hammocks and tour desk. $

WHERE TO EAT BELIZEAN & GARIFUNA FOOD IN HOPKINS

Semiti Giffiti
Old-school eatery where you'll consistently find *gibnut* stew, barbecued pigtail and other true-blue Belizean dishes. $

Hopkins Smokey Grill
Superb coconut-encrusted snapper and stuffed jacks, burritos and jerk chicken, made by a husband-and-wife team. $

Innie's
Hands down, the best *hudut, darasa, bundiga* and other traditional Garifuna dishes, plus Belizean classics. $

KNOW YOUR GARIFUNA DISHES

Bundiga
Snapper, coconut-milk and banana stew with herbs, lemongrass, cinnamon, cardamom, peppers.

Darasa
Garifuna tamal. Green bananas, spices, coconut milk and sometimes chicken boiled in banana leaf.

Ereba
Flatbread made from cassava root.

Fulita
Hash-brown-like green banana fritters.

Hudut
Whole fish and mashed plantain cooked in coconut milk and spices.

Sahou
Eggnog from cassava root, coconut milk, condensed milk, vanilla, cinnamon, nutmeg.

Sere
Coconut fish stew with onions, garlic, cilantro, spices, occasional potatoes, cassava, okra.

Tapou
Fish, root vegetable and green-banana stew, colored red with achiote paste.

Marie Sharp's Hot Sauce

When it's dark, and Uwahnie paddles you back across the occasionally bioluminescent river, you'll see fish dart through the dark water like luminous green torpedoes.

Uwahnie can cater cultural experiences to individual interests and to families. Besides cooking lessons and dinner, you can talk about Garifuna history and culture, see the impressive drum collection and take a drumming lesson. You can even stay in one of three snug, solar-powered cabins, kayak on the river or lagoon at night to experience the unearthly phosphorescence, and watch the star-filled sky on a sultry night.

Drums of Our Fathers

LEBEHA DRUMMING SCHOOL

An integral part of Garifuna culture that refused to be erased during Belize's oppressive colonial period, drumming is not just about music – though the **Lebeha Drumming School** (lebeha.com) at the north end of Hopkins has resulted in some notable drummers – but is also an essential spiritual connection to African ancestors. Run by local Garifuna drummer Jabbar Lambey, the school no longer operates on a walk-in basis. If you're lucky, you might catch local boys having an impromptu drumming session at night or on weekends at this educational and cultural center. Call ahead for an introduction to the bass drum and essential Garifuna beats, including *punta* (traditional Garifuna dance), and lose track of time as you jam with the master.

WHERE TO HAVE BREAKFAST IN HOPKINS

Thong Café
Belizean-style breakfast, French toast or eggs Benedict at this beachside Caribbean-meets-Euro-style cafe. **$$**

Kat's Coffee
This tiny shack serves Hopkins' best filter and espresso coffee, plus bagels, epic smoothies and juices. **$**

Siomara's
Pillowy fry-jacks, refried beans, eggs, tortillas and other belly fillers await at this breezy spot. **$**

Sugar & Indentured Servitude

GLIMPSE INTO BELIZE'S DARKER HISTORY

Serpon Sugar Mill, 1 mile (1.6km) from the Southern Hwy south of Hopkins, or via a bone-shaking route through cane fields, was set up in 1865 by American Confederates who fled to Belize following their defeat in the American Civil War. At its peak, the mill produced and shipped 1700 pounds of sugar a month. It used indentured Chinese and East Indian labor, not unlike plantation slavery in spite of paltry wages, but went out of business in 1910 when northern Belize sugar production became more profitable. The small interpretative center explains the sugar-production mechanics, but the real attraction is the machinery, including a steam-powered engine and the crusher and boiler, scattered through the park, shaded by giant fig trees, and slowly becoming one with nature.

Shopping for Garifuna & Maya Crafts

FIND QUALITY CRAFTS AT GARIMAYA

Your one-stop shop for quality Garifuna and Maya crafts is **GariMaya Gift Shop**. Browse full-size and compact Garifuna drums, Guatemalan carnival masks, hardwood carvings of birds and animals, rough-hewn bowls made of rosewood, ironwood and mahogany, hammocks, Belizean chocolate, cacao beans and coffee, Guatemalan coffee, embroidered Maya clothing, an array of Marie Sharp's hot sauces and Maya textiles.

Fish Torpedoes & Glistening Waters

BIOLUMINESCENT LAGOONS

The boat chugs along Sittee River as daylight fades, the jungle opens and you emerge in **Anderson's Lagoon**. You drag your hand through the water and your skin seems to glow, while torpedo-like fish shoot through the darkness in an unearthly blue-green blaze. The phosphorescence phenomenon is caused by harmless micro-organisms called dinoflagellates that emit a blue-green glow when disturbed; the brackish lagoon, where saltwater and river water meet, is saturated with them during dry season. **Get to Know Belize Adventures** (gettoknowbelizeadventures.com) runs frequent tours in spring, outside the full moon. You can also see bioluminescence in the Freshwater Creek and nearby lagoon of Kalipuna Island (p149).

MARIE SHARP'S LEGENDARY ABANERO SAUCES

If there's one thing that defines Belize from a culinary perspective, it's Marie Sharp's hot sauces that grace the tables of most Belizean restaurants.

In 1981, Marie Sharp began bottling hot sauces from her farm's own produce. Today's international enterprise employs 80 locals (mostly women), while Ms Marie's sauces range from mild to the inferno-like Red Hornet.

Guided factory tours (7am–5pm, Mon–Sat; BZ$20), are 17 miles (28km) north of Hopkins, down an unpaved road off the Southern Hwy. You'll feel the acrid chili pinch in your throat as workers stir vast pots of habanero, salt and vinegar mix before it's aged in giant vats. You can also watch the fiery stuff being bottled and labeled before sampling all 16 sauces. All products are available for purchase.

WHERE TO GO FOR DINNER IN HOPKINS

Driftwood Beach Bar
Popular Driftwood cooks Hopkins' best pizza, and hosts occasional Garifuna drumming sessions and beach BBQs. **$$**

J&J Cool Spot
Lobster, barbecued chicken, fried fish with rice and beans and key lime pie served at this beachside crowd pleaser. **$**

Coconut Husk
Fish sandwiches, seafood platters, coconut curries, wraps, and cocktails served on a seafront terrace. **$$**

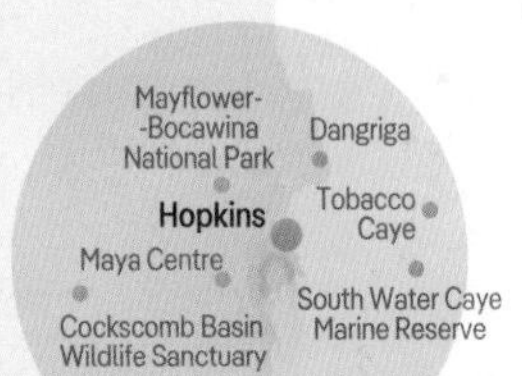

Beyond Hopkins

Continue your Garifuna cultural immersion, sample hot sauce, make chocolate with the Maya, and go in search of jaguars near Hopkins.

A short drive north of Hopkins, the somewhat scruffy, languid town of Garifuna is the place to commune with expert Garifuna drum-makers, musicians and artists. For those wishing to head out to the Central Cayes independently, Dangriga's boaters are your best bet, while Hopkins is the day-trip gateway for snorkeling and diving off South Water Caye, among other slivers of land. Near Dangriga, lovers of capsicum-induced endorphins make pilgrimages to Marie Sharp's hot-sauce factory; dirt roads branching off the Southern Hwy near Hopkins lead to Mayflower-Bocawina and Cockscomb Basin national parks, both with well-marked trails for day hikes and waterfall dips in the jungle, and the latter particularly renowned for jaguar-spotting during night visits and overnight stays.

TOP TIP

You need a car with high clearance to access the two national parks; guides are mandatory for some hikes and activities.

South Water Caye (p157)

DUARTE DELLAROLE/SHUTTERSTOCK ©

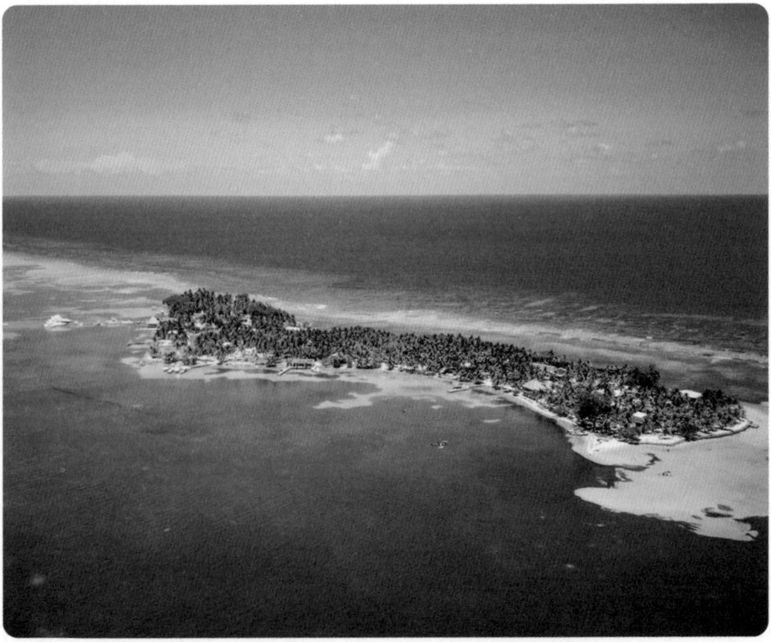

Garifuna Settlement Day celebration

Dangriga's Garifuna Culture

GARIFUNA MUSEUMS, GALLERIES AND MUSIC WORKSHOPS

Some 19 miles (31km) north of Hopkins, Dangriga's ramshackle appearance – clapboard houses on stilts, trash-strewn river mouth – all belies the name, meaning 'sweet water' in the Garinagu language. Yet as you walk around the original Garifuna port of entry into Belize, engaging locals in conversation, its charm reveals itself. On the western outskirts, **Gulusi Garifuna Museum** has exhibits charting the 17th-century arrival of the Garinagu in southern Belize and highlighting traditional thatch-roofed *büdürü* homes and household implements. Special attention is given to *beluria* (the nine-night wake when someone dies) and to traditional music, dance and drumming. Free guided tours liven up a visit.

Inside the workshop of Pen Cayetano – the creator of *punta* rock (a fusion of acoustic Garifuna and electric instruments), and one of Belize's foremost painters and musicians – you'll be struck by the portraits, rendered in bold colors and strokes, and recognizable for their unique style, as well as the dramatic renditions of the Garinagu arrival in Belize by boat. Also on display is textile art by Pen's wife, Ingrid, plus assorted musical instruments, from turtle-shell drums to ankle

GARIFUNA SETTLEMENT DAY

On November 19, Dangriga hosts Belize's biggest celebration, re-enacting the arrival of the Garifuna on Belize's shores in 1832.

During the whole week there are art exhibits, live-music gigs, plus drumming and *punta* rock dancing in the evenings at various 'sheds' around town until the wee hours of the morning.

On the morning of the 19th, take your place at 7am among the spectators on the main bridge overlooking the Stann Creek River to welcome the dugout canoes filled with costumed revelers and mounds of cassava and plantain.

After you're done cheering them on, follow the crowd in a colorful procession to the nearby church, then join the crowds lining the main street for the afternoon parade and further revelry.

WHERE TO STAY & EAT IN DANGRIGA

Bonefish Hotel
Opt for a spacious upper-floor room with air-con at this waterfront motel-style place. **$$**

Tuáni Garifuna
Garifuna dishes such as *hudut* and *darasa* join Belizean standards at this lovely waterfront restaurant. **$**

Island Breeze Bar & Grill
Munch on quesadillas and fish burgers at this open-sided beach bar while watching boats enter Stann Creek. **$**

MATYAS REHAK/SHUTTERSTOCK ©

Tiger Fern Trail, Cockscomb Basin Wildlife Sanctuary

WILDLIFE & THRILLS IN MAYFLOWER-BOCAWINA

The knowledgeable guides at Bocawina Rainforest Resort run two-hour birding tours early in the morning, pointing out toucans, parrot varieties and other feathered life.

Two-hour night tours are great for spotting kinkajou, possums and the occasional fer-de-lance snake.

Some of the accommodations packages include tours and activities; otherwise they are available as add-ons.

At the resort, with the help of Bocawina Adventures & Eco-Tours guides, you can fly screeching through the air along Belize's longest zipline (2300ft), rappel down either the 1500ft/457m Antelope Falls or the smaller 125ft/38m Bocawina Falls amid pummeling spray, or go on a guided trek to Antelope Falls, with the bonus of being helped with the rope-climb up to the spectacular viewpoint at the top.

Scan this QR code to book with Bocawina Adventures & Eco-Tours

shakers. There are occasional music shows and drumming workshops, and you might find Pen cooking *hudut* in the open-air kitchen beneath the mango and cashew trees.

If you'd like to see how Garifuna drums are made, look for the tiny workshop of master drum-maker Austin Rodriguez, who makes drums from mahogany, cedar, mayflower wood and deer skin by the water's edge, southeast of Dangriga Central Market. You can also buy his drums at the **Garinagu Crafts & Art Gallery** on Tubroose St.

Mayflower-Bocawina Jungle Adventures

WILDLIFE-SPOTTING, JUNGLE TREKKING

Some 13 miles (21km) northwest of Hopkins, the beautiful 11-sq-mile (28.5-sq-km) **Mayflower-Bocawina National Park** comprises dense jungle, mountains, waterfalls, hiking trails, swimming holes and Maya ruins, and is home to over 300 bird species, water opossums, howler monkeys, Baird's tapir, ocelots, endangered rain frogs and Belize's most spectacular big cat – the jaguar. There's a 3.7-mile (6km) unpaved access road to the ranger station, where

WHERE TO STAY & EAT IN OR NEAR MAYFLOWER-BOCAWINA

Bocawina Resort
Eco-resort with six lodge rooms, traditional thatch *cabañas* and family suites; wi-fi and breakfast included. $$

Wild Fig
Thatch restaurant with Belizean breakfasts, salads, buffets and awesome cheesecake. $$

Maya Heights
This hilltop restaurant cooks tacos, fajitas and seafood chowder with a side of incredible coastal views. $$

you pay the BZ$10 entry and peruse the map. Opposite the station is the partly excavated Mayflower Maya site, with two pyramids and nine other structures, occupied in the late 9th and early 10th centuries.

A little way toward the **Bocawina Jungle Lodge**, the most popular trail crosses the Silk Grass Creek. It's a 10-minute walk past the larger, unexcavated, partly tree-covered Maintzunun temple mound (800 CE) to a Y-junction (a jaguar has been spotted here in broad daylight!). The right fork is a narrow, moderately strenuous trail that undulates through the jungle to the small New Waterfall (35 minutes). Taller and more impressive, the Antelope Falls are reached via the broader left-hand trail (25 minutes) that climbs to the base of the falls. It's a steep 10-minute ascent to the deep bathing pool at the top of the waterfall; from the pool itself, you can scramble up to the viewpoint using ropes for terrific jungle and coast vistas.

The park's longest hike is the demanding loop that starts at the end of the access road, 1 mile (1.7km) past the lodge, reachable on foot or by 4WD. A 15-minute, mostly flat hike gets you to Lower Bocawina Falls, with a short detour to the top of the falls 10 minutes later and Upper Bocawina Falls just beyond. Some ups and downs along a narrow trail get you to the Tears of the Jaguar Falls (35 minutes), then Pecks Waterfalls (1½ hours), with a short, steep detour to the impressive Big Drop Falls with swimming hole halfway along the loop (2½ hours). Allow seven hours, including detours.

In the Pawprints of Jaguars

COCKSCOMB BASIN WILDLIFE SANCTUARY

Belize's most celebrated wildlife sanctuary, **Cockscomb Basin** (6am to 10pm daily) – the world's first jaguar sanctuary in 1984, thanks to the efforts of American zoologist Alan Rabinowitz – encompasses a 154.5-sq-mile (400-sq-km) swathe of tropical rainforest that's part of a biological corridor, critical to the jaguar's future in Central America. It's home to an estimated 40 to 50 jaguars, and other furred and feathered life. Jaguar sightings are likely on the access road in the very early morning, or during night walking tours.

The sanctuary is also home to Belize's four other wild cats, the puma, ocelot, margay and jaguarundi, all nocturnal, as are kinkajous and possum. Dawn and dusk are the best times to spot tapirs, anteaters, armadillos (the jaguar's favorite prey – crunchy on the outside, soft and chewy on the inside), brocket deer, coatimundis, otters, gibnuts, plus black howler monkeys

BEST PLACES TO STAY & EAT IN SITTEE POINT

Hamanasi Resort
Top-class dive resort with sea-view rooms, secluded tree houses, excellent restaurant and plethora of inland tours. $$$

Lodge at Jaguar Reef
Local artwork adorns the thatch-roofed *cabañas* and colonial-style suites at this 'cash-free' luxury beach resort. $$$

Chef Rob's
Opt for multicourse chef's table meals on Fridays or come for imaginative seafood and hot-rock-grilled steak. $$$

Bahay Fiesta Restaurant
Belizean classics are well executed, but the Asian dishes – Filipino *lechon kawali* (pan-roasted pork) and *pancit* (rice noodles) – really shine. $$

WHERE TO STAY IN COCKSCOMB BASIN

Campgrounds
Three well-maintained campgrounds: by the ranger station, on Tiger Fern Trail, and on Victoria Peak trail. $

Dormitory
Five spartan bedrooms by the ranger station, with hot water and communal kitchen access. $

Cabins
Two solar-powered four-person cabins, one with a beautiful veranda, private bath and kitchenette. $$

SUMMITING VICTORIA PEAK

Cockscomb Basin's toughest hike is the three-day, 30-mile (48km) round-trip trek up Victoria Peak, Belize's second-highest mountain. You can summit between February and May (dry season) but require a permit and guide. Experienced guides include Francisco Alvarado (501-602-3103) and Benedicto Coc (501-667-7780).

From the ranger station, take the broad trail, passable by ATV; for the first 8.7 miles (14km), it's a steady and mostly flat trek through the forest.

Beyond, the trail narrows and the next 3 miles (5km) are fairly relentless ups and downs until you reach the rudimentary campground at Km 19, where you sleep in hammocks beneath an awning, listening to the chirps and roars of the night jungle.

An occasionally scrambly and steep day ascent brings you to the summit, with incredible views of the surrounding mountains and valleys.

that live near the visitors center. When you're hiking, a strong unpleasant smell and rustling in the undergrowth indicates the presence of peccaries (small wild pig); with babies present, they can be aggressive. Bird-wise, over 290 feathered species have been spotted in the sanctuary, including the keel-billed toucan, king vulture, great curassow and scarlet macaw, while reptiles include boa constrictors and the highly venomous and nocturnal fer-de-lance.

From Maya Center, 5 miles (8km) south of the Hopkins turnoff on the Southern Hwy, an unpaved, winding and rutted road brings you to the ranger station (8am to 4pm), run by the Audubon Society (belizeaudubon.org), responsible for community conservation outreach. Pay the BZ$10 entry and peruse the map of the park's 20.5 miles (33km) of marked trails. Of the dozen or so branching off the access road, most are short loops, so you can hike several in one day. Bring a swimsuit for waterfalls and also to float along the clear, shallow Stann Creek River on an inner tube (BZ$15).

You need to hire a guide in Maya Center to hike the rigorous 1.2-mile (2km) Tiger Fern Trail (45 minutes) that crosses a creek, becoming steeper and narrower as it climbs to the twin falls with a dipping pool, rewarding you with a fantastic view of the Cockscomb Range. You can gaze upon Victoria Peak (3675ft/1120m) – Belize's second-highest mountain – from Ben's Bluff by taking the moderately strenuous Ben's Bluff Trail that passes by a smallish waterfall and dipping pool (30 minutes) before the path climbs steadily out of the dense forest for 15 minutes to a pine-fringed outlook.

Night hikes, run by local Maya Center guides or organized by tour operators such as **Get To Know Belize Adventures** (gettoknowbelizeadventures.com) in Hopkins and **DTourz** (placenciadtourz.com) in Placencia stick to the shorter trails near the South Stann Creek River.

A Morning in Maya Center

MAYA CULTURAL EXPERIENCES

A small village at the junction of the Southern Hwy and the access road to Cockscomb Basin Wildlife Sanctuary, **Maya Center** is home to Mopan Maya who were relocated here in the 1980s when the sanctuary was established. While some make their living from the sanctuary as park staff, guides or taxi drivers, for others, tourism is the only way to avoid working for paltry wages at nearby citrus and banana farms.

Maya Center is the sanctuary's closest base so if you stay overnight, you can consult Aurora at her clinic **Nu'uk**

WHERE TO STAY & EAT IN MAYA CENTER

Nu'uk Che'il Cottages
Simple rooms in a verdant garden, knowledgeable Maya hosts and *palapa* restaurant with traditional Maya dishes. $

Tutzil Nah Cottages
Four spacious, simple rooms with queen beds and fans; meals on request. Numerous outdoor excursions. $

Southern Highway Cafe
Great roadside spot for baked chicken with rice and beans, *salbutes*, tamales, *garnaches* and burritos. $

South Water Caye Marine Reserve

SOUTH WATER CAYE'S DIVING RESORTS

It's worth staying on South Water Caye for terrific diving and snorkeling.

Pelican Beach Resort
Solar-powered, palm-shaded wooden cottages, veranda-facing guest rooms, guest kayaks and hammock-strung beach, plus undersea outings. $$

Blue Marlin Lodge
Choose from *cabañas* or wallet-friendly guestrooms at this popular dive lodge with its own PADI dive center. Excellent restaurant. $$$

IZE South Water Caye
International Zoological Expeditions hosts marine-biology students and guests in log cabins. Three-night minimum includes snorkeling, kayaks and meals. $$

Che'il Cottages about traditional Maya medicine that treats everything from gastric misadventure to emotional distress, since she learned her skills from legendary Maya healer Eligio Panti. You can also buy local slate carvings, jungle jewelry, woven baskets and handmade textiles at **Maya Center Women's Crafts**; arrange taxis and guides here, or with the Chun family who run **Tutzil Nah cottages** (p156). At **Che'il Chocolate Factory**, master chocolate-maker Julio Saqui can walk you through the bean-to-bar process during a two-hour tour that includes a trip to the local cacao plantation. Cockscomb Basin day tours tend to stop here; otherwise call ahead for a tour. **Ya'axkin Butterfly Farm**, south of Maya Center, offers a fascinating insight into the lives of blue morpho butterflies. Be sure to stroll through the butterfly house.

Hopkins' Marine Adventures

DIVING AND SNORKELING

Based in Sittee Point, 1.2 miles (2km) south of Hopkins, PADI-certified dive shop **Belize Underwater** (belizeunderwater.com) offers diving courses, private charters to Glover's Reef (p164), Turneffe Island (p85) and the Blue Hole (p86), and superb diving and snorkeling at **South Water Caye Marine Reserve**, a 184-sq-mile (477-sq-km) protected area that

WHERE TO STAY ON TOBACCO CAYE

Tobacco Caye Paradise Cabins
Overwater *cabañas* with bathroom, cold-water shower, hammock and veranda. $$

Reef's End Lodge
Lodge-style rooms, beachfront *cabañas*, onsite dive shop and excellent overwater restaurant. $$

Windward Lodge
Waterfront place. Beach hammocks and six simple, beach-facing, en-suite rooms with veranda and fan. $$

ESCAPE TO THATCH & COCO PLUM CAYES

Accessible via boat from Hopkins or Dangriga, these two tiny islands are worth your time.

Coco Plum Caye has a luxury resort with 14 colorful ocean-front *cabañas*, a three-bedroom villa, excellent meals and staff, a Serenity Spa with deck, middling snorkeling (compared with other cayes) and a nude beach around the back of the island – a rarity in Belize!

A stone's throw from Coco Plum, Thatch Caye hosts an adventure lodge with 13 beautiful thatched-roof, air-con overwater *cabañas* on stilts, connected by paths winding through native mangroves.

While off-beach snorkeling is limited, there are numerous marine activities and an excellent overwater bar-restaurant, open to non-guests with reservation.

Tobacco Caye

encompasses some of the most abundant marine life along the Belize Barrier Reef, plus Tobacco Caye and South Water Caye.

Sitting right on the barrier reef, 12 miles (19.3km) from Dangriga, tiny **Tobacco Caye** – an island you can circumnavigate in 10 minutes – is the budget destination among the central cayes. There's ample scope for decent beach snorkeling, diving, fishing and hanging out in a hammock, but some of the best diving and snorkeling sites are found off and around the larger, 15-acre (0.5-sq-km) South Water Caye. Snorkeling above the forest of fan coral and elkhorn coral off the south end of the island, you're likely to spot eagle rays, yellow rays, pufferfish, trumpetfish, lobsters, barracuda, angelfish and stoplight parrotfish, among others. Two top dive sites include the Abyss – a beautiful wall dive plummeting to 130ft (40m), along which nurse shark, eagle ray and turtle sightings are common; and Parrot Reef – a 70ft (21m) wall attracting barracuda, hawksbill turtles, spotted rays and schools of creole wrasse.

If you stay at South Water Caye, take advantage of diving and snorkeling at nearby Aquarium, Tobacco Cut, Angel Reef, Forereef Drift, Carrie Bow Patch and other top sites.

GETTING AROUND

Daily buses connect Hopkins and Dangriga (45 minutes). For the Marie Sharp factory you can drive or get a Belize City bus to the turnoff. Hopkins buses heading south pass the Maya Center. For Cockscomb Basin or Mayflower-Bocawina, join one of the frequent (pricey) tours or use your own high-clearance wheels.

A daily boat runs from Dangriga's river mouth to Tobacco Caye (40 minutes) around 9am, returning mid-morning. Accommodations on South Water, Coco Plum and Thatch cayes include transportation to/from Dangriga. You can also reach South Water Caye via a tour from Hopkins. Otherwise, agree on a price with local boat owners, either at Dangriga or Sittee Point, south of Hopkins.

PLACENCIA

Framed by the Placencia Lagoon and the Caribbean Sea, the narrow, sandy, 19-mile (31km) long Placencia Peninsula runs parallel to Belize's mangrove-and-beach coastline. The road ribbons its merry way through the laid-back village of Maya Beach with its low-key resorts, and the Garifuna settlement of Seine Bight, all the way down to the compact, highly walkable Placencia village at its tip – 'the caye you can drive to.' Its single main street and parallel pedestrian sidewalk is lined with some of southern Belize's best restaurants, bars and mostly inexpensive lodgings. Placencia village exudes a relaxed, ramshackle vibe, though it's increasingly popular as a low-key celeb getaway, mangroves have been cut back to make room for a marina, and golf carts roam the street. Stay awhile – for the superb diving and snorkeling, the day tours, the seemingly endless happy hours and music events at Placencia's clutch of watering holes, and the genuine sense of bonhomie.

TOP TIP

During the March to June full moons, divers are drawn to whale sharks feeding nearby. The 27-mile road from the Southern Hwy is paved (with speed bumps). Some businesses close September and October – the height of hurricane season.

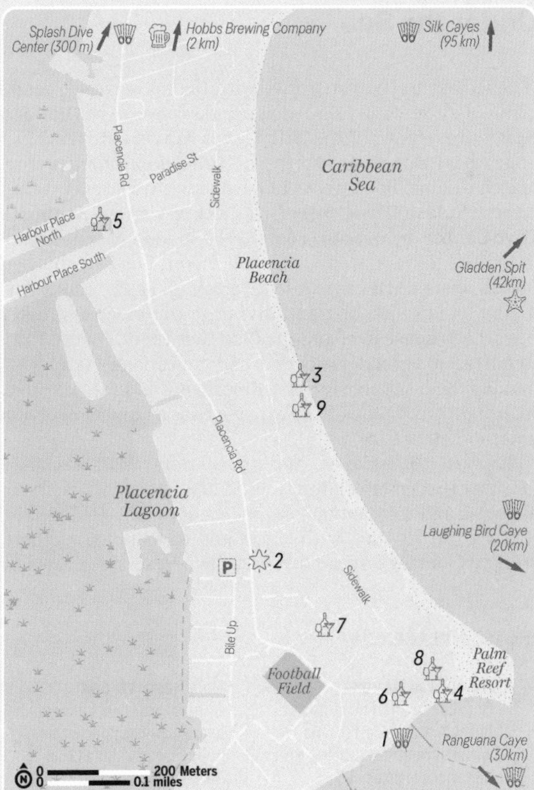

ACTIVITIES, COURSES & TOURS
1 Seahorse Dive Shop
2 Taste Belize Tours

DRINKING & NIGHTLIFE
3 Barefoot Beach Bar
4 Big Titty Rum Bar
5 Buba Wuba's Grill & Smokeshack
6 Little Wine Bar
7 Pickled Parrot
8 Point
9 Tipsy Tuna Sports Bar

BEST PLACES TO EAT IN PLACENCIA

Rumfish & Vino
Romance your sweetie at this gastro-bar with lionfish crudo, conch ceviche, plus red-curry snapper and braised short-rib lasagna. $$

Secret Garden
In a garden strung with fairy lights, dine on an eclectic mix of creole shrimp, Caribbean gumbo and jerk chicken. $$

Mare Restaurant
Book ahead for beautifully executed Italian and seafood dishes, or the full Indonesian *rijsttafel* (rice dishes) spread on Mondays and Thursdays. $$$

SmoQiz Bistro
International menu with the chef executing everything with aplomb, from buttermilk pancakes and Texas-style brisket to fish tacos. $$

Ranguana Caye

Under the Sea

SNORKELING AND DIVING EXCURSIONS

If you'd love to snorkel or dive with the magnificent, gentle giants of the sea, 60ft (18m) whale sharks converge on **Gladden Spit** – the 'elbow' of the **Silk Cayes Marine Reserve**, an hour's boat ride from Placencia – to feed on snapper from March to June. Book weeks in advance with Placencia's dive centers: **Splash Dive Centre** (splashbelize.com) and **Seahorse Dive Center** (belizescuba.com), as the window of opportunity is limited to days around the full moon. Long-established Splash offers PADI courses to divers of all levels, and Nitrox diving, plus snorkeling and diving to the inner and outer reefs, Lighthouse Reef and the Blue Hole (p86). Owner Patty Ramirez and her staff are patient and professional instructors, making them suitable for first-time divers and experts alike. Also highly recommended, Seahorse runs a number of diving and snorkeling trips.

Photogenic **Silk Cayes** – three small sandy islands – makes for superb underwater adventures. While snorkeling you'll spot angelfish and sergeant majors, but the standout site is Shark, Ray and Turtle Alley, with lemon and reef sharks, southern stingrays and loggerhead turtles, drawn by scraps thrown by

WHERE TO STAY IN A HOTEL IN PLACENCIA

Elysian
Crisp, glassed-in monochrome suites with air-con overlook beach and pool. Excellent rooftop restaurant-bar. **$$$**

A Belizean Nirvana
Belizean-owned boutique hotel. Art-adorned rooms with kitchenette, rooftop grill, hammocks, bikes. **$$**

Naïa Resort & Spa
Contemporary art adorns the luxuriously appointed beach houses and villas at this destination spa resort. **$$$**

lobster fishers. Top dive sites include White Hole – with eagle rays, nurse sharks and yellowtail snappers among gorgonians and coral walls; North Wall, dropping to 80ft (24m), with eagle rays, manta rays, moray eels, hawksbill turtles and reef sharks; and Turtle Canyons, renowned for hawksbill and loggerhead-turtles. A 45-minute boat ride from Placencia, **Laughing Bird Caye** is a picture-perfect spit of sand in the heart of its namesake national park, with a ranger onsite. Snorkel along the reef to see spectacular fan coral, lobster, hogfish, stoplight parrotfish, barracuda, blue-striped grunts and black jacks, trumpetfish, bonefish, nurse sharks and even rays. Splash runs night snorkeling trips outside peak season. With superb visibility, **Ranguana Caye** has decent snorkeling from shore, while excellent dive sites a couple of miles out include Fox Hole, a wall dive dropping to 100ft (30m), where you'll likely see queen triggerfish, hawksbill turtles, nurse sharks and barracuda.

Day snorkeling trips cost from BZ$230, while two-tank dives on an inner-reef site will set you back from BZ$350.

Tasting Belize

FOODIE TOURS

On Placencia's main street, **Tasting Belize**, a cheerful local outfit, caters to foodies wanting hands-on experiences. Take a half-day tour of an organic cacao farm, learn about the bean-to-bar process, or combine a cacao tour with waterfall swimming. Cook classic Garifuna, Kriol or Maya dishes in a local home; learn about local rums and cashew wine; or just wander around with a fun group on a bar crawl or sampling Placencia's street food.

Paint Placencia Red

PLACENCIA'S BEST BARS

Placencia's nightlife belies its compact size. Just outside the village, microbrewery **Hobbs Brewing Company** (hobbsbeer.com) gives the ubiquitous Belikin some serious competition with Blue Marlin Coffee Stout, Toucan Mango Hefeweizen, Wildcat IPA and other small-batch brews. Swing by for a weekend brewery tour or relaxed evening at the brewpub near the airstrip. In Placencia's north, **Buba Wuba's Grill & Smokeshack** is a cross between an Irish pub and local diner, with Guinness-fueled games of Chicken Drop (where participants bet on where on the outdoor bingo board the chicken will, erm, annoint). Expat haunt **Pickled Parrot** has a

WHERE TO EAT & DRINK IN PLACENCIA

Jana Belknap, owner of the Little Wine Bar

Momolicious
A shack just off the Sidewalk, serves fast, inexpensive food: empanadas, *salbutes* (mini tortillas, usually stuffed with chicken), fried tacos. Try a selection of everything.

D'Tatch
For my money, this is the best spot for the classic Belizean breakfast: eggs with refried beans and fry-jacks.

Dawn's Galley
Fresh fish and seafood prepared Belizean- or Creole-style, plus Placencia's best key-lime pie. $

Barefoot Beach Bar
Everything is great: the location, the vibe, the fact that it attracts locals and tourists alike, and the excellent (strong) drinks.

Shak
If you want good vegetarian food, this place by the dock serves big portions of plant-based dishes. Excellent breakfasts, too.

WHERE TO SLEEP CHEAPLY IN PLACENCIA

Sea View Suites
Rambling pink edifice overlooking the beach. Nine large rooms with air-con, fridge and coffee maker. **$$**

Anda di Hows Hostel
The original beachfront hostel, with a 10-bed dorm, camping, hammocks, full kitchen and small veranda. **$**

Sea Glass Inn
Six spotless rooms with fans, fridges, air-con and verandas looking out over the beach. **$**

PLACENCIA'S BEST SHOPPING

Lola's Art
Gallery on an unpaved street in Seine Bight, 5 miles (8km) north of Placencia, showcases cheerful, life-affirming acrylic paintings of local women and beach scenes, plus hand-painted cards and gourd masks by locally renowned artist Lola Delgado.

Art'n'Soul
On the Sidewalk, has bright canvases by local artists.

Denyse's Original Gift Shop
Sells funky, offbeat jewelry made by Denyse herself (though be wary of buying black-coral items), plus fun coconut pod fish.

Among the Sidewalk sellers of beautiful bowls and home decor from native rosewood and ziricote wood, the works of Bob & Tyrone Lockwood stand out, while Leo works magic with driftwood and mahogany at Made in Belize.

PAUL HARDING/LONELY PLANET ©

Tipsy Tuna

legendary Thursday-night quiz, while **Little Wine Bar** makes for an intimate evening as you sample Californian, Italian and other wines, while munching on cheeses and cold cuts not found elsewhere in Belize. By the marina, the **Big Titty Rum Bar** action kicks off later, fueled by signature Ginger Habanero daiquiris and Grace Jones cocktails. At the **Point** next door, partake in karaoke and read customers' graffiti opinions regarding what 'the point' is. Proceed up the Sidewalk to beachside **Tipsy Tuna** for nightly specials and live events, including Garifuna drumming on Wednesdays, or head to **Barefoot Beach Bar** for Placencia's best rum selection, and cocktails that'll leave you happily horizontal.

Reel it In

WORLD-CLASS FISHING

Placencia is world-renowned for sportsfishing, and the fly-fishing off the cayes is the best in the country. Catch-and-release deep-water fishing is great for sailfish, wahoo, marlin, kingfish and dolphinfish, while the mangrove lagoons are terrific for tarpon and snook. For the best bonefish flats, head out to the cayes. Most better hotels, plus **Destinations Belize** (destinationsbelize.com), can hook you up with self-taught, serious local fishing guides, who'll take you out on their *pangas* (skiffs).

WHERE TO HAVE BREAKFAST IN PLACENCIA

Above Grounds
Sip Placencia's best (organic Guatemalan) coffee while munching on a smoked fish bagel or muffin. $

Brewed Awakenings
Decent espressos supply an early-morning caffeine fix; uber-healthy seaweed shakes (unique to Placencia) also. $

Wendy's Creole
Try stuffed fry-jacks and traditional Belizean breakfasts at this established spot with a people-watching veranda. $

Glover's Reef
Red Bank
Placencia
Monkey River

Beyond Placencia

Head out to world-class diving destinations, look for scarlet macaws and jaguars, and boat down a jungle river, serenaded by howler monkeys.

Two words: Glover's Reef. If you're a diver, Placencia is the most convenient gateway to one of Belize's (and the world's!) most remarkable underwater worlds, along with a supporting cast of cayes – some inhabited, some not – that are terrific day-trip destinations. South of Placencia, reachable via an exhilarating ride along the coast and through mangrove tunnels, the fishing village of Monkey River entices wildlife-spotters and those in search of genuine remoteness in jungly surroundings. Off the Southern Hwy, near the turnoff for Placencia, Red Bank's endangered scarlet macaws draw twitchers, and Placencia is as good a base for ventures into Cockscomb Basin National Park in pursuit of jaguars as Hopkins is (though the drive is a bit longer).

TOP TIP

Give yourself plenty of time in Placencia if you have your heart set on Glover's Reef, due to temperamental sea conditions.

Glover's Reef

YOUR OWN SLICE OF PARADISE

Play out your castaway dreams a short boat ride from Placencia.

Tarpon Caye Lodge (tarponcaye.com) Family-owned, Belizean-operated fishing lodge on the edge of tarpon lagoon with superb angling. Three solar-powered cabins on stilts, excellent snorkeling and home-cooked Belizean meals at the Pesky Permit restaurant. $$

Ranguana Caye (ranguanacaye.com) Stay in one of three rustic-chic *cabañas,* fill your days with snorkeling, kayaking, and paddleboarding or come for a day visit, a 90-minute boat ride from Placencia. $$

Coral Caye (thefamilycoppolahideaways.com) Tiny spit of land owned by Francis Ford Coppola. The Great House has lounge, kitchen, bar and fishing dock, two rustic-chic cottages, its own beach and a great reef for snorkeling. Ideal for a group of up to 10. $$$

CAMPHOTO/GETTY IMAGES ©

Coral, Glover's Reef

Glover's Reef

WORLD-CLASS DIVING

Its very name inspires awe in divers in the know. The names of its spectacular dive sites – Manta Reef, Turtle Tavern, Emerald Forest Reef, Shark Point, Octopus Alley – speak for themselves. A Unesco World Heritage Site along with the **Belize Barrier Reef**, and considered the second-best place to dive in Belize after Lighthouse Reef (p86), **Glover's Reef** is unmissable. The southernmost of Belize's three atolls has a ring of almost continuous shallow reef, enclosing a 50-sq-mile (129-sq-km) lagoon with stunning drop-offs, superb visibility of over 150ft (46m), and over 700 coral heads, ideal for snorkelers and rookie divers. To the east, the drop-off plummets to the 15,000ft (4500m) depths of the Caiman Trench – one of the deepest in the world.

In the northern part of the atoll, anglers fish for marlin, wahoo, snapper and grouper, while waters around the four cayes in the southern part are Belize's largest no-take zone, with frequent sightings of dolphin pods, eagle rays, sea turtles and plenty of grouper, parrotfish and other reef fish. Southwest Caye, Long Caye and Northeast Caye diving lodges have week-long packages. **Splash Dive Centre** and **Seahorse** in Placencia offer day-long, three-dive outings, well worth the two-hour boat ride each way.

LIGHTHOUSE REEF & THE BLUE HOLE

If you want to learn more about world-class diving, read our feature on Lighthouse Reef: **'Blue Hole: Beyond the Myth & Mystique'** (p229).

WHERE TO STAY ON GLOVER'S REEF

Glover's Atoll Resort
Wallet-friendly resort with 16 overwater and beachside cabins, dorm, camping, restaurant and dive center. **$$**

Off the Wall
Week-long diving packages at this intimate five-star resort include oceanfront *cabañas* and watersports. **$$$**

Isla Marisol Resort
Upscale diving resort with 11 luxe cabins, overwater restaurant, kayaking and fishing outings. **$$$**

Escape to Monkey River

WILDLIFE-WATCHING TOUR

The boat bounces on choppy water along Placencia's coastline, where pelicans hover on the stiff sea breeze, before ducking into a green tunnel of mangroves, docking 20 minutes later at Monkey River village. A popular half-day tour from Placencia, this tiny fishing community of 300 residents is the jumping-off point for boat cruises up the river, at the mouth of which it sits. Your guide will point out assorted wildlife: tiger herons, tree-dwelling bats, basking crocodiles, kingfishers, and you'll dock for a half-hour wander through the jungle (pack bug spray), where you'll likely spot giant land crabs and howler monkeys. On the way back to Placencia you'll have a solid Belizean lunch at **Alice's**, the village's only restaurant, and then look for manatees in the shallow waters near the private island of Harvest Caye. You can linger longer at the eight-room **Monkey Beach Retreat** – a secluded eco-resort offering snorkeling, kayaking, jungle hikes and more.

In Search of the Scarlet Macaw

BIRDWATCHING IN RED BANK

As you walk along the narrow trail through the forest that fringes the Maya village of **Red Bank**, the guide hands you birding binoculars so you can watch the rare, spectacularly plumaged scarlet macaws up close as they feed on the annatto fruit growing on top of the polewood trees. The macaws – sometimes as many as 100 – gather in the nature reserve a mile from the village from December to early March. Run by local guides Florentino and Miguel, the thatch-roofed **Scarlet Macaw Guesthouse** by the village entrance is a terrific base for birding year-round. Accommodations are basic but comfortable: spartan doubles and bunk rooms with shared bathroom, and meals provided. Besides birdwatching, Florentino, Miguel and other villagers involved in Red Bank's community-based ecotourism industry offer cacao-farm tours and day treks into the surrounding jungle, where you can splash in swimming holes and spot wildlife, such as tapirs, jaguars, gibnuts and agoutis.

COPPOLA'S HIDEAWAY

The Turtle Inn, 1.8 miles (3km) north of Placencia, is movie producer Francis Ford Coppola's labor of love.

At this Balinese-style resort where the Coppola family and assorted celebrities vacation, the thatch-roofed cottages and villas have soaring ceilings, hand-carved Balinese doors and handmade textiles, and are clad in bug netting, leaving them to catch the sea breeze (no air-con necessary), with a signature 'shellphone' in each one.

Splurge on the modernist, Laurent Deroo-designed Sofia's Beach House or dine on fine Italian fare, seafood and Indonesian *rijsttafel* at Mare Restaurant, plus Belize's best pizza or at the Pizzeria (open to non-guests). Two pools, a PADI shop and Thai day spa seal the deal.

GETTING AROUND

Visit Glover's Reef as a day diving trip from Placencia. Glover resort prices include boat pickup. If you're on Glover's Reef for less than a week, you can charter a boat from Dangriga or Sittee River (BZ$900 one way). Reach Monkey River via an unpaved, 12-mile (19km) road, 19 miles (31km) south of the Southern Hwy Placencia turnoff.

Drive to the boat landing opposite Monkey River village and take a boat to stay in a low-key local village guesthouse. The Red Bank turnoff is off the Southern Hwy, 10 miles (16km) south of the Placencia turnoff; buses can drop you at the junction, but you need to arrange transportation in advance for the 3 miles (5km) to the village.

PUNTA GORDA

'I ❤ Peini' proclaims a rainbow-colored sign next to a ramshackle pier with *palapa*-covered (open-air shelter with a thatched roof) huts at its tip, where locals picnic while kids splash in the choppy waters of the Gulf of Honduras. Another sign on the outskirts of windswept, palm-tree-dotted, mellow Punta Gorda (PG to friends) points you to the Confederate cemetery.

The only town of any size in Toledo – Belize's Deep South – has no beaches and few sights, but has laid-back charm. Locals strike up conversation, genuinely interested in what you have to say, and you'll want to linger over a plate of *salbutes* at the waterfront market while watching a lively parade of Maya, Garifuna, creoles, descendants of ex-Confederate immigrants from the US who settled here in 1867, and Mennonites with their beards and bonnets, who make up the population of this eclectic place. Should you be fortunate enough to get out on the water, the Gulf of Honduras, east of PG, is home to some of the least-visited, most spectacular cayes.

TOP TIP

Hourly buses run to Belize City via Dangriga and Belmopan from the King St bus station. PG is spread out yet walkable; guesthouses rent bicycles. Boats run daily to Puerto Barrios in Guatemala. Beyond the paved Southern Hwy, roads are bumpy or potholed.

Punta Gorda

IAN PETER MORTON/SHUTTERSTOCK ©

Garifuna Rhythms

WARASA GARIFUNA DRUM SCHOOL

Ronald Raymond ('Ray') McDonald began his drumming career when he was three years old. 'I was given a full-size bass drum,' he'll tell you, 'and just started playing.' A thatch-roofed space on New Rd (about a 15-minute walk out of town) hosts the **Warasa Garifuna Drum School**, where he begins his teaching sessions with a brief introduction to Garifuna history and culture.

After he explains the difference between the larger bass drum – *segundo* – and the smaller, higher-pitched *primero*, beginners start with a basic *paranda* rhythm on the *segundo* while Ray plays a complex rhythm on the *primero* while singing traditional Garifuna songs. You then proceed to more complex traditional rhythms, losing track of time as your palms hit the taut deer skin in time to the *punta, chumba, hungu-hungu* and other rhythms, listening to Ray's haunting Garifuna refrains. Ray can also arrange group drumming sessions, Garifuna dance lessons, traditional Garifuna meals and even drum-making sessions.

DRUMMING IN HOPKINS

You can also jam with the masters in Hopkins at **Lebeha Drumming School** (p150), run by local Garifuna drummer Jabbar Lambey.

SIGHTS

1 Golden Stream Corridor Preserve

ACTIVITIES, COURSES & TOURS

2 Belize Spice Farm
3 Copalli Rum Factory
4 Cotton Tree Chocolate Factory
5 Eladio Pop's Farm
6 Ixcacao Maya Belizean Chocolate
7 Mahogany Chocolate Factory
8 Port Honduras Marine Reserve
9 Sapodilla Cayes

ENTERTAINMENT

10 Warasa Garifuna Drum School

WHERE TO STAY IN PUNTA GORDA

BlueBelize Boutique B&B
Fantastic waterfront guesthouse. Six breezy apart-suites, friendly dogs, excellent breakfast and staff. **$$**

Coral House Inn
Vast colonial-style rooms overlook the lovely garden, pool and the sea at this sublime seaside inn. **$$**

A Piece of Ground
Four-story guesthouse/hostel with dorms, spotless rooms and American-style top-floor restaurant-bar. **$**

COPAL TREE LODGE

Some 4.3 miles (7km) north of PG, Copal Tree Lodge enjoys a superb hilltop setting overlooking miles of protected jungle stretching down to the Gulf of Honduras.

Comprising 12,000 acres of coffee, cacao and citrus farms as well as jungle, this unique space offers 12 spacious and luxurious tree-house suites with private veranda overlooking jungle and sea, plus four signature Canopy Suites fanned around a private infinity pool. You're likely to spot howler monkeys and local birdlife from your bedroom window.

Activities include fishing, snorkeling, cacao-farm and rum-factory (p169) tours and visits to Maya ruins.

A cable tramway leads down through the jungle to the hotel gym, while the onsite farm-to-table restaurant is one of the best around and open to non-guests.

Open cacao pod

Sweet Dreams are Made of This...

CACAO TOURS AND CHOCOLATE MAKING

To the ancient Maya, the cacao plant – the key ingredient in chocolate – was 'the food of the gods.' Much of Belize's cacao is grown in the Toledo District, making Punta Gorda and around the best place in the country to witness traditional methods of fermenting, drying, roasting and hand-grinding the cacao beans, then tasting the final product, either in liquid form, or as the best chocolate bars of your life.

In central Punta Gorda, the small, delicious-smelling **Cotton Tree Chocolate Factory** is a good place for a short tour of the chocolate-making process, after which you can buy milk- and dark-chocolate bars, produced onsite. Beans are sourced from Toledo Cacao Growers Association, promoting both fair trade and local production.

A five-minute walk north of Cotton Tree along the waterfront brings you to the **Mahogany Chocolate** (mahoganychocolates.com) factory, which handcrafts a greater variety of chocolate bars and, if you contact them in advance, offer more hands-on experiences, with visitors witnessing the seed-to-bar process and having a go at making chocolate themselves.

WHERE TO GO FOR DINNER IN PUNTA GORDA

Asha's Culture Kitchen
Choose from lobster, cracked conch or grilled lionfish and have it with two sides at this colorful waterfront deck. $$

Garden Table Restaurant
Fish tacos, *pibil* tostadas and nightly international dishes on a jungle-view terrace. Book ahead. $$$

Seafood Infusion
Fish burgers, fried snook and creole-style shrimp at a Maya-run waterfront spot, along with fruit juices. $

A half-hour away from Punta Gorda, you can learn all about the Maya chocolate-making process at **Ixcacao Maya Belizean Chocolate** (ixcacaomayabelizeanchocolate.com), Juan and Abelina's beautiful cacao farm and chocolate factory (reserve a couple of days in advance). Of the available tours, the most interesting option is the five-hour tour that includes a walk around the farm. After the walk, Juan will take you through the traditional chocolate-making process – from harvest and fermentation to drying and roasting, and on to deshelling and grinding, tasting as you go, followed by a traditional Maya lunch. Camping and farm stays are available for those wishing to linger longer.

Finally in San Pedro Columbia village, a 45-minute drive from PG, Mopan Maya local **Eladio Pop** and his children – Feliciano and Victoria – take you on a tour of his 30-acre farm. Half of the land is given over to the cultivation of cacao; you'll see it in pod form and get to suck the sweet membrane off the cacao seeds inside, then follow your host uphill to a breezy open-air kitchen beneath a thatched *palapa*. The cacao seeds will be roasted over a fire, then split open to reveal the cacao nibs within. You may have a go at crushing them using a traditional stone grinder, after which the paste will be combined with boiling water, with the resulting 'food of the gods' imbibed from a carved calabash shell. You can opt for a traditional Maya lunch and purchase homemade chocolate bars. While you can visit as a half-day trip, the family also offers homestays (US$50 per room) in a basic but well-equipped guesthouse.

Savor Belize's Organic Rum

VISIT THE COPALLI RUM FACTORY

In recent years, **Copalli**, a high-end, smooth rum has been making waves around the country and beyond as Belize's sole organic, carbon-neutral rum. While rum production in Belize is nothing new, this rum distillery is unique, because the process skips the molasses stage completely, and the machinery is powered almost entirely with the desiccated cane waste. After cane juice is squeezed from the sugarcane, it's fermented with rainforest water and organic yeast, rather than molasses, before being distilled and matured in aged bourbon barrels – the white rum and cacao-infused rum for six months, and the golden-colored aged rum for at least 12 months.

FIESTA TIME!

PG and surrounding villages host some of Belize's most interesting festivals.

Toledo's biggest event is the Chocolate Festival, held on the Commonwealth Day holiday weekend in Punta Gorda's main park. There's Maya and Garifuna music, chocolate tasting and chocolate-infused cocktails, plus a craft fair along Front St.

On the weekend before November 19 (Garifuna Settlement Day), PG hosts Battle of the Drums, an exuberant Garifuna cultural fest with competing drumming teams from all over Belize and Honduras, plus concerts, dancing and a Garifuna feast.

Head to San Antonio in August for the Deer Dance Festival and witness the ritual dance re-enacting the hunting of deer to the accompaniment of Maya violins and harps, alongside a showcase of Maya food and crafts.

Scan this QR code for more about the chocolate festival.

WHERE TO EAT CHEAPLY IN PUNTA GORDA

Grace's
Old-school restaurant excels at Belizean specialties like stew chicken, fry-fish, and rice and beans. $

Gomier's
Moreish barbecued tofu, imaginative organic vegetarian and vegan dishes, conch soup and fresh juices. $

Fi Wi Food
Stuffed fry-jack, smoked ribs and tacos alongside coconut fish curry at this thatch-roofed waterfront joint. $

HICKATEE COTTAGES

Less than 1.2 miles (2km) out of PG, this award-winning, solar-powered, expat-run resort leaves as light an ecological footprint as possible, and is popular with birders and nature lovers.

It has two spacious suites, three furnished cottages and the detached Hickatee Den unit overlooking a tiny plunge pool.

Chat to Allison and Eduardo about their horticultural activities (sans pesticides), join a Wednesday-night Garifuna drumming lesson with Ray McDonald (p167), or wander the 2 miles (3.2km) of nature trails through the surrounding rainforest in the hopes of spotting howler monkeys.

Borrow a bicycle to get to town, or opt for a fantastic home-cooked meal (don't miss the signature 'cacao three ways' dessert!). Hickatee feels wonderfully remote, located down a rugged dirt road.

Call ahead for a free pickup.

The factory is on the grounds of the **Copal Tree Lodge** (p168). The two-hour distillery tours and the two-hour mixology classes, during which you learn to craft impressive rum cocktails with farm-fresh ingredients, are open to non-guests with a reservation.

Ranger for a Day

JOIN A RANGER PATROL

Set up in 1997, the **Ya'axché Conservation Trust** (yaaxche.org) manages the forests, reefs and rivers of Toledo's 'Maya Golden Landscape' – a mix of protected areas (including the Golden Stream Corridor Preserve), private land and Maya communities that make up Belize's vital wildlife corridor, connecting the Maya Mountains with the forested coastal plains.

If you want to deepen your appreciation of Belizean nature, join some of Belize's best rangers for a half-day patrol in the **Golden Stream Corridor Preserve**. During the jungle trek along a riverside trail, you will learn how they detect illegal activities – such as hunting, contributing to the wildlife logs, learning to identify small wildlife species (such as the difference between jaguar, puma, and tapir tracks), and learning what the birdcall of the Montezuma oropendola sounds like, while spotting hummingbirds, toucans and curassows.

A less strenuous option involves joining the Ya'axché river patrol, paddling down the Golden Stream River, occasionally carrying your craft short distances and partaking in the same activities as during a trek.

EcoTourism Belize (ecotourismbelize.com) and **Tide Tours** (tidetours.org) organize both tours from Punta Gorda for a minimum of three participants.

Cayes of the Deep South

BELIZE'S REMOTEST DIVING AND SNORKELING

Unlike the northern or central cayes, the little-visited cayes of the Deep South are truly off the beaten path. Closest to Punta Gorda, the **Port Honduras Marine Reserve** is managed by the Toledo Institute for Development & Environment. **Tide** (tidetours.com) can arrange snorkeling trips via boat charter (around BZ$800 a day; up to six people). Trips take in Abalone Caye, where rangers give a short presentation; and the Snake Cayes, 30 to 45 minutes by boat from Punta Gorda. There's excellent snorkeling off East Snake Caye and South Snake Caye, with barracuda, dog snapper,

WHERE TO PAINT PUNTA GORDA RED

Rainforest Reggae
Makeshift-looking waterfront bar popular for cocktails and a laid-back soundtrack. Live reggae on Sundays. $

Leela's Bistro & Bar
Restaurant dedicated to *brukdown* singer Leela Vernon. Hosts impromptu drumming sessions and live music. $

Waluco's
This breezy *palapa* is well loved for its karaoke nights, plus Garifuna drumming some Fridays and Sundays. $

Lime Caye

porcupinefish and angelfish abundant among the coral gardens, while West Snake Caye is known for its white-sand beach.

The southernmost of Belize's protected marine reserves, **Sapodilla Cayes**, 90 minutes by boat from Punta Gorda, is seriously remote. Its boundaries protect the endangered manatee, three turtle species and the scalloped hammerhead shark. The coral gardens surrounding **Lime Caye**'s shipwreck teem with grunts, angelfish, butterflyfish and blue tang, while Lime Caye Wall attracts spiny lobster, moray eel, grouper and snapper. Vigilante Shoal, off Hunting Caye, is a shallow site ideal for snorkelers, where you swim among giant coral along with bluehead wrasse, stoplight parrotfish, dog snapper and spiny lobsters.

Tide can arrange basic accommodations (including camping) on Abalone Caye, while **Garbutt's Marine & Fishing Lodge** (garbuttsfishing.com) arranges diving, snorkeling and fishing trips to the Sapodilla Cayes, along with overnight stays.

OVERNIGHTING IN THE SAPODILLA CAYES

Staying the night (or three) in the Sapodilla Cayes is a unique experience.

The stars are brighter than anywhere else in Belize and some relish feeling like they're the only people on earth.

The only place to stay overnight is the remote outpost on Lime Caye run by Garbutt's Marine & Fishing Lodge in PG. It has three basic waterfront cabins, housing a mix of bunkrooms with shared facilities and en-suite doubles, plus two slightly plusher cabins on stilts affording terrific views of the reef.

Camping can also be arranged and meals are included.

Lime Caye makes an excellent base for diving, snorkeling and fly-fishing (all arranged through Garbutt's), and one of the caye's white-sand beaches is a designated turtle-nesting site.

WHERE TO SHOP IN PUNTA GORDA

Fajina Crafts
Carved hardwood bowls, handmade necklaces, belts, baskets and more, made by Toledo's indigenous peoples.

Maya Bags (mayabags.org)
Handbags, shoulder bags and clutches, handmade by 90 women from eight Maya villages; workshop by airstrip.

Punta Gorda Market
On Wednesdays and Saturdays, buy crafts or just people-watch along Front St and the central plaza.

FISHING FROM PUNTA GORDA

PG is a terrific place for fly-fishing, spin-fishing and trolling, all of which can be practiced year-round.

Fishing for snook, barracuda, kingfish, jacks and snapper is superb in the offshore waters and some coastal lagoons and inland rivers; the estuary flats in the Port Honduras Marine Reserve are good for bonefish and tarpon.

Tour operators, such as Tide Tours, can arrange fishing trips and a guide.

The beautiful sea-front rooms and stilt *cabañas* at Garbutt's Marine & Fishing Lodge (garbutts fishing.com) are PG's only waterfront accommodations and the number-one place for serious fishers; the Garbutt brothers offer guided fishing trips and know the best spots in Port Honduras and the Sapodilla Cayes.

IAN PETER MORTON/SHUTTERSTOCK ©

Lotus pond, Belize Spice Farm

Spice Up Your Life

VISIT THE BELIZE SPICE FARM

At the **Belize Spice Farm** near Indian Creek, an hour's drive from Punta Gorda, a tractor-pulled jitney does hourly 45-minute tours of the beautifully landscaped grounds. Your guide will point out mahogany trees, heliconia in bloom, non-native species, such as jackfruit, dragon fruit and cinnamon, and spices, such as black pepper, cardamom and clove, that are more commonly associated with India and Asia.

You'll get to handle samples of lemongrass (used as insect repellent), nutmeg covered in waxy mace, *morenga* (a superfood used to treat diabetes) and allspice leaves, chewed to combat toothache. You'll also get to witness the cultivation of native vanilla, pollinated by hand when it's outside its jungle habitat.

The lovely open restaurant serves breakfast and lunch for BZ$25.

GETTING AROUND

Punta Gorda is relatively compact and walkable; you might want to catch a taxi from Central Park to Warasa Drum School, though.

Hourly James Line buses departing between 4am and 4pm connect Punta Gorda with Belize City (seven hours) via Dangriga (3½ hours); some run via Belmopan (5½ hours) and Hummingbird Hwy rather than the more direct Coastal Hwy. Bus schedules fluctuate; stop by the BTB office in Punta Gorda for the latest.

Be very careful if driving the Southern Hwy after dark, when pedestrians, animals, cyclists without lights, cars with their headlights off and old-colony Mennonite horse-drawn buggies may be hard to spot.

Nim Li Punit
Lubaantun
Uxbenka
Big Falls
Río Blanco National Park
Toledo Distict
Punta Gorda

Beyond Punta Gorda

Maya villages, ancient ruins, waterfalls, cave networks and pristine jungle await beyond Punta Gorda's borders.

From the Southern Hwy intersection at delightfully named Dump, a paved road runs to the Guatemalan border, while minor roads, ranging from partially paved to hideously rutted and barely passable, lead to villages that make up Belize's Maya heartland. Some villages are Mopan Maya; others Kek'chi Maya, with distinct traditions and a rich culture you can delve into via ambitious community initiatives, from artisans' cooperatives to guesthouse networks and homestays. Beyond the villages, partially excavated Maya ruins, appealing ecolodges, cacao farms, vast caves – some with mighty stalactites and stalagmites, others with rivers running through them, and remote national parks with waterfalls vie for your attention.

TOP TIP

The scattered attractions are reachable either via tours or a high-clearance/4WD vehicle. Contact local guides in advance to arrange tours.

Maya Mountains from Lubaantun (p175)

MAYA MOUNTAIN RESEARCH FARM

This 70-acre organic farm and registered NGO, which is reached on foot or via a 1.8-mile (3km) river journey in a dory (dugout canoe) from San Pedro Columbia, is run by permaculture teacher Christopher Nesbitt (christopher.nesbitt@permaculture.bz) and promotes sustainable agriculture, climate-smart cultivation and alternative energy, and has over 500 plant species, including rare cacao varieties.

Internships are on offer to learn about sustainable food production.

Accommodations comprise rustic dorm-style *cabañas* and *palapas*. Interns help harvest fruits, vegetables, nuts and herbs, and cook over a wood-burning stove in the farm's outdoor kitchen, while doing short-term courses (one to three weeks) in permaculture design and renewable energy.

Rustic and beautiful in the extreme, the farm is remote, which is all part of its charm.

ROY PRENDAS/SHUTTERSTOCK ©

Maya tomb, Nim Li Punit

Nim Li Punit: Maya Ceremonial Center

ADMIRE AN ANCIENT MAYA CITY

The ruins of **Nim Li Punit** (8am–5pm daily; BZ$10) stand atop a hill half a mile north of the Southern Hwy, near the village of Indian Creek. Inhabited from 400 CE in the middle Classic period (250–1000 CE) until around 850 CE, it was probably a town of 5000 to 7000 people at its peak, and likely was a religious and ceremonial center of some importance in the region.

Preliminary excavations of the southern Plaza of the Stelea in 1976 unearthed 26 stelae, include Stela 14, which, at 33ft (10m), is the second-longest stela found anywhere in the Maya world (after Stela E from Quirigua, Guatemala). It depicts the ruler of Nim Li Punit in an offering or incense-scattering ritual, wearing elaborate headgear which gave the site its name ('Big Hat' in Kekchí Maya).

Don't miss the small onsite museum featuring elaborate ceramics, carved human bone used in bloodletting rituals,

WHERE TO STAY AROUND PUNTA GORDA

Chaab'il B'e Lodge
Rustic, thatch-roofed *cabañas* and deluxe rooms set amid jungly gardens delight orchid lovers and birdwatchers. **$$**

Sun Creek Lodge
Rustic ecolodge with thatch-roofed *cabañas,* two villas with outdoor showers and numerous excursions. **$$**

Laguna Maya Lodge
Maya-run, thatch-roofed accommodations, fringed by jungle. Birdwatching trips and delicious meals. **$**

jadeite-inland teeth from the Royal Family Plaza, circular and x-shaped eccentric flints, a replica of a T-shaped jade pendant, carved with hieroglyphs, and well-preserved stelae.

On the site itself, the most interesting part is the south end, comprising the Plaza of the Stelae and the Plaza of Royal Tombs. The Plaza of the Stelae is thought to have acted as a calendrical observatory: seen from its western mound, three of the small stones in front of the long eastern mound align with sunrise on the equinoxes and solstices. The Plaza of Royal Tombs, with three open, excavated tombs, was a residential area for the ruling family. Archaeologists uncovered four members of this family in Tomb 1, along with several jadeite items and 37 ceramic vessels.

Lubaantun: Ancient Maya Trade Center

DELVE INTO MAYA MYSTERIES

These ruins were unearthed in 1924 by Belize's then-chief medical officer Thomas Gann, an amateur archaeologist, who bestowed the name **Lubaantun** ('Place of Fallen Stones') on them. Lubaantun, 1.2 miles (2km) northwest of San Pedro Columbia, has an unparalleled location atop a conical hill, with views of the sea and the Maya Mountains.

Devoid of engraved stelae and displaying an unusual construction method of mortar-less, neatly cut, black-slate blocks (which distinguishes it from other Maya sites), Lubaantun is thought to have flourished during the late Classic Period, between 730 CE and 860 CE, as a trade center of up to 20,000 people.

Eleven major structures sit around five main plazas (18 plazas in total), while the tiered seating on the central plaza could have accommodated up to 10,000 spectators to watch the proceedings on the three ballcourts. The small onsite museum displays distinctive clay whistle figurines, mold-made ceramic figurines representing ancient ball players, obsidian blades, eccentric flints presumably used in rituals, and panels detailing the controversial 'crystal skull.'

To reach Lubaantun from the Southern Hwy, you have to drive either via Silver Creek (signposted just north of Big Falls) and San Miguel, or San Pedro Columbia; the dirt roads are in good shape outside rainy season. Village buses running between San Pedro Columbia and San Miguel can drop you at the turnoff to the site, then it's about half a mile further.

LUBAANTUN & THE CRYSTAL SKULL

In *Danger, My Ally* (1954), the British adventurer Frederick Mitchell-Hedges details how Anna, his daughter, made a remarkable find under an altar at Lubaantun during its excavation in 1926 – a crystal skull, carved of white quartz.

According to steamy newspaper copy at the time, Maya high priests focused their energies through the Skull of Doom to will their enemies' deaths. The subject of a 1990 documentary, *Crystal Skull of Lubaantun,* the skull is believed to be a hoax – one of several 19th-century commissions from German craftsmen by dodgy antiques dealer, Eugene Boban.

The late Anna Mitchell-Hedges resisted entreaties by the Belize government to return the infamous skull. It's presently owned by Bill Homann, her caregiver.

WHERE TO STAY & EAT IN BIG FALLS

Lodge at Big Falls
Birdwatchers love these thatch-roofed *cabañas* overlooking the Río Grande. Fine restaurant. **$$**

Big Falls Cottages
Two delightful, family-run cottages with kitchenettes, surrounded by a lush garden, just south of Big Falls. **$**

Coleman's Cafe
Excellent lunchtime buffet, with rice, beans and slaw. East Indian curries and Creole dishes for dinner. **$**

Cotton Tree Lodge

Named after the silk cotton tree, this partially solar-powered jungle lodge, several kilometers north of San Felipe village (along a bumpy, unpaved road) is a destination in its own right, and has been featured in *National Geographic*.

Connected by raised boardwalks along the bank of the Moho River, the 11 thatched-roof cabins on stilts orbit the excellent restaurant (open to non-guests by prior reservation), with the fruit and vegetables sourced from the onsite organic garden.

The cabins are luxuriously furnished in a jungle/hardwood motif and, while they're screened in, there's an exhilarating feeling of sleeping in the open. Multi-night packages include jungle hikes, horseback riding, kayaking, caving, canoeing and bird-watching, and from the 100-acre property there are terrific views of the nearby Maya Mountain Range.

Living Maya

IMMERSE YOURSELF IN MAYA CULTURE

In **Big Falls** village, join two Kekchí families for the Living Maya experience, organized with the help of Tide Tours (p171) in PG. The Maya families have opened their homes to culturally curious travelers who wish to learn about everyday life in a Maya village. Tour the Cal family home and self-sufficient garden, be introduced to traditional farming methods, and roll up your sleeves to make tortillas over a fire hearth. Nearby, the Chiac family teaches you the basics of woven Maya crafts – baskets, hammocks or bags.

With the help of **EcoTourism Belize** (ecotourismbelize.com) you can tour an organic farm with a Maya farmer to learn about climate-smart agriculture, get your hands dirty, and pick and taste fresh produce; or spend half a day in Indian Creek village with the Maya Arts Women's Group, learning to weave traditional *cuxtal* bags, engraving calabash bowls, wood carving, making fresh chocolate from cacao beans, helping to cook a traditional fire-hearth meal and learning the marimba or the harp dance.

This is a wonderful glimpse into a culture that has been part of this region for thousands of years, and your hosts are happy to cater to your specific interests. Plus, 100% of your money directly supports these communities and a unique way of life.

Uxbenka: Belize's Oldest Maya City

INVESTIGATE JUNGLE-COVERED MAYA RUINS

Belize's oldest Maya city, **Uxbenka** sits on a ridge close to Santa Cruz village on the road from San Antonio, signposted along the road from Dump to Jalacté. Believed to have been continuously occupied for at least 1000 years, Uxbenka dates to the Classic period, with stelae erected in the 4th century.

The visible part – the large Group A plaza with some excavated tombs and sweeping views to the sea – is merely the center of a larger, yet-to-be-excavated city. At the site entrance there's a small visitor center (9am to 4pm; BZ$10), housing some stelae fragments and other Uxbenka finds. Stela 11, with its elaborate depiction of an Early Classic ruler, features the name 'Jaguar Paw' – a personal epithet of the 14th ruler of the Tikal dynasty, Chak Tok Ich'aak I – providing evidence of a close relationship between Uxbenka and Tikal to the north. If the visitor center is not open, walk across the road to the Mopan Maya community of Santa Cruz and ask for a guide; Jose Mes (501-628-9535) can walk you around the site and also runs trips to other, little-visited Maya sites in the jungle.

WHERE TO SHOP IN INDIAN CREEK

Ixchel Women's Group
Small Kekchí Maya women's cooperative makes bracelets, bags, necklaces, *kalaba* shakers. Free craft demos.

Marigold Women's Cooperative
Kekchí Maya women sell traditional Maya food such as breads and cakes, plus crafts.

MAURITIUS IMAGES GMBH/ALAMY STOCK PHOTO

Blue Creek Cave

Go Below: Caving in Toledo District

EXPLORE TOLEDO'S SUBTERRANEAN WONDERS

A short drive from San Miguel and a 15-minute hike across private land, the **Tiger Cave** is a spectacular introduction to Toledo's subterranean world. From the hydroelectric station, it's a short scramble to the vine-hung cave entrance, with narrow, raised caverns leading to several roomy interior chambers. On a ledge, ancient pottery shards attest to the cave's use by the ancient Maya, and there's a stone platform believed to have been used for ceremonial purposes. Halfway into the cave, a vast cavern is lit by two natural skylights, beyond which it gets scrambly and muddy. It takes around an hour to reach the Maya Temple Room near the back of the cave. Another way to reach the cave is via a 45-minute forest hike from San Miguel village, fording a jade-green stream, ideal for a post-caving dip.

At the Mopan and Kekchí Maya community of Blue Creek, take a 20-minute walk along a jungle path from the bridge to **Blue Creek Cave**, one of the region's 'wet caves'. Arrange a guide with life jackets and waterproof flashlights in advance via **Toledo Cave & Adventure Tours** (tcatours.com). Inside, you periodically wade and swim some 600yd to a small waterfall. You can also explore the 'dry side' – a more strenuous venture involving scrambling, emerging at a different entrance.

MAYA HOME STAYS & GUESTHOUSES

Stay in the Maya heartland and enjoy jungle treks, caving, canoeing, bird-watching, dining on 'bush meat' (iguana, aka 'bush chicken' or roasted gibnut), and experience traditional Maya life while contributing to local communities.

Toledo Ecotourism Association (TEA; belizemayatourism.org) manages basic guesthouses in five Maya villages in San Antonio, San Jose, San Miguel, Santa Elena and Laguna, with visitors having meals in village homes.

Alternatively, you can opt for a home-stay in a thatched-roof Maya house, helping on the farms, exploring surrounding attractions, and enjoying traditional dancing and singing.

Contact Jose Mes (501-628-9535) in off-grid Santa Cruz; Justino Pec (501-668-7378) in San Jose and Louis Cucul (501-663-9954) in Aguacate. Tide (p171) in PG can also help.

WHERE TO STAY IN SAN ANTONIO & SAN MIGUEL

Bol's Hilltop Hotel
Spartan San Antonio guesthouse with basic rooms and shared facilities. Meals on request next door. **$**

Back-a-bush
Dutch-owned, chilled San Miguel jungle guesthouse with rustic rooms and meals with homegrown ingredients. **$**

San Miguel Guesthouse
Home-cooked Maya dishes, snug rooms and chocolate-making await at this thatched TEA guesthouse. **$**

MAYA OF THE DEEP SOUTH

Over 60% of the population in Toledo District is Maya.

This includes those driven into Guatemala by the British in the 18th and 19th centuries, before crossing back to southern Belize in the late 19th and early 20th centuries, fleeing forced labor and land grabs. There are also more recent arrivals who escaped from Guatemalan dictatorships in the 1980s.

The Mopan Maya settled in the uplands of southern Belize, while the Kekchi Maya, from the Alta Verapaz area of Guatemala, settled in the lowlands, though some Toledo villages are mixed Mopan and Kekchi Maya. The two speak distinct Maya languages, and sometimes Spanish.

While Maya men generally adopt Western styles of dress, most women wear plain, full-length dresses with bright trimmings. Rituals and folklore continue to play an important role in Maya life.

Río Blanco National Park

Do Go Chasing Waterfalls

FROLIC IN TOLEDO'S GLORIOUS CASCADES

At the 105-acre **Río Blanco National Park**, a compact protected wildlife area just west of Santa Elena village, pay the ranger the entry fee (BZ$10), then take the five-minute forest trail to Río Blanco Falls, a beautiful 20ft-high (7m) waterfall leading into a clear swimming hole that locals claim is bottomless. During rainy season, the falls are a thundering 100ft (30m) wide; during drier months, they're reduced to a dainty trickle. A concrete path leads to a rickety suspension bridge across the river, connecting to a 1.8-mile (3km) loop trail.

Near San Antonio village, splash in the jade-colored pool beneath **San Antonio Falls** – a popular weekend hangout for picnicking locals. Both falls are signposted just off the Southern Hwy.

GETTING AROUND

Frequent buses run between Punta Gorda, Belize City, Dangriga and Belmopan; transportation from PG to Toledo villages is not so frequent.

One morning bus from PG connects the villages of Eldridge, Dump, Mafredi, San Antonio, Santa Cruz, Santa Elena and Pueblo Viejo before reaching Jalacte near the border with Guatemala. The beautifully paved Southern Hwy runs all the way to the border, but the border crossing is unofficial, done on foot and only used by locals.

For Guatemala, catch a daily boat from PG. Any northbound bus leaving PG will drop you at the Dump or Lubaantun intersections, from where people often hitchhike to the villages. Hitchhiking is popular among locals, but there are potential risks.

THP CREATIVE/GETTY IMAGES ©

Río Blanco Falls

Tikal (p184)

TIKAL & FLORES (GUATEMALA)

MAYA MAJESTY, ISLAND PARADISE

Guatemala's finest ruin, Tikal, lies nestled deep in thick jungle. Travelers often stay in nearby Flores, where hotels and restaurants abound.

For many visitors to Belize, Tikal, a quick hop across the border into neighboring Guatemala, is simply a bucket-list must-see. It is arguably the greatest Maya city yet uncovered, and certainly the crown jewel of Guatemala's Maya patrimony. With its iconic temples rising so dramatically out of the surrounding verdant jungle, and the fact that so much about the Maya civilization is yet to be known, Tikal is the reason many tourists visit this region in the first place.

Yet the Petén region is far more than just Tikal. In fact, there are so many ruins, each of them as unique and individual as modern cities today, that it's a shame so many people think they've 'seen it' when they leave Tikal. Tikal is only the beginning, and to fully see the wealth of sites here would take more time than most travelers have, yet it's certainly worth exploring.

There's also far more than just ancient history to uncover: modern Maya traditions light up streets on colorful festival days, the thick jungles host a myriad of special animals and plants, and the Lago de Petén Itzá region offers delightful, tranquil, relaxed lakeside living, whether on the island of Flores (pictured) or the El Remate area. South, the hills, valleys and lagoons of Sayaxché and Petexbatún lend themselves to leisurely river rides and hikes to ruins few tourists find the time for.

THE MAIN AREAS

TIKAL
Majestic Maya ruin.
p184

FLORES
Relaxed island paradise.
p188

Find Your Way

El Petén is a vast place, much of it (thankfully) protected by amazing national parks. Tikal and Flores are easily accessible, but remoter ruins may require a 4WD, horse, or helicopter.

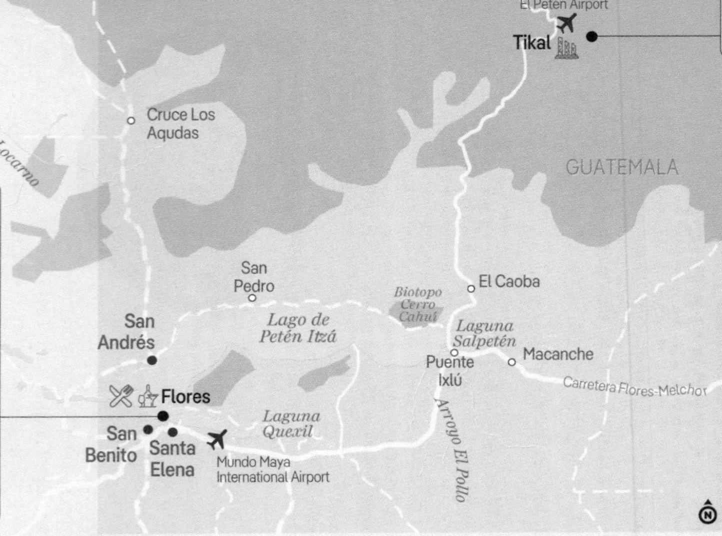

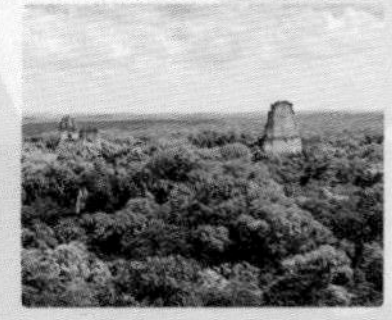

Tikal, p184

This majestic Maya ruin is a top spot not only for Guatemala, but for the entire Maya world.

Flores, p188

Flores is connected by a thin bridge to its sister city, Santa Elena. Flores is the tourist hub; Santa Elena is cheaper and more local.

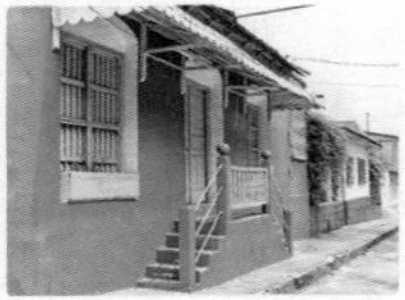

BUS

Long-distance express buses serve all major parts of El Petén, and smaller microbuses zip (often at hair-raising, knuckle-whitening speeds) to most smaller towns and villages. To reach the more remote tourist spots requires a private vehicle.

CAR

You'll be well served if you rent a vehicle. The freedom to roam where you want and when you want will allow you to make the most of your time. Even so, certain regions may be out of reach.

0 30 km
0 15 miles

FROM LEFT: MILOSZ MASLANKA/SHUTTERSTOCK ©, BRESTER IRINA/SHUTTERSTOCK ©

Flores (p188)

Plan Your Time

This region will seduce you with its variety of things to do and see. You can hike through the jungle, laze on the shores of lakes and follow rivers far upstream to swim or explore.

If You Only Do One Thing

It's **Tikal** (p184). Even though there are other Maya ruins that compare with Tikal both in historical value and scale, if you visit El Petén and don't see Tikal it's like going to Paris and not seeing the Eiffel Tower. The sunrise tour is particularly awe-inspiring, especially if you're lucky enough to see the sun. No joke, it's cloudy or raining on up to 80% of mornings.

More Time to Explore

Base yourself at the quaint island town of **Flores** (p188). Take a day trip either just to **Tikal** (p184) or to other ruins too. The next day, take a boat tour of Lago de Petén Itzá, visiting the **El Mirador** (p189) lookout, then the often-flooded town of **San Miguel** (p189). Finally, laze about at **Jorge's Rope Swing** (p189) or check out animal-rehab-center **Arcas** (p189).

Seasonal Highlights

APRIL TO JUNE
By April's end, the dry season is over: hikers and deep jungle explorers, pack up before you're mired in mud.

JULY TO SEPTEMBER
By some measures, the worst time to come: heat over 30°C (85°F), high humidity and rain.

OCTOBER TO DECEMBER
Christmas brings colorful decorations, trees, lights and classic 1950s carols. Just don't expect snow.

JANUARY TO MARCH
Beginning of the dry season in February: hikers and deep jungle explorers, the 'Go!' light just turned green.

TIKAL

BELMOPAN

Tikal

Few people can see images of Tikal's majestic temples rising up out of verdant jungle without feeling their heart beat faster, and unlike so many tourist spots, Tikal is just as magical as the photos...if not more so. Catch the first rays of morning sun as howler monkeys clamor in the treetops, or meander mazelike passages of a lost and once-forgotten world. Yes, other tourists – even busloads of them – will join you, but the ruin is so vast that it's easy to duck away and find a part that feels like you might just be the only person to have been here for centuries. Mossy steps beckon, ancient glyphs tell stories of conquests and kings, and astronomical structures still point to the stars as they did so many centuries ago. Though it's a challenge to get here, nobody leaves thinking it wasn't worth the time.

TOP TIP

Be sure to buy your tickets (even for sunrise and sunset tours, as well as for Uaxactun if you're going) before you enter the park. No tickets are sold inside, meaning a sunrise tour ticket must be chosen – and paid for – in advance.

Temple complex, Tikal

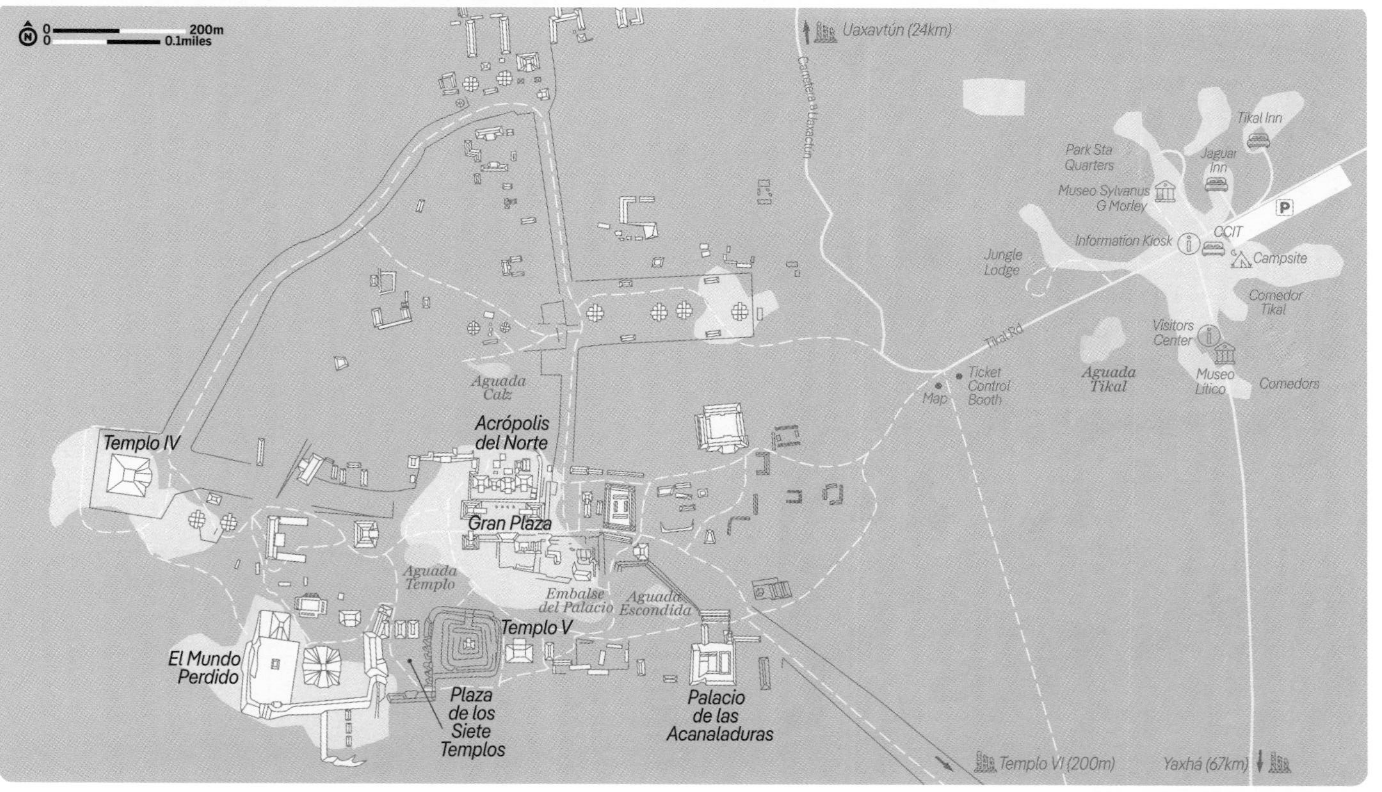
0 200m
0 0.1miles
Uaxavtún (24km)
Carretera a Uaxactún
Tikal Inn
Park Sta
Quarters
Jaguar
Inn
Museo Sylvanus
G Morley
P
CCIT
Information Kiosk
Campsite
Jungle
Lodge
Comedor
Tikal
Visitors
Center
Tikal Rd
Map
Ticket
Control
Booth
Aguada
Tikal
Museo
Lítico
Comedors
Aguada
Calz
Templo IV
Acrópolis
del Norte
Gran Plaza
Aguada
Templo
Embalse
del Palacio
Aguada
Escondida
Templo V
El Mundo
Perdido
Plaza
de los
Siete
Templos
Palacio
de las
Acanaladuras
Templo VI (200m)
Yaxhá (67km)

MEUNIERD/SHUTTERSTOCK ©

Scan this QR code for prices and opening hours.

TOP SIGHT

Tikal

At Guatemala's most impressive ruins, archaeology continues to reveal fascinating discoveries even today. The massive temples honored rulers who governed a feared, powerful capital for centuries. Like many cities, it was eventually burned and abandoned, covered by the jungle until relatively recently.

DON'T MISS

- Templo IV
- Gran Plaza
- Acrópolis del Norte
- El Mundo Perdido
- Templo V
- Palacio de las Acanaladuras
- Templo VI
- Plaza de los Siete Templos

Excavations began in 1956, uncovering hundreds of structures, ballcourts, temples and residences.

Templo IV

One of the ruin's most impressive temples and – thrillingly – one of the few you can ascend, Temple IV looks out across the rest of the site with a commanding view that is both picture-worthy and breathtaking. Whether you're here for the sunrise tour or later in the day, it's a delightful climb up above the treetops to stare across at the temples poking out of the jungle the way mountains poke out above the clouds. Star Wars fans will enjoy seeing a spot that was used in *A New Hope*, and if you're lucky, you'll hear or see monkeys cavorting in the treetops.

Gran Plaza

If there's one place you need to be sure to visit, it's the Gran Plaza, where the incredible Templo I and Templo II stand facing each other. If you have a brochure image of Tikal in your head, chances are it was taken here. You cannot climb Templo I, but across the plaza wooden walkways lead you up Templo II, where you can take fantastic photos, that must-have selfie, strike a yoga pose (while those around you roll their eyes), and so on. In the center, near where the ceremonial offerings are burned, you can clap your hands and hear a quetzal-like sound in the echo. It's not too far off to imagine that just like today, much of the action and focus of the ancient Maya revolved around this sacred plaza.

Built by the son of Tikal's ruler Jasaw Chan K'awiil I to honor his memory, Templo I, also known as Temple of the Great Jaguar, rises 41m vertically; a stately, commanding presence that spoke to the ruler's greatness even after death. It is not possible to climb this one, but the nearly as impressive Templo II faces it, and has stairs to a viewing area that overlooks the entire plaza.

Templo II, 125 feet (38m high), looks across at Templo I and was built by Jasaw Chan K'awiil to honor his wife, and the construction was completed after both of their deaths by their son.

Birders, take note: the *ramón* trees attract both aracari toucans and slaty-tailed trogons. Keep your zoom lenses at the ready!

El Mundo Perdido (The Lost World)

El Mundo Perdido is one of the most fascinating areas of Tikal, as it was used as an astronomical observatory and still functions today. Perhaps more interestingly, it shows many links to Teotihuacán, the famous ruin outside Mexico City: its stepped *talud-tablero*-style structures clearly show the influence of the latter. *Talud-tablero* is a style of architecture that begins with an inward slope, then has a front-facing 'table,' that is followed by another inward-facing slope.

Like the Acrópolis del Norte, it's believed that for a time, El Mundo Perdido also served as a funerary and possible necropolis, in addition to its astronomical value. Surprisingly, even when parts of the grand city were going into decline in the Terminal Classic period, El Mundo Perdido continued to be used. Some believe that was due to it being close to one of Tikal's great reservoirs.

TO SUNRISE OR NOT TO SUNRISE

If you're willing to get up at 3:30am and hike for half-hour in darkness, your spectacular reward is the morning sun waking the howler monkeys as it rises over the towers of Tikal. It's a photographer's dream, but frequent cloud cover means mist or rain. Get sunrise tickets prior to entering the park.

TOP TIPS

- If you do the sunrise tour you'll not only see the sunrise, but you'll also have two to three hours of extra time to explore before the temperatures rise.
- Late afternoon or early-morning light is best for photographs.
- Make sure you bring mosquito repellent, as well as plenty of water and snacks.
- Leave the ruin cleaner than how you found it. Don't be afraid to grab that water bottle someone has long forgotten and put it in the trash.
- Be sure to bring plenty of sun protection: a hat, sunscreen and even an umbrella.

FLORES

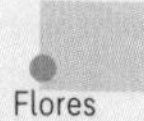

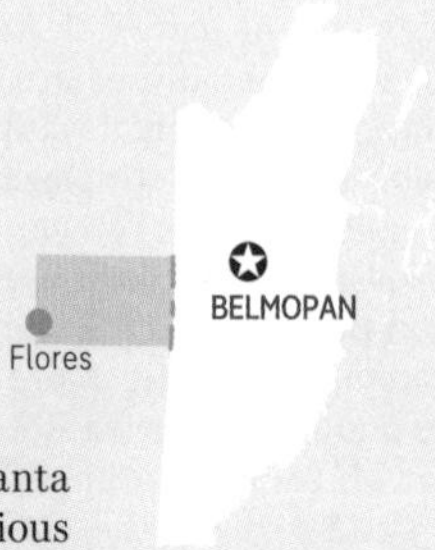

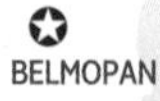

Tiny island Flores, along with its nearby 'sister' city, Santa Elena, is a delightful gem in the Petén region, with delicious restaurants, a lively night scene, great bars and a host of activities. Yes, you'll almost certainly visit Tikal, but the town is a great base for all sorts of day excursions to other parts of the region. Evenings can be spent calmly with a glass of wine, watching the sunset, or in a bar filled with boisterous dancers. The entire island takes less than 10 minutes to circle by car and less than 30 by foot, unless you're distracted by the shops, cafes or restaurants that beckon. Access to a hospital and airport are pluses, but most people won't need the former and will be sad when they have to use the latter, since it's likely you won't want to leave.

TOP TIP

If you plan to stay in Flores, choose a hotel that's on either the east side (sunrise) or the west side (sunset), as the views will be spectacular at the respective time of day. If Flores is full, look for vastly cheaper, nontouristy hotels in Santa Elena.

Calm Lake, Flores

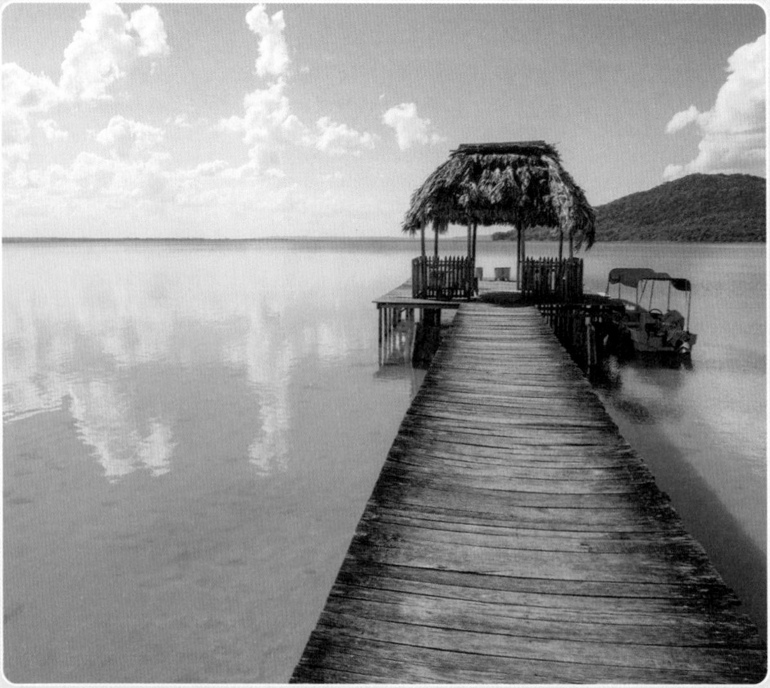

SIMON DANNHAUER/SHUTTERSTOCK ©

Life on the Lake

WATER BY DAY OR NIGHT

It's impossible to spend time in **Flores** and not end up out on the lake, even if you hate boats. The water is mostly calm and glassy, and even a 10-minute zip out and back lifts the spirits: who could resist feeling happy when the sun is tickling the lake's surface, turning the entire vastness into glitter and sparkles like a ballerina's gown. It's delightful. There's little chance of feeling queasy when the lake surface is so placid.

It's also a method of transportation: you'll hop on a *lancha* (skiff) to reach places like **El Mirador**, a commanding lookout atop an unexcavated Maya structure, and nearby **San Miguel**, both across on an isthmus opposite Flores' north shore. A little further away you can visit **Arcas**, an organization dedicated to preserving trafficked wildlife and educating the public about this heinous crime. Learn about wildlife trade and see animals and birds that can no longer be released to the wild due to trafficking crimes. If lazing about is your fancy, just stop at **Jorge's Rope Swing** to swing, splash, or sunbathe.

At night, the party boats depart for cruises through the darkness, with neon and strobes and music. Crowds of

BEST PLACES TO EAT IN FLORES

Maple y Tocino
Delightful spot on the west side of Lago de Petén Itzá with seating that overlooks the lakeside. $$

Casa Ramona
Great breakfasts served with a cheery smile at this spot on the lake's southeast side. $

Maracuya
A delightful dinner and late-night coffee or wine spot, with airy balconies and vine-entwined terraces. Also great for morning sunshine over the lake's east shore. $$

WHERE TO STAY IN FLORES

Casa Ramona
A bright, spanking-clean spot with a nice cafe on the 1st floor. $

Casa Azul
Blue is the theme here at this west-facing hotel with a pool. $$

Los Amigos Hostel
It's all happening here at centrally located Los Amigos, with dorms, private rooms and a great restaurant/bar. $

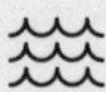

LAKE LEVELS

In some ways, geology has cursed Lago de Petén Itzá (pictured), for it is essentially a vast flat plain that eventually flooded when runoff from surrounding land had no exit.

At its deepest spot, a cenote has a depth of several hundred feet, but most of the lake is quite shallow.

Water levels rise and fall at the mercy of evaporation and rainfall. In the rainy season, streets that might be otherwise walkable can be several feet under water; in the dry season, it seems unthinkable that a shoreline so dry need worry.

The traffic patterns may change at times to account for flooded streets, but it's all part of what makes this island so unique. Go (pun intended) with the flow.

mostly tourists get to see the lake as a backdrop for socializing and perhaps a conversation or more. Crowds gather in rooftop bars to watch the dark, still water blend as the sun vanishes into the darkness of the sky. Perhaps a cool night breeze carries off a hat, which floats and tumbles downward to rest on the water and slowly be carried away from shore.

Flores Nightlife

LOTS GOING ON AFTER DARK

This island has a bit of a Dr Jekyll, Mr Hyde thing going on between its sleepy, easy, relaxed days and its pumped-up, frenetic nights, and there's no place but Flores for nightlife in all of El Petén.

Things start shortly after the stars come out, generally with people seeking spots on the west side of the island to drink, chat and mingle. Walk along the main circle (mostly **Calle Union** and **30**), and listen for music you like. Then follow your ears, sometimes up stairways or down narrow alleys, or even across flooded footbridges, and find the place that's right for you. It could be quiet karaoke in a dive bar, a hopping scene at a second-story terrace, or drinks and new friends at a youth hostel or hotel bar. After 10pm expect to hear the nightclubs and see lines, sometimes long ones, to get in on Fridays and weekends. Put in earplugs if you have them and plan on quite the party.

There's a bar for just about every lifestyle and most are within easy walking distance from each other. Your best bet is to start the night and wander, letting whatever happens happen. Don't expect the party to last all night though: things wrap up and shut down by 1am, and once revelers have stumbled back to their bunks, beds or homes, the island is quiet as a tomb until morning.

GETTING AROUND

Getting to Flores from Belize can be done several ways. Frequent bus tours head to Tikal as part of their circuit, and non-tour buses arrive from Belize as well.

If your pocketbook allows, consider flying into Flores' international airport.

For drivers, you'll want to cross at Melchor de Mencos. It's about four hours from the border to Flores.

Once there, Flores and Santa Elena are small, bustling spots where it's easy to flag a taxi or a tuk-tuk, which may even be easier than parking and re-parking a vehicle, if you have one.

Within Flores, you can easily walk across the island in 15 minutes, or circumnavigate it in half an hour.

Flores

TOOLKIT

The chapters in this section cover the most important topics you'll need to know about in Belize. They're full of nuts-and-bolts information and valuable insights to help you understand and navigate Belize and get the most out of your trip.

Barton Creek Cave (p128)

Arriving

Most visitors to Belize will arrive through the Philip SW Goldson International Airport (BZE), located about 10 miles (16km) from Belize City's center. All international flights arrive here, as well as many of the domestic ones. There are only two baggage-claim carousels, which are surrounded by a few duty-free stores. Other travelers may cross land borders from Guatemala or Mexico, or arrive by boat.

Visas

For most nationalities, visas are issued upon entry for up to 30 days. Visa extensions to stay beyond this time can be obtained at immigration offices.

SIM Cards

Local SIM cards can be used in most unlocked international cell phones, but they are not sold at the airport. They are easily found in most grocery stores, along with inexpensive phones.

Cash

Cash is king in Belize. Many hotels and restaurants will take cards, but taxis, shops and food stands won't. There are ATMs in the airport, as well as in the larger towns and villages.

Wi-Fi

Free wi-fi is available at the airport, though it's sometimes unreliable when many people are there. Most hotels and many restaurants offer wi-fi for free too.

Public Transport from Airport to Main Cities

	Belize City	San Pedro	San Ignacio	Placencia
FERRY		90 mins **US$31** (plus taxi to Belize City ferry)		
PLANE		15 mins **US$99**		25 mins **US$147**
TAXI	20 mins **US$25**		110 mins **US$150**	160 mins **US200**
SHUTTLE	20 mins **US$25**		110 mins **US$120**	150 mins **US$75**

BELIZE BUSES 101

While the iconic repurposed Bluebird buses that make up Belize's coach-based transportation can be spotted hauling passengers throughout the country, their routes do not include the international airport. There are a large number of private bus companies, but they share dedicated bus stations and stops, and most will stop on major highways if you flag them down. Schedules can be found online or by calling individual operators. Buses are quite a common way for locals to get around, and due to the lack of air-conditioning in them, being on board can be a hot, crowded affair.

Getting Around

Having your own vehicle maximizes flexibility, whether that's renting a car on the mainland or a golf cart on the cayes with roads. But there are many other ways to get around.

TRAVEL COSTS

Rental
From BZ$130 per day

Gas
Approx. BZ$14 per gallon

Bus ticket from Belize City to Cayo
Up to BZ$10

Flight from Belize City to San Pedro
From BZ$170

Hiring a Car

Generally, renters must be at least 25 years old, have a valid driver's license and pay by credit card. Most car-rental companies have offices at the international airport, and there are golf-cart rentals near the airport in San Pedro.

Road Conditions

Belizean roads are riddled with speed bumps, especially within villages, and can often have potholes. Roads may change noticeably after it rains. Passing in the oncoming lane is common, and drivers may make up their own rules as needed. Staying vigilant while driving is highly recommended.

TIP

When getting around on foot, a parasol can work wonders in mitigating the sun's rays.

AN UNWANTED IMPACT

Large populations of wildlife is one of Belize's greatest assets, but this means animals risk being struck by cars. From tapir to dogs to jaguars, there's very little stopping creatures from crossing the road, made harder to see at night due to a lack of streetlights. Avoid collisions by driving the speed limit and keeping eyes on the road. If the unfortunate occurs, the authorities must be contacted. If the animal is still alive, call Belize Wildlife & Referral Clinic (belizewildlifeclinic.org) for help. For birds, contact Belize Bird Rescue (belizebirdrescue.com).

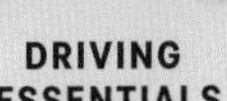

DRIVING ESSENTIALS

Drive on the right

Speed limit is 25mph in towns and villages, and 55mph on highways

Look out for marked and unmarked speed bumps (aka 'sleeping policemen')

Hitchhiking

Hitchhiking is a fairly common way for Belizeans to get around, especially off the main highways, but like anywhere else, it's never entirely safe. Avoid doing it at night, and trust your instincts. Buses can be flagged down too, especially at bumps where vehicles must slow down.

Boats

Individual island destinations offer their own boat transportation, but San Pedro and Caye Caulker are best accessed using the water taxi from Belize City. The San Pedro Belize Express also goes to Chetumal, Mexico, and there is a water taxi traveling from Punta Gorda to eastern Guatemala.

Domestic Flights

All domestic flights are on small propeller planes operated by either Tropic Air or Maya Island Air. They serve most of the major towns including San Pedro, Placencia and Punta Gorda. Flights in and out of Belize City use both the international airport and the municipal airport, so note which one when booking.

Money

CURRENCY: **BELIZEAN DOLLAR (BZ$)**

Belizean Dollar

The Belizean dollar (BZ$) is pegged to the US dollar at two to one (BZ$1 = US$0.50). Nearly every business in Belize accepts US dollars and prices are often quoted in US dollars at resorts and hotels – always check in advance whether you're paying in Belize dollars or US dollars. ATMs are easily found throughout the country. Paying through smartphones and apps is not yet commonplace.

Best Ways to Pay

Restaurants, shops and hotels are generally credit-card-friendly, but it's best to have cash for businesses that aren't; this can include taxis, tours and food stands.

Tipping

Tipping is not obligatory but is always appreciated by guides, drivers or servers. Some hotels and restaurants add a service charge to your check (usually 10%).

Haggling

Bargaining is not common in Belize with the notable exception of outdoor souvenir markets, where everything is negotiable.

HOW MUCH FOR...

Maya ruin entry
BZ$10–15

national park entry
BZ$5–10

golf-cart rental
BZ$90 for a 24-hour period

ferry from Belize City to San Pedro
BZ$33.50 for a one-way ride

HOW TO... Avoid Scams

Belize is not particularly rife with scammers, except for when it comes to real estate. Many tourists fall in love with Belize and want to buy a piece of it, then end up buying a faulty title that has been sold to similar tourists multiple times. Beware of deals that seem too good to be true, and hire a lawyer to facilitate the paperwork.

LOCAL TIP

Belizean banks will not take torn or written-on bills, so please do not pay or tip using them, as they are useless to locals.

BUDGET TRAVEL

Belize is one of the most expensive destinations in Central America, though it's still cheaper by international standards.

Budget travel here is possible, especially by staying in hostels, eating where locals go, and traveling during slower seasons like May and November.

Taking the bus can also significantly cut down on travel costs, as the cost of gas is high and transfers and taxis reflect this. Because haggling is uncommon, getting discounts on hotels and tours is unlikely. Budget travelers should expect to pay BZ$150 to BZ$200 a day at least.

Accommodations

Private Islands

If you've ever dreamed of renting a private island, then Belize is the place to do it. They range widely in price and amenities offered – some are very basic, while others have a private chef – so there's really a caye for everyone. Divers and people who love fishing have been visiting Belize for decades due to the ability to stay in a place surrounded by the Caribbean Sea.

Jungle Lodges

Sleeping in comfort surrounded by the Belizean jungle is one of this country's specialties. Most of them are on the luxury end of the accommodations spectrum and have everything a guest might need on-site since they're typically some distance from town. Waking up to birdsong and having the best inland tours at your doorstep are just some of the perks.

Family-Owned Hotels

Belize is boutique by nature, with international brands being a rare sight to see in any industry. However, as the country grows in popularity, major hotels are setting their sights on the Jewel. Family-owned properties embody the hospitable spirit of the country, creating a tangible connection for travelers to maintain visit after visit.

Maya Village Homestays

Several Maya villages in the Punta Gorda area generously participate in a homestay program enabling visitors to experience modern Maya culture up close. Guests will participate in the daily activities of their hosts, from harvesting corn to doing laundry in the nearby creek. It doesn't cost a lot to do this, but the opportunity is valuable.

HOW MUCH FOR A NIGHT IN...

a jungle lodge
Approx. BZ$600-1000

a cave
BZ$500-4000

a Maya homestay
BZ$15-20 per person

WELCOME

Hostels

Backpackers love Belize for its laid-back attitude and friendly locals, which is why there is a wealth of accommodations catering to this crowd. They are generally quite clean, inviting and at the center of the action wherever they're found. Hostel staff tend to go above and beyond when making recommendations and arranging tours.

WHERE ARE THE ALL-INCLUSIVES?

Caribbean destinations might be known for all-inclusive resorts, but that's never been Belize's style. Hotels, and Belizeans in general, encourage their guests to explore the country, thus it's uncommon to hear tales from visitors who never left their resort. This is largely because such accommodations don't exist. While some places – especially remote cayes – do provide packages including everything a guest would need, such as meals, transportation, rooms and tours, traditional all-inclusives should be sought elsewhere.

CLOCKWISE FROM TOP LEFT: TATIANA POPOVA/SHUTTERSTOCK ©, LAURA.H/SHUTTERSTOCK © RYAN MCVAY/GETTY IMAGES ©, NUTCD32/SHUTTERSTOCK ©, NREDMOND/GETTY IMAGES ©

Family Travel

Belize has some special ingredients for a family holiday. It's both affordable and safe, especially compared with other Caribbean destinations, and it's small and easy to navigate. Belizeans are famously friendly, and traveling with kids will often break down barriers between tourists and residents, sometimes opening doors to local hospitality. Belizeans love kids and will go out of their way to accommodate them

Best Spots for Families

Attractions in Belize – sea life, exploring caves, climbing ruins, watching for birds, wildlife and bugs – will delight kids as much as grown-ups. Jungle lodges around San Ignacio are well equipped to keep kids entertained, while the seaside towns of San Pedro and Placencia are rich with things for kids to do. Many activities, however, are not suitable for babies or toddlers.

Facilities

Some hotels will offer discounts for children, but arranging cots and high chairs for kids should be done prior to arrival. Babysitting services are very uncommon, so be sure to check with your hotel prior to making plans to leave your kid alone. Changing-tables in restaurants and other public places are also uncommon.

Pram Unfriendliness

Plan on carrying infants and toddlers around Belize: most of the tours and activities can't accommodate prams, and road surfaces and sidewalks are typically uneven, if they are paved at all.

Eating

Your kids will probably be happy to eat most typical Belizean and Mexican foods, such as sandwiches, rice and beans, fried chicken, hamburgers and tacos. Bakery goods, pasta and pizzas are additional favorites. Tropical-fruit smoothies and fresh juice are delicious and healthy, and found everywhere.

CHILD-FRIENDLY PICKS

Belize Zoo (p57)

Kids between 12 and 17 years old can attend Conservation Camp, a five-day program exploring the waterways and wildlife of the Sibun River. A regular visit to the zoo is also delightful.

Ayala's Natural Pools (p143)

Seven ziplines make up this progressively challenging course, which adventurous kids will love. It costs BZ$30 to use the zipline, and BZ$10 to enter the park and use its water slides and pools.

Mountain Equestrian Trails (p133)

MET is well versed in teaching kids the equestrian arts, and has a stable full of horses to safely escort them on an adventure through the jungle.

UP CLOSE WITH WILDLIFE

Because of the many opportunities visitors have to get up close and personal with animals in the wild, Belize is a great place for teaching kids appropriate and ethical behavior when it comes to animals. Generally, guides on animal-centered tours will provide education on the importance of looking but not touching (or feeding), including at the Belize Zoo. Wild animals present a real danger, especially to children, so this is a great chance for kids to find out that looking on respectfully is also the best way to stay safe.

Health & Safe Travel

ROAD ACCIDENTS

Belizean driving habits can be unpredictable, and intoxicated driving is common. Road accidents are common, especially with intermittently maintained roads and unexpected obstacles, so be sure to wear a seatbelt and stay vigilant. Call the police if you're involved in an accident.

Hurricanes

Belize's hurricane season is from June through November, and they sometimes make landfall in the country. It's a small target, but a target nonetheless. The coast is more susceptible to damage, but floods can occur inland. Pay attention to alerts and updates, which can be found online and via local radio stations.

Wildlife

Conflict with wildlife is uncommon in Belize, and when it does occur, a human is typically at fault. Give animals like crocodiles and sharks plenty of space, and never allow anyone to talk you into feeding them for a fee: this is illegal and unethical. Be cautious when walking in forested areas where snakes might blend into the foliage, and avoid stepping on anthills.

TAP WATER

Avoid drinking tap water, particularly on Ambergris Caye. Ice and washed vegetables could be from tap water as well. Ask if unsure.

WILDLIFE ROAD SIGNS

Crocodile

Tapir

Jaguar

Coatimundi

Monkey

Drugs

Possessing up to 10 grams of marijuana on private property is legal in Belize, however there is no legal market to obtain it: buying, selling and growing it are all illegal. Police are unlikely to bust you with it, but other drugs like cocaine are fair game to them: they are quite clearly illegal.

BOTFLIES

Bugs abound in Belize, and one of the scariest is the botfly. While far from the most dangerous, the botfly is a skin burrower, and can hitch rides on unsuspecting tourists enjoying the jungle. Most locals have advice for coaxing it out or suffocating it, but the larva can be surgically removed too. Larva gets inserted into skin via mosquito bites, so bring bug spray.

Food, Drink & Nightlife

When to Eat

Breakfast (7–9am) Belizean breakfasts can be large or small, but usually include coffee.

Lunch (11:30am–2pm) Lunch is commonly a plate of rice and beans with stewed chicken.

Siesta (2–4pm) A time to rest and digest. Best done in a hammock.

Dinner (6–10pm) Dinner usually features more elaborate dishes with varying origins.

Where to Eat

Restaurants Any sit-down eatery with a kitchen and menu.

Cafes Bakeries and small shops selling pastries and coffee.

Street carts Moveable carts open usually for lunch and dinner.

Beach shacks Small, usually wooden huts on beaches serving takeaway meals.

Roadside snacks Seasoned fruit or corn sold in bags by people waiting at speed bumps on roads.

Bars Spots open at night selling mostly alcohol, but can have extensive food menus too.

MENU DECODER

Rice and beans Rice and beans cooked together

Beans and rice Rice served with beans separately

Chicha Fermented drink

Pepper or peppa Hot sauce

Royal rat Gibnut

Bamboo chicken Iguana

Fast food Anything fried

Pear Avocado

Tambran Tamarind

Sorrel Roselle fruit from the hibiscus plant

Fry-jack Puffed-up flour dough ready to be filled

Culantro A cilantro-like herb that grows locally

Johnnycake Cornmeal flatbread

Black Dinna Chirmole, aka a chicken soup made with black recado

Salbutes Puffed corn tortillas topped with shredded meat

Panades Like salbutes but stuffed

Fufu Mashed half-ripe plantains

Hudut Fish stew made with fufu

Bile Up Kriol boil-up of eggs, protein and starch

Quita pone Hair of the dog

Stretch mi guts Candy made with coconut

HOW TO...

Pay The Bill

Every restaurant in Belize seems to make its own rules, which is especially noticeable when it comes to paying the bill.

Typically the bill is paid once you have finished your meal, but on occasion you may be expected to pay before being served. This is more common at quick, casual spots, just like in the United States.

At other restaurants, the bill is to be paid once dining is finished. However, there's no consistency on what this looks like. In some cases servers will wait to be called over to bring the check. Elsewhere, a check will be brought out without asking. It's anyone's guess whether you can pay at the table, or whether you will need to go to the restaurant's cash register to pay. As is the case with other aspects of traveling in Belize, clarity is most easily gained by asking for it.

HOW MUCH FOR...

an ice cream
BZ$3

a serving of fry-jacks
BZ$4

a serving of ceviche
BZ$10

a lunch with fried beans and chicken
BZ$15

a coffee
BZ$6

a Belikin beer
BZ$5

a rum punch
BZ$6

HOW TO... Enjoy Belizean Dining

Most American travelers will find themselves very much at home when dining out in Belize. The schedule of meals, the amount of food served on a plate, and even many of the dishes will feel familiar to Americans in particular.

Overall the country is very casual, so there's no unique dining etiquette to adhere to, other than that it's suggested you finish what's put on your plate. Dressing up is uncommon, and usually based on the diner's discretion. Locals will don nicer clothes for celebratory meals at higher-end restaurants, but there's nowhere in the country where a suit and tie or ball gown is necessary.

The pace of service can feel somewhat slow, as meals are typically cooked from scratch, and Belizeans are not culturally prone to rushing anyway. While some luxury resorts might have quiet dining areas, that's not typically the case at restaurants in town, where locals and tourists often gather for raucous get-togethers that inevitably incorporate other diners looking to have fun.

Feel free to ask your server what they recommend, but beware that they might at first tell you what other tourists like to order. If desired, clarify that you're looking for local flavor, and you will surely be eating like a Belizean. And while locals aren't expected to tip, tourists should budget 10% to 15% gratuity after a good meal.

Catching Your Own Fish

Catching your own fish and having it cooked for you is a quintessentially Belizean experience. Most coastal restaurants will do it at a cost, and fishing tour operators can help facilitate that.

MAKING RESERVATIONS

When traveling to popular destinations during high season, it is recommended to make reservations at sit-down restaurants. The pandemic enabled many restaurants to create reservation systems online and through WhatsApp, making it fairly straightforward to create a booking digitally with those establishments which have opted in to the technology.

In Belize, finding contact information to make a reservation can be slightly challenging, however. Businesses in Belize, other than hotels, are likely to use Facebook in lieu of a website. Updated menus, contact information and upcoming specials are usually listed on their pages, but oftentimes they are not. Facebook Messenger is also a common portal for communication with guests, and some restaurants take reservations over dedicated WhatsApp lines as well. There is no country-wide app or website for making restaurant reservations in Belize.

The best way to make a reservation (besides asking your hotel to do it for you) is to check a restaurant's Facebook page and call the number listed. This is also beneficial for ensuring they're open, as most restaurants are family-operated and won't necessarily stick to strict hours if business is slow. Calling is also the most reliable way to get up-to-date information on menus, accessibility options, or anything else you might be wondering about.

Now, making reservations isn't always required, especially at more casual or local spots. If you do go this route, the polite thing to do is to arrive for your meal, or at least cancel if plans change. Reservations can be canceled through the same medium through which they were booked.

TOOLKIT

Responsible Travel

Climate Change & Travel

It's impossible to ignore the impact we have when traveling, and the importance of making changes where we can. Lonely Planet urges all travelers to engage with their travel carbon footprint. There are many carbon calculators online that allow travelers to estimate the carbon emissions generated by their journey; try resurgence.org/resources/carbon-calculator.html. Many airlines and booking sites offer travelers the option of offsetting the impact of greenhouse gas emissions by contributing to climate-friendly initiatives around the world. We continue to offset the carbon footprint of all Lonely Planet staff travel, while recognizing this is a mitigation more than a solution.

Choose Sustainable Lodging

Conservation is at the core of Belize's culture, making it easy to find accommodations that support the country's eco-outlook. Jungle lodges and resorts on remote cayes tend to be off-grid, solar-powered, and deeply committed to operating sustainably.

Skip the Flight

Flying domestically is the fastest way to get around, but Belize is a small country, and it's fast enough to get around. Consider taking a bus or shuttle with other passengers to reduce airplane fuel use.

Seasonal Cuisiner

Indulging in Belize's cuisine is as tasty as it is sustainable. By sticking to seasonally available fruits and vegetables and locally ranched meats, you ensure that the massive ecological impact of shipping is irrelevant to your meal.

Visit Maya Communities

Experiencing Maya culture up close is a wonderful opportunity to support communities without many other means of earning income while learning about a beautiful facet of Belize's multiculturalism.

Belize has the highest concentration of jaguars in the world, with 60 to 80 cats living in their wildlife corridor.

Belize was the first country to ban offshore oil drilling in 2018. Citizens are hoping it sticks.

Eat Lionfish

This invasive fish species is preying on Belize's coral-reef ecosystem, so visitors are encouraged to spear the venomous creatures and let an expert cook them up. The good news is they're delicious.

Tourism is a major driver in protecting Belize's coastline;. 25% of Belize's tourism is based on the reef alone, while tourism overall makes up nearly half the country's GDP. Visiting the reef is a great way to protect it.

Help Plant Coral

Placencia-based coral restoration organization, Fragments of Hope, is reseeding the Caribbean with coral. Donate to their cause, or take a kayak tour that helps support their critical work.

Scan this QR code to donate.

Buy Belizean

Artisans abound in Belize, their wares available at farmers markets and craft fairs. Buy a unique souvenir that directly supports a local artist, enabling them to grow Belize's cultural footprint.

Try Birdwatching

Walking slowly and quietly in the wilderness is one of the lowest-impact ways to enjoy any destination, and Belize's capable birdwatching guides will enthusiastically show you how to do it so birds stay put to be seen.

The Belize Audubon Society (p142) manages seven natural areas in Belize, both on- and offshore. Consider volunteering with them on various bird-protecting projects.

In 2021, 236,000 acres of Belize's Selva Maya tropical forest were purchased for conservation, bringing the country's total percentage of protected lands to nearly 40%.

Scan this QR code to find out more.

Don't Feed the Wildlife

There are options when booking tours that bring you up close and personal with wildlife. Choose operators that avoid baiting or feeding wildlife to help minimize the impacts of tourism.

RESOURCES

travelbelize.org/ sustainability
Travel Belize's website has many sustainability recommendations.

belize.oceana.org
Protecting the Belize Barrier Reef.

belizeaudubon.org
Belize's Audubon chapter is saving birds and their ecosystems.

CLOCKWISE FROM TOP LEFT: BEARFOTOS/SHUTTERSTOCK ©, ERNI/SHUTTERSTOCK ©, ERNI/SHUTTERSTOCK ©, BLUEHAND/SHUTTERSTOCK ©

LGBTIQ+ Travelers

Male homosexuality only became legal in Belize in 2016, when the Supreme Court found the anti-sodomy laws to be unconstitutional. The country's first official Pride march was held in 2017. Generally speaking, Belize is a tolerant society with a 'live and let live' attitude. But underlying Central American machismo and traditional religious belief mean that same-sex couples should be discreet.

PDA

Public displays of affection and explicit shows of sexuality are frowned upon in Belize in general, but more so when those involved are of the same gender or appear queer. Discrimination toward LGBTIQ+ tourists existing or moving through Belize is unlikely, however that can change when PDA is involved. It's best to be somewhat cautious, especially around more conservative communities like the Mennonites. Even when outright hatred isn't a factor, people may make it clear that they're uncomfortable.

UNDERSEA EXPEDITIONS

This gay and lesbian scuba-diving company sometimes offers liveaboard trips to the Blue Hole. Get added to their list to be alerted of new trips being scheduled. While discrimination underwater isn't going to happen, it can be helpful to travel with guides knowledgeable about what could potentially be faced on land.

The Power of Tourism

Because tourists are held in fairly high regard in Belize, travelers wield a lot of power in reducing stigma around being queer. Simply showing up and being a good tourist can affect the future of queer rights in Belize.

Belize Gay Pride Week

A newly hatched celebration in Belize that takes place in August, with the bulk of events in Belmopan. It's not guaranteed to happen every year, since fundraising is required, but there is generally some effort by the local queer community to put it on. It's very much a radical act given the overarching attitude toward LGBTIQ+ people, thus there is a risk of danger when attending.

CHANGING THE LAW

When Belize overturned its sodomy law in 2016, it became the first British colony in the Caribbean to do so. This was largely thanks to Caleb Orozco, who fought to end discrimination against people for their sexual orientation.

Bars

There are no dedicated LGBTIQ+ bars in Belize, as most queer Belizeans live under the radar, even using aliases. The best places to encounter and enjoy queer culture are places where tourism is heavy, particularly around San Pedro. There are numerous bars on Ambergris Caye and Caye Caulker, and they are generally queer-friendly. Placencia is also home to nightlife that is fun for queer travelers.

Accessible Travel

Belize lacks accessibility regulations and many buildings are on stilts or have uneven wooden steps. You won't see many ramps for wheelchair access and there are very few bathrooms designed for visitors in wheelchairs. Visitors with restricted sight and hearing will find a similar lack of accessibility.

Airport

Philip Goldson International Airport does not have staff or services dedicated to assisting passengers with disabilities: they recommend arranging assistance with your airline. There are no jet bridges, so planes unload passengers down stairs: airlines are responsible for assisting passengers.

Accommodations

There are a range of wheelchair-accessible hotels in Belize, but not all accommodations fit the bill. Still, there is at least one option in every major destination. Call ahead to find out what accessibility entails at a given hotel.

RESOURCES

There are no on-the-ground resources for travelers with disabilities in Belize. Contacting local resources designed to support Belizeans living with disabilities may be the best way to find relevant information. The Belize Council for the Visually Impaired (501-822-3541) and the Cayo Deaf Institute (501-638-3323) are two such organizations.

Transportation

Finding a wheelchair-friendly car or taxi will be challenging, however shuttle services often operate large vans. Domestic flights don't require advance notice of wheelchairs, but they can't fit some powered wheelchairs on small planes, so it's best to call ahead.

BELIZE ZOO

The first truly accessible nature destination in Belize, the zoo was designed to be step-free. It offers tours specifically for wheelchair users, but it can be navigated independently as well.

Helpful Locals

What Belize lacks in accessible travel facilities it makes up for in helpful locals who are generally willing to assist travelers with special needs in getting around or, say, reading a menu.

Activities & Tours

Belize's accessible activities are limited. ROAM Belize is recognized as a particularly helpful operator curating trips for travelers with disabilities, and has the transportation to accommodate wheelchairs.
Scan this QR code to find out more.

The Belize Water Taxi asks passengers using wheeled devices to contact them in advance to make arrangements. Service dogs are also welcome on board. Check with sailing operators for their accessibility offerings.

Not every road in Belize is paved, and those that are often have chips and potholes in them. The same is true for sidewalks, where they can be found. Wheelchair users and everyone else should be cautious on the roads.

Hurricane Watch

Hurricanes have long bedeviled the Belizean coast, and the effects of these tropical storms are not only physical: hurricane season is ingrained in the brains of the residents who long remember the last evacuation and always anticipate the next one. Any visitor to Belize is likely to engage in at least one conversation about the most recent tempest. Here are a few of the lowlights from Belizean hurricane history.

Hurricane Five (1931)

One of the deadliest seasons in Atlantic Coast hurricane history. Hurricane Five hit the coast of Belize on a national holiday, so emergency services were slow to respond. The entire northern coast of the country was devastated, and around 2500 people were killed.

Hurricane Hattie (1961)

This history-making hurricane killed 275 people and destroyed much of Belize City. Afterward, survivors moved to refugee camps, which later morphed into permanent settlements – the origins of the town Hattieville. The popular Split on Caye Caulker was created by Hattie, and it also motivated the Belizean government to build a new inland capital at Belmopan.

Hurricane Iris (2001)

This devastating Category 4 storm made landfall in southern Belize, destroying many rural Maya villages and leaving upward of 10,000 people homeless. Off the coast south of Belize City, a liveaboard dive ship capsized, killing 20 people. Joe Burnworth recounts the tragic tale in his book *No Safe Harbor*.

Hurricane Richard (2010)

This Category 1 hurricane made a direct hit on the tiny community of Gales Point, severely damaging houses and isolating the village. The only loss of life on land was an expat American who was mauled by a jaguar which had escaped when a tree fell on its cage.

Hurricane Earl (2016)

Some in Belize are still recovering from this Category 1 that forever altered the country's landscapes and caused upward of US$100 million in damages. Around 80% of the homes in Belize District were flooded and countless structures on the cayes and coastline were destroyed.

Recent scientific evidence suggests that the strength of hurricanes increases with the rise of ocean temperatures. So as our climate continues to change, countries such as Belize are likely to experience more frequent and more intense hurricane hits.

WHAT TO DO IN EVENT OF A HURRICANE

The Atlantic Hurricane season is from June 1 to November 30. If a hurricane comes during your visit and leaving the region isn't possible, hurricane shelters will be made available. Hotel management will provide guidance to guests, and all major radio stations will share continuous updates. Travel insurance is advised especially when visiting Belize during hurricane season.

Nuts & Bolts

Christmas, San Pedro (p71)

OPENING HOURS

Banks
8am to 3pm Monday to Thursday and to 4pm or 4:30pm Friday

Pubs and Bars
Noon to midnight (or later)

Restaurants and Cafes
7am to 9:30am (breakfast), 11:30am to 2pm (lunch) and 6pm to 8pm (dinner)

Shops
9am to 5pm Monday to Saturday, some open Sunday

Smoking

Banned in many public indoor spaces such as government buildings, banks and bus stations, but it's still permitted in bars and restaurants with designated smoking and non-smoking areas.

GOOD TO KNOW

Time zone
GMT - 6 hours

Country code
+501

Emergency number
911

Population
407,900

PUBLIC HOLIDAYS

There are 13 official annual public holidays in Belize. Some businesses and public services will be unavailable on and around these days, particularly Easter and Christmas. Holidays like Independence Day can cause road disruptions.

New Year's Day January 1

Baron Bliss Day March 9

Good Friday March or April

Holy Saturday March or April

Easter Monday March or April

Labor Day May 1

Sovereign's Day May 24

National Day September 10

Independence Day September 21

Day of the Americas October 12

Garifuna Settlement Day November 19

Christmas Day December 25

Boxing Day December 26

Toilets

Public toilets are rare in Belize, although many businesses will lend you their services without a fuss. Airports and museums generally have toilets, but not all bus terminals have facilities.

Electricity 110V/60Hz

Weights & Measures

The imperial system is used. Note that gasoline is sold by the (US) gallon.

Wi-Fi

Wi-fi is generally available for free at hotels and restaurants.

THE BELIZE

STORYBOOK

Our writers delve deep into different aspects of Belizean life

Mask Temple, Lamanai (p108)

Maya ruins, Cahal Pech

A HISTORY OF BELIZE IN 15 PLACES

Don't be fooled into believing that Central America's youngest independent nation is short on history. Long before independence came in 1981 (peacefully, we might add), there were pirates, loggers, and looters, and ancient peoples. From millennia ago to modern times, the people of Belize have been making their mark for generations.

BELIZE'S UNIQUE LOCATION bridging the gap between the Caribbean and Central America means this small country has seen big things. Civilization isn't new to Belize, with evidence of flourishing Mesoamerican communities seen as far back as 2400 BCE. Over the millennia, populations have come and gone, some seeking their fortunes, while others sought freedom.

The country has been shaped by those who have landed here, some even generating disputes which persist to this day: Guatemala maintains a claim over much of Belize due to centuries-old treaties.

Today's culture is a legacy of diverse populations from long ago, found in the language and the food. Even the spirit of the country hearkens back to the day of pirates, in which seaworthiness was a value and personal freedom reigned supreme.

Many people alive today will know Belize better as British Honduras, a name shed in pursuit of independence. As a sovereign nation, Belize continues to identify as a melting pot of multiculturalism found in few other places.

There's a delightful undercurrent of British humor even in the most welcoming displays of Caribbean hospitality, and a reverence for Maya knowledge when it comes to the outdoors.

1. Cuello

BELIZE'S FIRST PEOPLE

The earliest known settlement in Belize is at Cuello in Orange Walk. It predates even the Preclassic period, and some archaeologists attribute the settlement to Maya predecessors. It's estimated that humans were here around 2400 BCE, with inhabitants likely living in thatch houses built upon platforms. There are remains of a steam bath dating to around 900 BCE. Structure 350, a nine-tiered pyramid, is the most interesting remnant for visitors to explore. Ceramics found at this site are even said by some archaeologists to indicate the beginning of a new type of pottery.

For more on Cuello, see p104.

2. Cahal Pech

MAYA CIVILIZATION SETTLES

This serene Maya site overlooking the town of San Ignacio has deeper roots than it appears. Between 2000 BCE and 250 CE, the earliest sedentary Maya communities formed during the Preclassic period. This is when the tallest temples were constructed. Among the earliest settlements was Cahal Pech in Cayo, built as an enclave for the Maya elite. Archaeologists have excavated 34 structures at this site, including a temple reaching 77ft (23m) high. The name translates to 'place of the ticks,' but only because cattle grazed here in the 1950s. It is otherwise tick-free.

For more on Cahal Pech, see p129.

3. Corozal Town

THE FIRST MESTIZO

Skip ahead to the early 1500s, when Spanish conquistadors arrived in Belize. Maya civilization was on the decline by this point, but still numbered a quarter of a million people. The Spanish left a bloody trail beginning in northern Belize, where Corozal is today, reducing the Maya population by at least 90%. Spain's conquest produced the 'First Mestizo,' the mixed-race Spanish and indigenous children of a shipwrecked Spaniard who married a Maya chief's daughter and later organized Maya resistance against the Spanish. The invaders were held off for 20 more years due to his efforts.

For more on Corozal Town, see p111.

4. Belize City

A PIRATE'S LIFE FOR ME

Belize emerged as one of several Caribbean outposts for Britain's maritime marauders. In the early 17th century, British sea dogs first began using the Bay of Honduras as a staging point for raids on Spanish commerce; henceforth the Brits in the region came to be known as Baymen. The official founding date of a British settlement at the mouth of the Belize River is 1638, when Scottish pirate captain, Peter Wallace, decided to organize the building of a new port town. Legend has it that he laid the foundations of what became Belize City with wood chips and rum bottles, presumably empty.

For more on Belize City, see p48.

Belize City

5. St George's Caye

BELIZE'S NEW BEGINNING

The British settlement of Baymen began harvesting the many rich hardwoods found in Belize, and as the settlement became more profitable, the Spanish monarch became more irritable. Spain's armed forces made several unsuccessful attempts to dislodge the well-ensconced and feisty squatters. With the 1763 Treaty of Paris, Spain instead tried diplomacy, and when that failed, they burned down Belize City. It came to a head at the seven day Battle of St George's Caye in 1798, when the nimble Baymen fought back 30 Spanish warships, inspiring a national holiday and ushering in the next phase of Belize's history.

For more on St George's Caye, see p53.

6. Dangriga

A PLACE OF CULTURE

In 1832, a group of Garifuna led by Alejo Beni came from Honduras and settled in present-day Dangriga, a coastal town that continues to be rich in Garifuna culture. This ethnic enclave was previously deported from the British-ruled island of St Vincent, after being defeated in the Carib Wars. They arrived in what was called British Honduras at the time, and maintained a population size second only to Belize City for many decades. Today Garifuna Settlement Day marks their arrival and celebrates their rich culture, which has persisted despite the odds.

For more on Dangriga, see p153.

7. San Pedro

RICH HISTORY, RICHER PRESENT

San Pedro, Belize's most popular town for tourism, was founded in 1848 after the Guerra de Castas on the Yucatán Peninsula, one of the most successful indigenous uprisings in the Americas. Refugees fleeing conflict settled here, continuing their farming and fishing practices, establishing San Pedro as a reliable source of produce for the nearby Baymen. Later, it was coconuts that drove the economy of Ambergris Caye, before the spiny lobster became a popular menu item. Now it's a hot spot for tourism, always growing and changing, but never losing sight of its provincial roots.

For more on San Pedro, see p71.

8. Sittee River

WEALTH AND PROGRESS

Logging was well underway by 1865, but Belize had not yet established itself as an economically viable place in the long term. That changed with the erection of the Serpon sugar mill – the country's first steam-powered mill. Built on the Sittee River, the mill ushered in an era of economic development, and later became the country's first historical reserve. For 30 years the mill fueled Belize's economy, shipping 1700 pounds of sugar a month at its peak. Today, remnants of the steam-powered contraption can be found in the jungle 1 mile (1.6km) from the village of Sittee River.

For more on Sittee River, see p151.

9. Spanish Lookout

TITANS OF INDUSTRY

One facet of Belize's multicultural population is the Mennonite community, which first arrived in Belize in 1958, settling Spanish Lookout. They brought agricultural equipment and maintain a strong farming tradition today. Many of Belize's most essential crops are grown in this area. Despite their traditional dress and habits, Spanish Lookout appears more modern than other villages around it. In fact, it almost looks like a rural district in the American Midwest. Spanish Lookout provides many essential services, like car repair and homebuilding.

For more on Spanish Lookout, see p135.

10. Belmopan

MOVING THE CAPITAL

Belize is no stranger to hurricanes, and the country bears the scars of volatile Atlantic weather. The very existence of the country's capital, Belmopan, is the direct result of the devastation wrought by Hurricane Hattie in 1961. The name is a portmanteau of Belize and Mopan, a reflection of the country's desire for unity. Belmopan was established as an inland base for the government after Hattie partly wiped out Belize City, which was the former capital. On the highway between the two, a town called Hattieville is so named because it's where refugees of the hurricane were moved to when their homes were lost.

For more on Belmopan, see p137.

Placencia

ATLANTIDE PHOTOTRAVEL/GETTY IMAGES ©

11. The Blue Hole

SCIENCE AND DISCOVERY

There is no site more iconic in Belize than the Blue Hole, a perfectly round sinkhole off the coast that is a major destination for divers and snorkelers. Before 1971, however, the Blue Hole lived in relative secrecy, known only to locals and diehard tourists of then-British Honduras. That all changed when famed oceanographer Jacques Cousteau took his research ship *Calypso* to the Blue Hole, bringing unprecedented publicity and kicking off a level of popularity that persists today. It also serves as an important scientific site, and is the face of marine conservation in Belize.

For more on the Blue Hole, see p86.

12. Cockscomb Basin Wildlife Sanctuary

WILDLIFE WINS

Today, Belize has the honor of being home to the largest concentration of jaguars in the world, and that is partly thanks to the establishment of the world's first jaguar preserve in 1986. Located in the Cockscomb Wildlife Basin, this 150-acre expanse of jungle is a place where jaguars and other wild animal species are able to thrive. Some 200 jaguars are said to call this area home, and while tours to Cockscomb are available (and fun), it's very unlikely you would spot one of the majestic jungle cats. Although, there's a chance they might spot you.

For more on Cockscomb Basin Wildlife Sanctuary, see p155.

13. Placencia

A NEW BEGINNING

Today, Placencia is known for its elegant beachfront resorts, but in 2001 the area was a more humble fishing village, until it was devastated by Category 4 Hurricane Iris. Around 75% to 85% of the structures in Placencia came down, and many residents were left homeless. After the immediate impact, the region was economically devastated, resulting in a real-estate situation that caught the eye of foreign investors. Able to buy land at lower-than-usual prices but still ideally situated by the sea, Placencia became a boomtown for expats, who remain a noticeably large part of the population.

For more on Placencia, see p159.

14. Mountain Pine Ridge

CLUES OF CLIMATE CHANGE

A visit to Mountain Pine Ridge begs the question: where are all the pine trees? The answer is in the bellies of dead pine bark beetles, a plague of which devoured 80% of the forest around 2003. The real culprit was climate change, which caused drought that then weakened the trees and made them vulnerable to the tiny beetles. Today the Mountain Pine Ridge is in a state of regrowth, with pines working their way back towards the sky, but they are not the towering trees that defined the place prior to the infestation.

For more on Mountain Pine Ridge, see p132.

15. Belize Barrier Reef

A TREASURE PRESERVED

The Belize Barrier Reef is the second-largest reef system in the world, and undeniably the pride of Belize (as well as the employer for one in two Belizeans). In 2018 the government took the historic step of banning offshore oil activity, the first time a developing nation has done so. The reef was removed from Unesco's list of endangered World Heritage Sites, a win for ocean conservation worldwide. It's an indicator of the global shift toward addressing climate change, and that betting on nature wins in the long run.

For more on Belize Barrier Reef, see p34.

MEET THE BELIZEANS

Characters welcomed! And don't be intimidated by the ones you meet along the way. Before long you'll feel like a local, in on the jokes and among family. Carolee Chanona introduces her people.

BELIZEANS TALK FAST – Belizean Kriol, our lingua franca, is spoken rapidly and includes well-timed facial expressions, lip-pointing for emphasis, and animated hand gestures. With eight main cultures represented, a wealth of languages and dialects shape our accents and favorite words. Consonants fall off and vowels flow under a familiar Caribbean lilt. Listen for a 'Cho!', the universal Kriol slang to express delight, surprise and disdain – all depending on its tone and delivery. Even if things get lost in translation, be sure to bid strangers the time of day, even at night, or at least offer a friendly nod to stave off a 'You nuh got no manners!' scold. Politeness is instinctive, and reciprocation is expected. First-time introductions include a 'Where you from?' in search of a connection, though we need no excuse to treat you like one of our own.

In a country with less than half a million residents, everyone is either family, working with family, married to family and so on. Social media platforms only helped to formalize our interconnectedness. Just by asking, you can get the skinny on the best street food, the cheapest ways to get around, or even land an impromptu guide to a once-in-a-lifetime experience.

Our culture of caring for others likely stems from strong religious faith. About 80% of the population is Christian and most take Sabbath very seriously. Sundays are for relaxation, not business. But even workdays are unapologetically structured on 'Belize time', making patience a virtue.

The capital city, Belmopan, is often labeled as boring, but residents, myself included, love its quiet, unassuming glory. If you're looking for nightlife, head to Ambergris Caye, an island abuzz with golf carts and beach bars until the wee hours. Belize City remains our largest municipality and commercial capital, despite its sea-level location increasing its vulnerability to hurricanes. Belizeans don't joke about hurricanes. We're people of the reef: the second-longest barrier reef in the world is our first line of defense against intensifying storms.

REWILDING BELIZE

It's fitting that mahogany is a symbol of Belize, featured on the flag and referenced in its coat of arms: 'Under the shade, I flourish.' Post-colonization, Belize has shifted from extraction to conservation, having since retained 61% of its 3423 sq miles (8867 sq km) as forest

Belizeans are proud people who need no convincing of the richness of the country's assets, both natural and cultural, we inherit by simple birthright. We boast about our rich ethnic diversity and world-renowned biodiversity, preferably over a cold drink during a hot game of pitty-pat (cards), or feech (dominos).

The bonds made over singular experiences or random encounters stick. Repeat visitors or even folks who never left are the norm, not the exception. With only anecdotal proof, I'd argue Belize's natural beauty brings you here, but the unbridled ease of fitting in – just as you are – is what makes you want to stay.

KEEPING THE PEACE

I have my ancestors to thank for my tranquil childhood growing up on my family's farm on the outskirts of Belmopan.

Like thousands of other Mestizos, they fled the Caste War of Yucatán (1847–1915) to find peace in Belize. Fortunately, my home nation has eluded the kinds of civil unrest and war that have ravaged our Central American neighbors in the century since.

Yet we are not people to shy away from a good debate, and the noise level is only bested by passionate positions. We're quick to defend the good, bad and even the ugly. And we're not afraid to dive into hard conversations about crime, overdevelopment and poverty because, deep down, we share the same values – almost like family. Even Belizeans in the diaspora – an estimated 300,000 of us live abroad – connect to the Kriol saying 'You could tek me outta Belize, but yuh kya tek the Belize outta me.'

El Castillo, Xunantunich (p129)

JANE SWEENEY/ROBERTHARDING/GETTY IMAGES ©

ANCIENT MAYA: THE MYTHS & THE MAGIC

Belize's rich history begins with the ancient Maya and their centuries of rich stories.

THOUGH THE MAYA population of Belize is small (around 10% of the nation's total), imagining contemporary Belize without them would be difficult. From the Cayo District's Caracol (which covers more area than Belize City and still boasts Belize's tallest human-made structure) and Xunantunich to smaller archaeological sites stretching from the nation's far north into its deep south, remnants of ancient Maya glory abound.

Creation Stories

Nearly all aspects of Maya faith begin with their view of the creation, when the gods and divine forebears established the world at the beginning of time. From their hieroglyphic texts and art carved on stone monuments and buildings, or painted on pottery, we can now piece together much of the Maya view of the creation. We can even read the precise date when it took place.

In 775 CE, a Maya lord with the high-sounding name of K'ak' Tiliw Chan Yoat (Fire Burning Sky Lightning God) set up an immense stone monument in the center of his city, Quirigua, in Guatemala. The unimaginative archaeologists who discovered the stone called it Stela C. This monument bears the longest single hieroglyphic description of the creation, noting that it took place on the day 13.0.0.0.0, 4 Ahaw, 8 Kumk'u, a date corresponding to August 13, 3114 BCE in the Western calendar. This date appears over and over in other inscriptions throughout the Maya world. On that day the creator gods set three stones or mountains in the dark waters that once covered the primordial world. These three stones formed a cosmic hearth at the center of the universe. The gods then struck divine new fire by means of lightning, which charged the world with new life.

This account of the creation is echoed in the first chapters of the Popol Vuh, a book compiled by members of the Maya nobility soon after the Spanish conquest in 1524, many centuries after the erection of Quirigua Stela C. Although this book was written in their native Maya language, its authors used European letters rather than the hieroglyphic script. The book gives a fuller account of how they conceived the first creation: "This is the account of when all is still, silent and placid. All is silent and calm. Hushed and empty is the womb of the sky. These then are the first words, the first speech. There is not yet one person, one animal, bird..." The Sacred Book goes on to describe the world as it was before anything else existed, a place enshrouded in darkness and stillness.

It then describes the great sages – the Framer and the Shaper, Sovereign and Quetzal Servant – brought to the world to conceive of life and bring forth the world that then surrounded. The Maya saw this pattern all around them. In the night sky, the three brightest stars in the constellation of Orion's Belt were conceived as the cosmic

hearth at the center of the universe. On a clear night in the crisp mountain air of the Maya highlands, one can even see what looks like a wisp of smoke within these stars, although it is really only a far-distant string of stars within the M4 Nebula.

Maya Cities as the Center of Creation

Perhaps because the ancient Maya of northern Belize didn't have real mountains as symbols of the creation, they built them instead in the form of plaza-temple complexes. In hieroglyphic inscriptions, the large open-air plazas at the center of Maya cities are often called nab' (sea) or lakam ja' (great water). Rising above these plastered stone spaces are massive pyramid temples, often oriented in groups of three, representing the first mountains to emerge out of the 'waters' of the plaza. The tiny elevated sanctuaries of these temples served as portals into the abodes of gods that lived within. Offerings were burned on altars in the plazas, as if the flames were struck in the midst of immense three-stone hearths. Only a few elite people were allowed to enter the small interior spaces atop the temples, while the majority of the populace observed their actions from the plaza below. The architecture of ancient Maya centers thus replicated sacred geography to form an elaborate stage on which rituals that charged their world with regenerative power could be carried out.

Many of the earliest-known Maya cities were built in Belize. The earliest temples at these sites are often constructed in this three-temple arrangement, grouped together on a single platform, as an echo of the first three mountains of creation. The ancient name for the site known today as Caracol was Oxwitza' (Three Hills Place), symbolically linking this community with the three mountains of creation and thus the center of life. The Caana (Sky-Place) is the largest structure at Caracol and consists of a massive pyramid-shaped platform topped by three temples that represent these three sacred mountains.

The Belizean site of Lamanai is one of the oldest and largest Maya cities known. It is also one of the few Maya sites that still bears its ancient name (which means Submerged Crocodile). While other sites were abandoned well before the Spanish

Hieroglyphic text, Caracol (p129)

Conquest in the 16th century, Lamanai continued to be occupied by the Maya centuries afterward. For the ancient Maya, the crocodile symbolized the rough surface of the earth, newly emerged from the primordial sea that once covered the world. The name of the city reveals that its inhabitants saw themselves as living at the center of creation, rising from its waters. The massive pyramid temples include Structure N10-43, which is the second-largest pyramid known from the Maya Preclassic period and represents the first mountain and dwelling place of the gods.

Maya Creation of Humankind

According to the Popol Vuh, the purpose of the creation was to give form and shape to beings who would 'remember' the gods through ritual. The Maya take their role in life very seriously. They believe that people exist as mediators between this world and that of the gods. If they fail to carry out the proper prayers and ceremonies at just the right time and place, the universe will come to an abrupt end.

The gods created the first people out of maize (corn) dough, literally from the flesh of the Maize God, the principal deity of creation. Because of their divine origin, they were able to see with miraculous vision: "Perfect was their sight, and perfect was their knowledge of everything beneath the sky. If they gazed about them, looking intently, they beheld that which was in the sky and that which was upon the earth. Instantly they were able to behold everything..." The Sacred Book goes on to describe how their vision was more than just sight as we know it, godlike in their abilities.

In nearly all of their languages, the Maya refer to themselves as 'true people' and consider that they are literally of a different flesh than those who do not eat maize. They are maize people and foreigners who eat bread are wheat people. This mythic connection between maize and human flesh influenced birth rituals in the Maya world for centuries.

The Belizean site of Lamanai is one of the oldest and largest Maya cities known. It is also one of the few Maya sites that still bears its ancient name (which means Submerged Crocodile).

How the Maya Calendar Worked

The ancient Maya used three calendars. The first was a period of 260 days, known as the Tzolkin, likely based on the nine months it takes for a human fetus to develop prior to birth. The second Maya calendar system was a solar year of 365 days, called the Haab. Both the Tzolkin and Haab were measured in endlessly repeating cycles. When meshed together, a total of 18,980 day-name permutations are possible (a period of 52 solar years), called the Calendar Round.

Though fascinating in its complexity, the Calendar Round has its limitations, the greatest being that it only goes for 52 years. After that, it starts again and so provides no way for Maya ceremony planners to distinguish a day in this 52-year Calendar Round cycle from the identically named day in the next cycle. Thus the Maya developed a third calendar system that we call the Long Count, which pinpoints a date based on the number of days it takes place after the day of creation on August 13, 3114 BCE.

Let's use the date of Saturday April 1, 2023 as an example. The Maya Long Count date corresponding to this day is 13.0.10.7.13, 13 B'en 1 Pop.

The first number, '13,' of this Long Count date represents how many *baktúns* (400 x 360 days or 144,000 days) that have passed since the day of creation (thus 13 x 144,000 = 1,872,000 days). The second number, '0,' represents the number of *katuns* (20 x 360 or 7200 days) that have passed, thus adding another 0 x 7200 = 0 days. The third number, '10,' is the number of *tuns* (360 days), or 3600 days. The fourth number, '7,' is the number of *uinals* (20 days), or 140 days. Finally the fifth number, '13,' is the number of whole days. Adding each of these numbers gives us the sum of 1,872,000 + 0 + 3600 + 140 + 13 = 1,875,753 days since the day of creation.

The Maya then added the Calendar Round date: the Haab date (1 Pop) and the Tzolkin date (13 B'en).

Garifuna drums, Battle of St George's Caye Day celebrations (p53)

IAN PETER MORTON/SHUTTERSTOCK ©

RHYTHMS OF A NATION

Belize is a musical powerhouse, its repertoire encompassing unique *punta*, *punta* rock, *brukdown,* traditional Maya music and assorted musical mélanges. By Anna Kaminski

FOR SUCH A compact country, Belize grooves to an exceptional range of musical styles, from the uniquely homegrown *punta* rock, *paranda,* brukdown and the percussion-and-wind melodies of the Maya to the pan-Caribbean calypso, soca (an up-tempo fusion of calypso with Indian rhythms) and reggae. The most complete catalogue of Belizean music is Stonetree Records (stonetreerecords.com), covering all manner of genres.

A Melting Pot of Musical Styles

Prior to the arrival of the Spanish, the Maya had been using a range of percussion instruments – bones, rattles, turtle shells, drums made of hollowed-out logs covered in deerskin, along with horns made from conch shells, whistles and flute-like ocarinas (ancient wind instrument with a wider body and 10 to 12 finger holes) – in ceremonial and recreational music. The arrival of each new immigrant group – the Europeans, the Creoles, the mestizos, the Garifuna – added a new layer of musical styles and influences that are alive today.

Mestizo Music

Mestizo music combined Maya ceremonial music with the guitar, violin, harp and other instruments brought from Spain. Marimba bands are particularly popular among Mestizo communities, including the Mopan Maya in the north and west of Belize, with several musicians playing the marimba – a percussion instrument that resembles a xylophone, made of wood and producing a mellower sound – accompanied by the drums and a double bass, while in the south of Belize you may hear refrains of ancient Maya melodies, recreated using Kekchi violins, harps and guitar. Belize's best-known marimba group, Alma Belicena, was led by the legendary Maya healer, Elijio Panti, while other renowned traditional musicians include Pablo Collado, a Maya flautist originally from Guatemala whose new-age-style music often incorporates sounds that mimic nature, and harpist Florencio Mess who makes harps by hand in the traditional style, and whose album *Maya Kekchi Strings* – based on age-old melodies and rhythms – has been called 'a living connection to ancient Maya culture.

Brukdown & Beyond

The British brought with them church music and brass bands, while West African rhythms, melodies and chants arrived indirectly as a result of the slave trade. Belize's most prominent Creole music, brukdown, was born in the logging camps of the Belize River valley in the 1800s, when enslaved Africans soothed their weary bodies and souls by drinking rum and using anything at hand – pig jawbones, coconut shells – as percussion instruments,

with layered rhythms and call-and-response vocals accompanied by an ensemble of accordion, banjo and harmonica.

Predominantly a rural folk tradition that is rarely recorded, brukdown was kept alive thanks to the likes of legendary Wilfred Peters and his band Mr Peters' Boom & Chime, who were making music for over 60 years, and Punta Gorda–born Leela Vernon, a high-energy Creole dancer and chanteuse, whose song 'Who Say Creole Gat No Culture?' is a source of national pride – both have been posthumously recognized as Belizean icons. As music legends pass on and the Creole community changes, the folksong tradition is kept alive by the likes of guitarist Brad Pattico, while Brother David Obi, better known in Belize as Bredda David, is responsible for the creation of kungo muzik, a fast-paced fusion of Creole, Caribbean and African styles, infused with rock guitar and lyrical wit on his album *Raw*.

More recently, African elements in Creole music have been expressed through pan-Caribbean styles, such as soca, reggae (Caribbean Pulse, Tanya Carter), calypso (Lord Rhaburn) and dub poetry – with Leroy 'The Grandmaster' Young's *Just Like That* winning international acclaim.

Paranda

Speaking of African elements, shortly after the Garifuna arrived in Belize in 1802, they started melding African percussion – wooden Garifuna drums and other percussion instruments, such as shakers and turtle shells – and raw, gritty vocals with Spanish-style acoustic guitar and Latin melodies, creating paranda. Named after a traditional African rhythm that is often at the root of the music, paranda is an unplugged genre that has recently enjoyed a bit of a resurgence, with the album produced by the Paranda Project showcasing the best of parandero talent in Belize, Honduras and Guatemala. While the Belizean master of paranda was the late Paul Nabor, who was born in Punta Gorda in the 1920s, the paranda torch has been passed on to younger generations. Recent releases include *Garifuna Soul* by Honduras-born Aurelio Martínez, who also served as Belize's first black congressman, and the eponymous *Garifuna Women's Project*. While paranda is nonetheless a genre in danger of disappearing, *punta* and *punta* rock that incorporate it, are not.

Punta & Punta Rock

Unlike traditional Maya, Mestizo and Creole music, *punta* is a traditional Garifuna drumming style, with master drummers Isabel Flores, Lugua & the Larubeya Drummers, and the LeBeha Boys showcasing the full range of Garifuna drumming styles and call-and-response

IAN PETER MORTON/SHUTTERSTOCK ©

Garifuna drummer, Punta Gorda (p166)

vocals alive; Bumari and BIAMA are particularly worth a listen.

Punta underpins *punta* rock, Belize's most popular music style, born in the 1970s, when *punta* musician Pen Cayetano (p153), conscious of Garifuna traditions withering away, wanted to inspire young Garifuna people to embrace their own culture instead of copying music from elsewhere – and so he added the electric guitar to traditional *punta* rhythms, with *Beginning,* his 1982 recording with the Turtle Shell Band, throwing down a gauntlet picked up by other musicians, including Black Coral, Mohubub and Titiman Flores. Frenetic or mellow, it has fast rhythms at its base, designed to get the hips swiveling, accompanied by lyrics in Garifuna or Kriol. No one has done more to popularize *punta* rock than Andy Palacio, known for mixing the Garifuna sound with pop, salsa and calypso beats, and turning it into the (unofficial) national music of Belize. Palacio's last album before his untimely death in 2008, *Watina,* a collaboration with the Garifuna Collective, consists of tracks based on traditional Garifuna rhythms, with all the songs in the Garifuna language.

OUT OF ONE, MANY PEOPLE: THE CULTURES OF BELIZE

Belize's exceptional diversity is reflected in the many peoples – and languages – that come together to make one whole. By Anna Kaminski

EXTRAORDINARILY DIVERSE FOR a small nation, Belize's population of 407,900 falls largely into four main ethnic groups – Mestizo (53%), Creole (26%), Maya (11%) and Garifuna (4%). The remaining 6% comprises East Indians (people of Indian subcontinent origins), Chinese, Spanish, Arabs (generally Lebanese), Mennonites, and North Americans and Europeans who have settled here in the last couple of decades.

While English is the main language, other languages used in Belize include Kriol – an English-based patois with influences from Maya and West African languages – as well as Spanish, Garifuna, Old German and three Maya languages.

The Maya

The Maya were here first, with settlements in various parts of Belize going back some 2000 years. They resisted both the Spanish conquistadors, and pushed back against British attempts to control and tax them in the 18th and 19th centuries, before being banished to Guatemala's highlands. In the late 19th century, Mopan and Kek'chi Maya began moving back into Belize's Toledo district. Maya culture is strongest in the south, where many continue to live largely traditional lives, practicing hunting and subsistence farming, with the women and elders wearing typical embroidered clothes, and holding arranged marriages. The three Maya languages spoken in Belize today are Mopan in Toledo, Kekchi in Toledo and western Belize, and Yucatec in the north.

The Garifuna

Out of all of Belize's peoples, the Garifuna have the most unique backstory. In the 17th century, shipwrecked African enslaved people washed ashore on the Caribbean island of St Vincent. They intermingled with the indigenous population of Caribs and Arawaks and formed a whole new ethnicity, now known as the Garifuna (plural Garinagu).

Having established a reputation as fierce warriors and expert canoe navigators, the Garinagu resisted French and British attempts to take possession of St Vincent until the latter tricked and

Garifuna Settlement Day celebrations (p153)

ROI BROOKS/SHUTTERSTOCK ©

killed the Garifuna leader and deported the Garinagu to the Honduran island of Roatan in 1796, from where the Garinagu migrated to different parts of the Mosquito Coast.

On November 19, 1832, the first Garifuna reached Dangriga, Belize in dugout canoes from Honduras and eventually settled in Dangriga, Hopkins, Seine Bight, Punta Gorda and Barranco. Apart from speaking the Garifuna tongue – a mix of West African, Amerindian and Carib languages – the Garinagu have a strong sense of community and ritual, and practice various West African traditions, such as the *dügü* ('feasting of the ancestors' ceremony), in which drumming and dancing play important roles in healing a sick individual. Other notable Garifuna ceremonies include the *beluria,* a nine-night wake for a dead person's soul attended by entire communities, and the *wanaragua* or *jonkonu* dance, performed during the Christmas-to-early-January festive season.

Mestizos

Belize's largest and quickest-growing demographic group, Mestizos comprise all Belizeans of mixed Spanish and indigenous descent. The first Mestizos arrived in the mid-19th century, when refugees crossed over from the Yucatán into northern and western Belize during the Caste War. More recent arrivals include thousands of political refugees from Guatemala, El Salvador and Honduras, with most settling between Corozal and Orange Walk, as well as in Benque Viejo and San Ignacio.

Creoles

Belizean Creoles are the descendants of enslaved Africans and British baymen, loggers and colonists. In the 1780s, after much Spanish-British conflict, an agreement was reached, allowing Brits to cut logwood and harvest the highly prized mahogany hardwood from the northern half of Belize. In return, Britain abandoned the Miskito Coast of Nicaragua and British buccaneers stopped using Belize's coastline to prey on Spanish ships.

After British attempts to force the Maya to do grueling logging work in insect-ridden swamps had failed, enslaved Africans were purchased from Jamaica to take their place from the 17th century onwards. Thus it was that mahogany played a key role in the creation of the Afro-Belizean population. The 'Creolization' of Belize's population began when the loggers – known as baymen – and other British colonists intermingled with enslaved Africans. Belize City is the epicenter of Creole culture, with pockets between Belmopan and San Ignacio, Placencia and Monkey River. Sounding familiar at first but not easily intelligible to a speaker of standard English, Creole-spoken Kriol is 'di stiki stiki paat,' or 'the glue that holds Belize together.'

Mennonites

If you're traveling in Toledo and Cayo, you will see horse-drawn buggies plodding along by the side of the road, carrying blond-haired, blue-eyed, bearded men in blue or sea-green shirts, denim overalls and straw hats, and women in drape-like frocks and black bonnets. These are the old-colony Mennonites, an enigmatic Anabaptist group that dates to 16th-century Netherlands and lives in agricultural communities according to strict, faith-based values that reject any form of mechanization or technology (though you'll sometimes see the men catching a bus or thumbing a ride). Speaking mostly Old German, these devout pacifists who reject political ideologies (including paying taxes) have taken a circuitous route to reach Belize, moving from the Netherlands in the late 17th century to Prussia, then Russia, then Canada, then Mexico, fleeing from military conscription and other societal demands. In 1958, the first Mennonite communities were welcomed by the

ADVENTURE
THEN

Belizean government due to their farming expertise, followed by later waves of more progressive, English-speaking Mennonite communities, mostly from Canada, that use tractors and other technology. Today, the Mennonites are responsible for much of Belize's dairy industry and furniture-making.

East Indians

Between 1844 and 1917, around 40,000 East Indians were brought to Belize as indentured laborers – mostly to work on the sugar plantations of the Toledo and Corozal Districts, but also to serve as policemen in Belize City. Indentured servitude contracts meant working for one 'master' for a set period of time, before either returning to India or settling in their chosen part of Belize. These contracts often proved to be a trap: paltry wages and being paid in goods from the company store meant having to reenlist for a greater number of years, just to make ends meet. Today there are East Indian communities in Calcutta (south of Corozal Town), Forest Home (near Punta Gorda), Belize City, Belmopan and Orange Walk.

Sugarcane truck, Orange Walk Town (p102)

THE BLUE HOLE: BEYOND THE MYTH & MYSTIQUE

This seemingly bottomless turquoise sinkhole beneath the waves has been beguiling marine explorers for decades.
By Anna Kaminski

VISIBLE FROM SPACE, the Blue Hole looks like a giant eye of fathomless sapphire blue, framed by 'eyelashes' of sandy, vegetation-covered spits and 'eye shadow' of brilliant turquoise and teal shallow waters. Long an open secret among Belizean fishers, in 1971 it was brought to global attention by legendary diver and marine explorer Jacques Cousteau, who declared it to be 'one of the world's greatest dive sites.' To date, it has claimed the lives of at least three divers, and sea monsters are rumored to dwell in its depths. But what is the Blue Hole, and what makes it so special?

An almost perfectly circular body of water, measuring 984ft (300m) across and 3140ft (957m) in circumference, the Blue Hole is located 62 miles (100km)off the coast of Belize, in the center of the Lighthouse Reef Atoll – Belize's premier diving destination. Believed to be the largest karst-eroded sinkhole (swallow hole) in existence, the Blue Hole is now known to have started out on dry land as a limestone cavern at the center of an underground cave and tunnel complex during the last glacial period, as far back as 120,000 years, when the sea was 397 feet to 500 feet (121–152m) below its present level. As the sea levels began to rise some 15,000 years ago, the cave complex flooded and the roof of the main cavern collapsed. Vast stalactite formations, as well as ledges and shelves carved by the sea into the limestone along the Blue Hole's complete interior circumference, provide irrefutable proof of its geological origins.

To add to the Blue Hole's mystique, evidence in the form of sediment and lagoon samples, found in its depths by underwater archaeologists from Rice and Louisiana State Universities, led them to solve the mystery of the collapse of the Maya civilization in Belize around 900 CE. In a 2015 study they concluded that the evidence strongly supports the theory that there were longer droughts and fewer cyclones during the era of the Maya decline, and that adverse climate conditions were the pivotal factor behind the civilization's demise.

In 1997, the Cambrian Foundation established the hole's depth at 407ft (124m), while 2018 saw an ambitious expedition led by Richard Branson and Fabien Cousteau – the grandson

Deep dive, Blue Hole

ANGELO GIAMPICCOLO/SHUTTERSTOCK ©

of Jacques – to the bottom of the Blue Hole, conducting over 20 dives in order to create a complete 3D sonar map of the underwater cave complex. Along with never-before-seen stalactites, the team came across unidentifiable tracks that fueled speculation regarding their origins.

Sea-monster myths and legends about the Blue Hole have abounded since the early 1970s, when a diving expedition from Caye Caulker claimed to have seen a 20ft-long (6m) sea serpent with red eyes in its depths. No such creature was seen again, with some divers suggesting that the diving team must have mistaken an oarfish or ribbonfish for a monster of the deep. The team can be forgiven this misidentification, since monsters (or pelagic creatures of grace and beauty, depending on your perspective) do lurk in the Blue Hole. Hammerheads are often spotted in its depths, while sea fans, sponges, and reef dwellers such as turtles, barracuda and an abundance of reef fish along its outer rim support a healthy population of lemon, black tip, reef and bull sharks that are found lurking in the caverns some 80ft (24m) below the surface.

Mythical and real monsters aside, there are genuine dangers to exploring the Blue Hole. Only experienced divers who have completed 24 prior dives are allowed to enter it, in spite of the lack of currents. The lack of natural light is a challenge during the descent, and even advanced divers have been known to become disoriented and muddled in the cave complex entered via the Blue Hole, feeling a numbing sensation of euphoria below 135ft (41m) because of nitrogen narcosis at such depths. Some reported seeing light emerging from tunnels and swam towards it, mistaking it for the surface. Yet in spite of all this, the Blue Hole draws scores of divers year-round, who come to witness its mysteries for themselves.

Aerial view of the Blue Hole

MLENNY/GETTY IMAGES ©

Keel-billed toucan

BIRDWATCHING IN BELIZE

Belize's unofficial national pastime is enjoying the rich avian life that calls the country's jungles and shores home.

By Ali Wunderman

IDEALLY SITUATED BETWEEN Central America and the Caribbean, Belize is home to nearly 600 species of birds – 20% of which are migratory. Besides being a draw to bird-loving travelers, Belize's avian life is a point of pride among those who live in the country, a cultural touchstone among Belizeans. Tour guides are inevitably chock-full of bird knowledge and birdwatching talent, from the pine savannas to the depths of the jungle.

Deep within the towering canopy of Chiquibul National Forest (p134), along Belize's western border, conservationists are celebrating. Summer is coming to an end, and all of the scarlet macaw chicks have survived to fledge, taking those first shaky steps and careful flaps of their wings outside the tree cavities where they've been nesting for the past few months. It's not predators that threatened these brightly colored babies, at least not natural ones: humans are the culprit behind population loss of scarlet macaws, but in Belize, humans are also the solution. Baby macaws are the target of poaching for the pet trade in Belize, and when coupled with habitat loss to make way for civilization, their numbers reached historic lows not too long ago.

Belize's devout love of birds is what is bringing the species back from the brink. Every summer, conservationists and volunteers spend weeks in the jungle camping beneath known nests, ensuring poachers can't get close enough to spirit away the young ones to almost certain death. The work isn't easy, but for Belizeans, there's no question that it's worth it.

Most bird-related activities in Belize won't be quite as life-or-death as the macaw protection program, but tourism plays a vital role in supporting conservation efforts. Plus, birdwatching gives passionate guides and locals an opportunity to share their love of Belize's species – a truly wonderful thing to witness.

It helps that Belize has such a breadth of species. From the colorful keel-billed toucan – the national bird – to a menacing selection of raptors and a whole selection of songbirds, there is a lot of avian life to enjoy.

Birding at Lodges

Birds can be found everywhere in Belize, including in its most densely populated areas, but ecolodges are particularly adept at facilitating birdwatching experiences. Often guests won't even need to travel off property to find a wealth of species. Despite Belize's size, it is home to numerous distinct ecosystems, each of which features its own selection of birds. Staying at a lodge out on a caye will yield different sightings than in the Mountain Pine Ridge (p132), which will be unique from those found deeper in the jungle.

Some of Belize's most talented birding guides are employed by these lodges, and guests reap the benefits of their experience and enthusiasm. One could spend an hour with a scope and binoculars surrounded by birdsong and not know which birds are singing or where to find them, but lodge guides will know which species are there from recall alone. There's nothing like a guide pointing out the tiniest glimmer of feathers among the foliage, identifying exactly which species it is, what kind of call it's making, and sharing even more facts about the creature from memory alone.

Lodges also go out of their way to ensure their properties don't get in the way of natural bird behaviors. At Turneffe Island Resort (p85), for example, they rope off a section of the beach used by nesting seabirds and keep curious guests far enough away to avoid a disturbance. While they are proud to offer such a close look at these birds, there's no question that the safety and well-being of the animals comes first.

eBird

eBird is a mobile app created by the Cornell Lab of Ornithology that enables birdwatchers around the world to upload data about which birds they've seen and where. It provides crucial data which can inform conservation programs and secure funding for essential survival programs.

Belize's birdwatchers are devotees of the app, creating checklists that rival much larger countries like Costa Rica. Guides compete to maintain the top spot of most species seen, or most checklists created, allowing Belize to give itself the moniker #BirdingNation. Given the country's small population size, the widespread use of eBird is indicative of just how much Belize loves birds. Additionally, local birders are often happy to share their eBird best practices, as the app is not always intuitive, and knowing which species are sighted is crucial. Taking a birding tour in Belize can be a great way to gain experience with eBird while actively enjoying the nearly 600 avian species that have been spotted in the country.

Merlin is an ideal app to pair with eBird, as it lists all known species for a region. This is especially helpful when a bird has been sighted and the species still needs to be identified before logging it in eBird.

Bringing Belize Together

Birds have at least cursory appeal to most Belizeans, but those who make a living in birdwatching have generated a subculture all their own. Facebook is the social-media platform of choice for the Belizean birding groups that are actively engaged in sharing sightings, eBird tips and suggestions with each other. Impromptu birding trips to difficult-to-reach destinations pop up in these groups often and always max out on capacity.

Belizeans will flock together to hear the slate-colored solitaire at the Natural Arch in Chiquibul National Forest, or climb the hills in Red Bank (p165) to see scarlet macaws. Roseate spoonbills and jabiru stork can be found in marshes near the coast, while everyone is always looking for the rare harpy eagle in the western parts of the country. Parakeets and Amazon parrots squawk overhead in the Cayo District, and many head to Mountain Pine Ridge to spot the rare orange-breasted falcon.

Scarlet macaw

INDEX

A

B

C

Map Pages **000**

Map Pages **000**

Map Pages **000**

'A lazy day spent snorkeling the Hol Chan Marine Reserve culminates spectacularly when you jump in at Shark Ray Alley and are immediately engulfed in a swirl of nurse sharks and sting rays.' (p76)

PAUL HARDING

'I can't think of a better way to end a day (and start a night) in San Pedro than watching the sunset from a lagoon-side bar – with a rum punch of course.' (p71)

PAUL HARDING

LEFT: PAUL HARDING/LONELY PLANET ©, RIGHT: PAUL HARDING/LONELY PLANET ©

Mapping data sources:
© Lonely Planet
© OpenStreetMap http://openstreetmap.org/copyright

THIS BOOK

Destination Editor
Sarah Reid

Production Editor
Claire Rourke

Book Designer
Norma Brewer

Cartographer
Bohumil Ptáček

Assisting Editors
Soo Hamilton, Kellie Langdon, Clifton Wilkinson

Cover Researcher
Mazzy Prinsep

Thanks
Sofie Andersen, Hannah Cartmel, Karen Henderson, Kate James, Katerina Pavkova, Gary Quinn

Paper in this book is certified against the Forest Stewardship Council™ standards. FSC™ promotes environmentally responsible, socially beneficial and economically viable management of the world's forests.

Published by Lonely Planet Global Limited
CRN 554153
9th edition – Dec 2023
ISBN 978 1 83869 679 5

10 9 8 7 6 5 4 3 2 1
Printed in China